A Full Plate of Retirement

A Full Plate of Retirement

Grandma Learns to Cook, Build Boats, Then Goes Cruising

**Dorothy Young
Hal Stufft**

**Outskirts Press, Inc.
Denver, Colorado**

The Great Blue Heron

The opinions expressed in this manuscript are solely the opinions of the authors and do not represent the opinions or thoughts of the publisher. The authors have represented and warranted full ownership and/or legal right to publish all the materials in this book.

A Full Plate of Retirement
Grandma Learns to Cook, Build Boats, Then Goes Cruising
All Rights Reserved.
Copyright © 2011 Dorothy Young and Hal Stufft
V3.0

This book may not be reproduced, transmitted, or stored in whole or in part by any means, including graphic, electronic, or mechanical without the express written consent of the publisher except in the case of brief quotations embodied in critical articles and reviews.

1. Cooking, learning to cook, European cooking, boat building in England, boat building in France, living in Europe, cruising in England, cruising in Europe 2. Dorothy Young, Hal Stufft

Outskirts Press, Inc.
http://www.outskirtspress.com

ISBN: 978-1-4327-7158-4

Outskirts Press and the "OP" logo are trademarks belonging to Outskirts Press, Inc.

PRINTED IN THE UNITED STATES OF AMERICA

Table of Contents

Introduction....ix

How I Learned to Cook....xi

Navigation Rules....xiii

I....Camping and Cruising in the United States....1

II....Building Our First Boat in England,
Cruising in England and on the Continent....21

III....Building a Sailing Yacht and Cruising
In the Western European Waters....51

IV....Building a Second Narrowboat and Continuing
to Cruise in England and on the Continent....81

V....Building a Wide-Beam Dutch Barge Replica and
Cruising in England and on the Continent....87

VI....Downsizing by Building a Tugboat
and Traveling Throughout France....95

VII....Additional Favorite Recipes,
Main Courses and Casseroles....115

VIII....My Favorite Foods That I Order
but Do Not Prepare....193

IX....Kitchen Utensils....199

X....Family Members and Friends....201

XI....Oops and Aahs and Ughs....205

XII....Index for All Recipes by Category....209

Acknowledgments

My husband Hal and I appreciate our family and good friends and the contributions they have made to this collection. We especially enjoyed their eagerness to try something from the author's kitchen/galley/camp stove. They should be thanked also for spreading the appreciation of the following recipes and stories around the United States, England, France, Belgium and Netherlands.

When you read this book keep in mind that Dorothy is the main writer and cook in the family. Hal is a kibitzer from time to time, contributor of a half dozen of the recipes. And, he assisted with the organizing, editing and preparing the manuscript for printing. Dorothy is the poet.

We wish to give a special thanks to daughter Sarah who offered to edit the book. She, more than anyone, is familiar with most of the recipes and helped in clarifying steps in recipe preparation. She is a competent cook and we have enjoyed sharing recipes for over thirty years.

We are also very appreciative to Dr. Evart (Bud) Cornell from Maryland who read an early manuscript of the book, including all the recipes and posed questions along the way. He was visiting us in Georgia for a week and graciously spent many hours poring over the contents. He probably would have preferred to be taking walks on the beach or reading his novel but he stayed with the project.

If you want to know more about our cruising years and where our boats took us, check out a book written mainly by my husband, Hal Stufft. His book is entitled: **"Let's Build a Boat Together and Go for a Sail in Europe."** The whole time we have been involved in cruising, Hal has written more than twenty articles for an English magazine, Waterways World.

Dorothy is the painter of the small black and white images made from her watercolors seen throughout the book. The inspiration for the cover was from a painting class given by Stephen Rothwell of Canada. He conducts watercolor classes on Jekyll Island, Georgia each winter. Other artists who have provided instruction are Ben Foster and Joyce Stokes at Jekyll Island and Stanley Rose in France. The photos were taken by us and friends. Hugh Potter and Richard Fairhurst, the editors of Waterways World magazine, have given us permission to use photos from Hal's articles in this book.

Introduction

The rationale for this book came about through the back door. My original intent was to make a copy of my favorite recipes for my daughter, stepdaughter, and daughter-in-law. I proceeded with this task and completed one set of recipe cards. Then, I realized how time consuming the project was going to be.

My second thought was that it would be nice to share these recipes with the grandchildren, also. And, following that thought was another. Will those children and grandchildren ever want to know in more detail how we have spent almost thirty years of our "retired" life and some of the places where we set up "boat or camp."

Following all these thoughts came the idea that maybe other boaters and campers would find my recipes appealing--simple to make and rich in taste. And, one last thought. A woman, who owned a beauty shop where my mother went each week, said to her: "If your daughter ever writes a book about her life abroad, I would like to read it."

So, my prospective audience keeps expanding exponentially. You don't have to be a camper. You don't have to be a boater. You don't have to have traveled outside the U.S. Hopefully, you will find my recipes meet your needs for serving good food with ease in preparation. And, I hope that you will find my stories that frame the recipes and the stories about boat building and traveling somewhat entertaining.

While most of our traveling involved cruising as we normally think of the word, on water, cruising for us also includes some land travel. As with most campers, we started out staying in a tent, then moved to a pop-up camper, then a Scotty trailer, and now a mid-size recreational vehicle. People continue to call it camping, but as I look around the campsite, I fail to see how one can classify it as camping when folks are living in such luxury. Our generation has turned camping into a quite-different lifestyle. Many northerners leave their homes and drive south, seeking the warmth of the sun. Some remain in one location for the entire winter; others travel from site to site. In my food stories, you will find us moving from place to place either by land or water, shopping in new markets, often with family members or friends. We continue to enjoy sharing our lifestyle with others.

While some of the recipes are made with rich ingredients, it does not mean that we consume high fat content and calories on a daily basis. For the most part, we eat salads two-to-three times a week for our evening meal. And, we consume lots of fruit and vegetables in our daily diets. However, when family or friends visit, we tend to serve, along with the salads, fruits, and vegetables, dishes taken from my favorites in this book.

How I Learned To Cook

I write about foods I like and how I prepare them to suit my own tastes. I wish to convey joy in the preparation and more importantly, in the eating. A simple dish I remember from my upbringing and the ability to transfer how it tasted have become my guide in learning to cook.

As a young person, I detested being indoors. When given the choice, I would go to the fields with my dad and brother rather than help my mother in the kitchen. As a teenager, I had put one meal on the table for my father and me when my mother had gone on a trip with her cousins. I don't recall how he and I ate the rest of the week. My mother would ask me to shine the hardwood floors on a Saturday morning, and I disliked the task. Ask me to mow the lawn or wash the car or raise a hundred chickens, or mow the wheat stubble, or drive the tractor to take the soybeans and wheat to the grain elevator, and I was a happy helper. They didn't really have to ask me to do these outdoor chores. I recall my father discouraging me when I widened the amount of lawn more and more each summer.

When I married at the age of twenty, I could not fry an egg properly. The first meal I made was that same one I had cooked for my father. Once away from home, married and with a career, I picked up the cooking routine quite easily. I have always believed it was because, as a teenager, I had sat on the kitchen counter visiting and watching my mother prepare meals, had been given the best-tasting food imaginable, and knew from those delectable flavors how good food was supposed to taste. And, with all my love for my mother still close at the surface that a tear has formed as I write this, she never insisted that I stay in the house and cook. To this day, I would rather be outside. I have to have a nice-looking lawn even if it winds a quarter mile to the road. Mom would be pleased to know that my tending the inside would meet with her expectations, though that task is not nearly as enjoyable.

For unknown reasons, perhaps because someone had to do it, I became more and more interested in cooking. However, it wasn't until I retired from a career that I had time to move from following cookbook recipes, to experimenting and to making dishes that met my standard of good taste. When I was beginning to face my responsibilities in cooking and entertaining, my mother would send me a recipe or two when she knew that I was going to be expected to produce for a dinner party. I recall she sent me a possible menu with ideas on how to bring it off. Mostly with help from a cookbook or two, I grew in confidence over the years. I still recall my first go at pie baking. I wanted to take pies to a community gathering and I remember being very proud of the results.

Perhaps because my mother did not force me to take up cooking but allowed me to do other things, I did not develop a negative attitude toward it. It is now a joy, most of the time. Thanks to generous friends and family who have shared their recipes, many of which are included in this book and the result of experimentation over 50+ years, I am proud to present 180 favorite recipes, along with stories of how some have been received.

Over a 50-year time span, it is not always possible for me to recall the origin of a recipe; some have become lost. Some recipes were written on scraps of paper or written in letters from my mother; some were given to me by immediate family members. Some were derived from outstanding restaurant food that I tried to duplicate at home. Some came from people whom we met along the waterways from various countries who invited us into their home or boat for a meal. And, others I have created in the past 30 years of more concentrated cooking. To everyone, I thank you for your contribution, and I hope that you will take pleasure in the compilation of my favorites.

Lastly, I admit to an uncontrollable need to tear recipes from magazines with the thought that I want to try making a dish that combines such interesting ingredients. This habit goes back to when I was 20 years of age and first married, as I still come across these "must try" recipes. Now in my 70's, I always have in the back of my mind two or three dishes just waiting to be tried.

Navigation Rules

It is very important before you begin using any of the recipes in this book that you follow these guidelines. I have converted my European recipes into the below measurements to keep life simple.

1 T = 1 tablespoon

1 t = 1 teaspoon

1 cup = 1 cup of 8 ounces for both liquids and solids

1 Medium-sized can is in the range of 14.5 to 15.5 ounces

1 Large-sized can is in the range of 24 to 29 ounces

The ingredients for each recipe are listed in the order in which they are used in the directions.

French Fishing Boats

I

Camping and Cruising in the United States

Switching gears, inventing a new life
Entering retirement as a first mate and wife
Ending up cruising, camping, and cooking
The following, I hope, is worth your reviewing.

In the late 1970's Hal and I were first starting to plan for our retirement years. We married in 1980 and moved from Maryland north to Pennsylvania where Hal had inherited a bit of land, most of it woods. He had selected a spot for a house that he had designed. I was on the scene when the first bit of carpentry began. While still working in Maryland, we would leave work on Friday evening pulling a flat-bed trailer loaded with the materials we would need for the weekend. We didn't choose to visit a lumberyard on Saturday morning and miss out on productive hours. The house is octagonal and the flooring was assembled in segments on weekday evenings in Maryland, then carried to the site for installation. Before Hal retired, progress was slow except in the summer months. He had a month free for full-time house building and I, who had not yet resigned from my work, would assist on the weekends.

He is particularly proud of the kitchen design, which provides a flow in the food storage and preparation. The ingredients are pulled from a pantry closet and/or the refrigerator to the work area and sink, to the stove, and, then, to the serving table. The work area has one section that is lower than the rest of the counter, thereby giving the chef ease in mixing and/or kneading. Also, the kitchen/dining/living rooms are one large open space and that gives the chef the ability to see and hear what's going on with the rest of the family or friends. If the kitchen or galley were in a separated part, I would probably make fewer mistakes, but I prefer the openness.

Simplicity when cooking has always been a high priority with me. You can have all the special equipment available if that pleases you, but I find many of those items to be more bother than they're worth. My preference in selecting kitchen equipment for home or boat or camper is to keep it as simple as possible. For example, I like using a saw-tooth peeling knife for most purposes rather than the specialized cutters. The kitchen tools that I find necessary for my minimalist kitchen are listed in Chapter IX.

My initial preparation in compiling recipes and stories for this book was to review more than fifty log books covering our cruising life over the past thirty years. I selected writings dealing with food and food-related events, though occasionally I steer off course. Not only is food important to us but when traveling food is also a central part of our social and cultural experiences. The French culture seems to make the dinner hour the family's priority. Whether you are inviting people to join you for a cup of tea or a coffee or something more involved, the visit is usually enveloped in good conversation and good eating. My favorite foods that I have prepared and shared with guests are included herein. Fortunately for you who want to find a particular dish quickly, there is an index. You are required to read the body of the text just once. You may wonder about certain dishes and think, "Surely she has a recipe for that." Probably I do but it's not included herein because it's not a favorite or it's so often used that it seemed unnecessary. For example, I serve lots of fruits and vegetables (frozen if fresh are not available), but one doesn't need a recipe. Some of the recipes have been passed to me, upon request, usually after having enjoyed the cook's serving a dish in his/her own home. You will get to know some of our long-lasting friends who have contributed their recipes and ideas. Their names appear in Chapter X.

Our retired years have been anything but boring. The first time I heard the following statement, only a couple of years ago, it came from my brother, Lynn. He is a land lover and cares not for water sports or cruising. In response to a conversation about our lifestyle, he said: "Whatever floats your boat." Camping and boating were a part of our lives before Hal and I met. They just took center stage, especially as we moved from careers into retirement. When I met Hal, he owned a 34' sailboat called Sea Quester that he had built from a bare, fiberglass shell. Our camping at that time was limited to a tent. But, the cooking and dining part of our lives has been and remains one of the joyous experiences throughout our years together--that and our desire to be a good team in whatever we have decided to do.

For several years in the early 1980's, we habitually stationed ourselves in the U.S. either at home in Pennsylvania or in camping vehicles in search of warmer climate. At times it was difficult to separate our traveling from our homestead life. However, through amateur radio we were able to keep in touch with family and friends. One winter we decided to take Sea Quester to Florida. The boat needed some improvements and we decided it would be far better to be in the water in Florida than in the Maryland marina. For one month, we moored in an inlet near Stuart, took the boat to shore once a week for water and supplies, and enjoyed completing the chores.

On our way south one warm, autumn day in Beaufort, North Carolina we had stopped to have lunch and we put down a lightweight anchor. Much to our surprise, a fellow

CHEESE-ARTICHOKE APPETIZER

4 medium green onions
16-ounce can artichoke hearts
½ cup mayonnaise
½ cup grated Parmesan cheese
crackers or cocktail rye bread, if desired

1. Peel and chop the green onions.
2. Drain the artichoke hearts in a strainer; chop into small pieces.
3. Mix green onions, artichoke hearts, mayonnaise, and cheese in non-greased casserole.
4. Cover with lid or aluminum foil.
5. Bake @ 350 degrees for 20 to 25 minutes.
6. Serve with crackers.

(Makes 1½ cups.)

Grandma's Tip: If you prefer to use the microwave, cover with plastic wrap, folding back 2" from edge to vent. Microwave at 70% power 4 to 5 minutes, stirring after 2.

Mentioning the holidays brings other favorites to mind. It would not be the holiday season for us without these delightful cookies. Similar cookies, I notice, go by the names of Mexican Wedding Cakes and Festive Pecan Something or Other, but these are not the same. Their appearance is quite similar but once you have tried these, I think you will agree that they are a cut above most of their sisters. They are so easy to prepare that you will want to engage the children in their making.

Cookie Alert: It helps to place the unbaked cookie dough in the refrigerator during the time that you are baking. Keeping the dough cool allows the cookie to stay more light and airy rather than flat during the baking process. I find that turning the cookie trays around about half way through the baking helps to keep them evenly baked. My experience has been that they brown faster at the back of the oven.

ALMOND COCOONS

1 c. butter, soft
5 T. granulated sugar
2 c. flour
1 c. slivered almonds
1 c. powdered sugar + ½ c.
2 t. vanilla extract

1. Lightly grease a cookie tray
2. Beat butter until light and fluffy with mixer on high setting.
3. Add sugar and continue to beat.
4. On low speed mix in flour a small amount at a time or you can mix by hand.
5. By hand, add the almonds.
6. Shape dough into approximately 1 ½-inch diameter balls. Make into crescents or press down with the bottom of a cup.
7. Bake @ 325 degrees for 20 minutes.
8. Add vanilla extract 1 t. at a time to 1 cup powdered sugar. Mix by hand until vanilla is well

combined with the sugar. Add additional powdered sugar, ¼ to ½ cup. Once cookies are removed from oven, allow to cool 4 minutes. Roll cookies while still warm in this mixture.

(Makes 24 to 30 cookies.)

<u>Grandma's Tip:</u> Don't be overly concerned if the crescents appear a bit rough looking. The powdered sugar will cover much of any uneven surface. Set aside to cool completely before placing in a cookie tin. These cookies stay fresh up to three weeks.

Ruth, my sister-in-law, recently made cranberry bread for us, and it was much better than any I had previously tried. Guess it shouldn't be a big surprise to find out that the recipe appears on the package of Ocean Spray Cranberries. This is another recipe that I cannot prepare when "across the pond" in Europe. (That is the reference many folks use referring to the wide span of the Atlantic Ocean.) In Europe they do not sell the sauce or cranberries anywhere I have traveled. Cranberry juice, however, has in recent years started to surface on the grocery shelves and markets of Europe.

CRANBERRY NUT BREAD

2 cups flour
1 cup sugar
1 ½ t. baking powder
1 t. salt
½ t. baking soda
¾ cup orange juice
2 T. vegetable oil
1 T. grated orange peel
1 egg, well beaten
½ cup nuts, chopped
1½ cups Ocean Spray fresh or frozen cranberries, coarsely chopped

1. **Grease a 9x5-inch loaf pan.**
2. **Mix together flour, sugar, baking powder, salt, and baking soda in a medium-size mixing bowl.**
3. **Stir in orange juice, oil, orange peel, and egg. Mix until well blended.**
4. **Stir in nuts and cranberries.**
5. **Spread evenly in loaf pan.**
6. **Bake @ 350 degrees for 55 minutes or until a toothpick inserted in the center comes out clean.**
7. **Cool on rack for 15 minutes. Remove from pan; cool completely**

(Makes 1 loaf.)

This bread makes a nice gift at holiday time. I wrote the Ocean Spray Company seeking their approval to print their recipe. They responded that they were pleased to see it passed along. So, with the courtesy from Ocean Spray, I think you will find that you will be pleased with the results and happy to make it part of your holiday presentation or any other time of the year for that matter.

There is one cookie, however, that is a family favorite any time of the year. In fact, I feel somewhat guilty if I know the family is coming for a visit and I have not made at least enough for their visit and enough for them to take home. Once when the Kraft family arrived home having consumed all the cookies along the way, they called to request the recipe as they wanted to make more that same day. If a vote was taken among the children and grandchildren, I daresay this cookie would receive the star rating. I cannot duplicate it in Europe because the candy bar is not known there but within the U.S., it's a must in our household.

Granddaughter Christina says that when she marries, beside the wedding cake she wants to have a plate of this recipe, four dozen cookies.

PEANUT BUTTER AND CHOCOLATE COOKIES

½ cup butter or margarine, softened
¾ cup sugar
2/3 cup firmly packed, light brown sugar
2 egg whites
1¼ cup chunky peanut butter
1½ t. vanilla extract
1 cup flour
½ t. baking soda
¼ t. salt
5 (2.1 ounce) chocolate-covered crispy peanut-butter candy bars, cut with scissors into ½-inch pieces. I suggest using Butterfinger bars.

1. Beat butter at medium speed with an electric mixer until creamy.
2. Gradually add ¾ cup sugar and 2/3 cup brown sugar, beating well.
3. Add egg whites, beating well.
4. Stir in peanut butter and vanilla. Set aside.
5. Combine flour, soda, and salt; gradually fold into peanut butter mixture, mixing well.
6. Stir in candy.
7. Shape dough into 1½-inch balls and place 2 inches apart on lightly-greased cookie sheets.
8. Bake at 350 degrees for 11 minutes or until starting to brown around the edges. Cool 5 minutes on cookie sheets. Transfer to wax paper to cool completely.

<u>*Grandma's Tip:*</u> I find that one needs to use plain aluminum cookie sheets. Those coated with Teflon have left me with cookies that baked too quickly. After 9 minutes, the cookies were flat and too brown. On aluminum, they bake the full 11 minutes and raise well. However, after the 5 minutes of resting, they do flatten somewhat.

There are four lasagnas in my recipe file. And, they are all favorites. Lasagna seems to be liked by everyone. The only concern that I have when serving it is to be sure that there are vegetarian choices. Perhaps the family has grown tired of the beef version as it has been a favorite in my kitchen for a long time. Because our children are all busy with their careers and we are retired from ours, I sometimes take a meal when we go visiting. The lasagna freezes well and can be carried in a cooler for quite a spell. Be sure to remove the dish a day ahead and place it in the refrigerator if using it at home, as it takes a long time for the frozen dish to thaw.

On one occasion, I prepared three different lasagnas to serve to a group of 12 or so amateur radio club members whom we had invited to our home. Most of the guests were from Pennsylvania and Maryland, but one couple had come all the way from Belgium. We are both amateur radio operators and it is through this medium that we have met many of our good friends in the U. S. and in Europe. There was space on the property for our visitors to park their recreational vehicles. It's a bit ironic that all those hams had RV's. They were invited for the evening meal and for breakfast the following day. When serving lasagna, one only needs a lettuce salad and a nice dessert to complete the meal.

Amateur radio was very popular when we began our cruising life. I remember one evening we were moored outside of London when Hal put up the radio antenna and started calling for a friend in Maryland. The friend responded with a clear signal. It was at that moment that I decided to earn a license, also. Now, of course, we utilize the radio just for fun. Other means of communication have superseded the need to rely on ham radio, though it is utilized in our county of Pennsylvania during times of flooding.

But, I digress. Returning to lasagna, the beef version has been served to most of our European friends. I usually start making the sauce in the morning and give it time to cook as we cruise the waterways. This dish comes in handy when serving a large group, approximately 12. On one occasion in France seated around the table were friends from Ireland, England, France, and New Zealand. Our boat table was not large enough so we did carry-out to the home of Jo Parfitt, the boatyard owner. Over the years, Jo has often provided the dining space, along with liquid refreshments, for our carry-in meals. I also remember that it was raining that evening and recall each gentleman in the party coming to our boat under umbrella to carry one course or another to the dining table. Somehow the rainy evening added to the fun of the party.

BEEF LASAGNA

1 pound Italian sausage, mild
½ pound ground beef
½ cup onion
2 cloves garlic
¼ cup parsley, divided
2 T. sugar
1 T. salt

1½ t. basil
¼ t. pepper
4 cups canned tomatoes, not drained
12 ounces tomato paste
water to cook noodles
12 noodles
1 pound ricotta or cottage cheese

1 egg
½ t. salt
¾ cup Parmesan
¾ cup mozzarella

1. Saute sausage, beef, onion, and garlic for approximately 20 minutes.
2. Add sugar, 1 T. salt, basil, pepper, and half of parsley.
3. Add tomatoes, tomato paste, and ½ cup water.
4. Simmer 1½ hours.
5. Boil lasagna 10 minutes.
6. Mix ricotta, egg, remaining parsley and ½ t. salt.
7. <u>Layer as follows</u> on a 13x9x2" baking dish; bake at 375 degrees for 1 hour.

1. 1½ c. meat sauce
2. 6 noodles
3. ½ of ricotta mixture
4. mozzarella, 1/3 of it
5. meat sauce, 1½ cups
6. Parmesan, 1/3 of it
7. 6 noodles
8. rest of ricotta
9. mozzarella, 1/3 of it
10. meat sauce, 1½ cups
11. Parmesan, 1/3 of it
12. Rest of sauce, mozzarella, and Parmesan.

(Serves 10-12.)

<u>*Grandma's Tip:*</u> I have found it quite helpful to have the layering ingredients in a list as you see above.

You may wish to try the no-boil lasagna. I prefer to use the regular that you boil. In the case of the chicken lasagna recipe included in this book, the use of the no-boil pasta did not turn out to my liking, perhaps because of the lack of moistness The pasta was too chewy and not sufficiently soft.

SEAFOOD LASAGNA

8 lasagna noodles
1 onion, large
2 T. butter
1 (8-ounce) cream cheese, softened
1 egg
1½ cups cream-style cottage cheese
2 T. basil
½ t. salt, ½ t. pepper
2 (10 ¾-ounce) cans cream of mushroom soup
1/3 cup milk
1/3 cup white wine, dry
1 pound prepared shrimp
1 (7 ½-ounce) can crab meat, drained
¼ cup Parmesan
½ cup sharp cheese, shredded

1. Cook noodles for 10 minutes, drain well and arrange half of the noodles to cover bottom of greased 13x9x2" baking dish.
2. Cook onion in butter and add softened cream cheese, egg, cottage cheese, basil, salt and pepper. Spread half onto noodles.
3. Combine soup, milk, and wine.

Stir in shrimp and crab. Spread half over cream cheese mixture.
4. Repeat layer of noodles, cheese mixture, and seafood mixture.
5. Sprinkle with Parmesan cheese.
6. Bake uncovered @ 350 degrees for 45 minutes.
7. Top with the sharp cheese and bake an additional 2 to 3 minutes.
8. Let stand 15 minutes before serving.

(Serves 10 to 12.)

VEGETABLE LASAGNA

2 t. vegetable oil
2 cups fresh broccoli, cut into small pieces
1½ cups carrots. chopped
½ cup red bell pepper, chopped
1/3 cup green onions, chopped
½ cup flour
3 cups 1% milk
½ c. Parmesan, divided
¼ t. salt, ¼ t. pepper
10 ounces frozen, chopped spinach, thawed and chopped
4 ounces mozzarella, shredded
½ cup Swiss cheese, shredded
1½ cups 1% cottage cheese
12 lasagna noodles

1. Saute' in olive oil the broccoli, carrots, pepper, and green onions for 7 minutes.
2. Place flour in a pan and gradually add milk, stirring until blended. Bring to boil over medium heat and cook 5 minutes until thick, stirring constantly.
3. Add ¼ cup Parmesan, salt and pepper and cook an additional 1 minute.
4. Stir in well-drained spinach and remove from heat, reserving ½ cup and set aside.
5. Combine mozzarella, Swiss, and cottage cheese.
6. Spread ½ cup spinach mixture in bottom of greased, 13x9x2" baking dish.
7. Order as follows: 4 noodles, ½ cheese mixture, ½ of vegetable mixture, and half of spinach mixture.
8. Repeat ending with noodles. Add the set-aside ½ cup of spinach on top, then, the ¼ cup of remaining Parmesan.
9. Bake @ 375 degrees for 35 minutes.

(Serves 10 to 12.)

Camping and Cruising in the United States

In more recent times, I have added a fourth lasagna which has become my favorite of the four lasagnas.

CHICKEN LASAGNA

8 ounces lasagna noodles
1 (10-3/4-ounce) can cream of chicken soup, undiluted
1 cup canned chicken broth
½ t. salt
6-ounces cream cheese, softened
1 cup cottage cheese
½ cup sour cream
½ cup mayonnaise
1/3 cup onion
1/3 cup green pepper, chopped
1/3 cup pimiento-stuffed olives, quartered
¼ cup fresh parsley
3 cups cooked chicken, bite-size pieces
½ cup dry breadcrumbs
1 T. butter, melted

1. Cook lasagna according to package directions. Rinse with cold water, drain well, and set aside.
2. Combine soup, broth, and salt, stirring until smooth; set soup mixture aside.
3. Combine cream cheese, cottage cheese, sour cream, and mayonnaise in a large bowl. Beat at medium speed with an electric mixer 1 minute or until smooth.
4. Stir in onion, green pepper, olives, and parsley—all finely chopped. Set cream cheese mixture aside.
5. Layer half of the well-dried noodles in a lightly-greased 13x9x2-inch baking dish.
6. Add a layer of cream cheese, chicken, and soup mixtures.
7. Repeat layers.
8. Combine breadcrumbs and butter; sprinkle over top.
9. Bake @ 375 degrees for 25 to 30 minutes.

(Serves 10 to 12.)

If you prefer to make the above into two meals for 6 persons each, you can adapt the quantities to fit 2 8-inch square baking pans. It requires a bit more calculating of the quantities that go into each pan but in the end, you have two lasagnas and two evenings' entertainment completed.

This apple dumpling recipe has been in my file for a very long time. My mother introduced me to it. One of the wives attending the amateur radio weekend brought a large tray of similar dumplings. Her adding to the meal was a nice gesture, and I'm sure the guests appreciated having two desserts. While visiting my good friend, Carla, in the Netherlands, she and I walked a short distance from her home to a small bakery that specialized in dumplings. They sold to bakeries and restaurants mostly but one could walk in and purchase these delights. What was interesting about them, besides the fact that they were tasty, was the fact that they were cooked and served upside-down, contrary to American style.

Apple Dumpling in Holland

APPLE DUMPLINGS

1½ cups sugar
1½ cups water
¼ t. cinnamon
¼ t. nutmeg
6 to 10 drops red food coloring
3 T. butter
2 cups flour
2 t. baking powder
1 t. salt
2/3 cup shortening
½ cup milk
6 medium apples (I recommend using Granny Smith apples.)

1. Combine sugar, water, spices, and food coloring; bring to boil.
2. Remove from heat; add butter.
3. Mix together the dry ingredients.
4. Cut in shortening until mixture resembles coarse crumbs.
5. Add milk all at once and stir just until flour is moist.
6. Roll on lightly floured surface to ¼-inch thick in 18 x 12-inch rectangle.
7. Cut into 6-inch squares.
8. Place whole, cored apple in each square.
9. Sprinkle each apple generously with additional sugar, cinnamon, and nutmeg. Dot with additional bits of butter.
10. Moisten edges of squares and fold in corners to center and pinch edges together. Place 1-inch apart onto ungreased baking pan.
11. Pour syrup over dumplings; sprinkle with sugar.
12. Bake @ 375 degrees for 35 minutes or until apples are done.
13. Serve warm with whipped cream or vanilla ice cream.

(Serves 6.)

A colleague of mine served a dessert similar to this next recipe in her home for the office staff and instantly, it became a favorite. She served it topped with a cranberry liqueur, but I prefer the chocolate syrup. It serves many and, of course, can be prepared in advance.

I have called the chocolate syrup "dope," because that was what it was called in my Ohio, childhood home. I have not a clue as to why. It can be made with cream as my mother did which makes the dope lovely and thick, or it can be made with varying fat-levels of milk. The flavor is still there but the result is a more liquid-type syrup. Again, its use is limited in our house because of the heavy amount of sugar. But, occasionally, it's a real treat. If serving it to guests, I would suggest using whole milk or cream. It's only when I make it for Hal and me that I substitute fat-free milk.

Be sure to remove the cake from the freezer some minutes before you intend to serve. If not, it will be too hard to slice.

ICE CREAM CAKE WITH CHOCOLATE SYRUP

2 (3-ounce) packages of ladyfingers
2 (9-ounce) packages thin, chocolate wafers
½ gallon vanilla/chocolate ice cream
½ gallon coffee ice cream
chocolate syrup recipe

1. Place the lady fingers on the bottom and sides of a 9" springform pan.
2. Place a layer of chocolate wafers on bottom over the fingers.
3. Layer as follows: half of each ice cream, 1/3 of wafers, then, repeat.
4. In a food processor or using a plastic bag and a rolling pin, mash the remaining wafers. Place crumbs on top of cake.
5. Cover cake with 3 layers of foil and freeze in springform pan overnight or for as long as you wish.
6. To serve, remove from freezer approximately 30 minutes prior to serving or until you can slice into the cake.
7. Top with chocolate syrup, warmed.

(Serves 16 to 18.)

<u>*Grandma's Tip:*</u> If you cannot locate coffee ice cream easily, soften vanilla ice cream sufficiently for mixing purposes and add some strong black coffee until it suits your taste, then, refreeze to desired consistency.

<u>*Grandma's Tip:*</u> If you cannot locate the chocolate wafers, I once substituted chocolate-fudge cookies, separated them, and scraped off the fudge that was in between.

CHOCOLATE SYRUP (DOPE)

¼ cup Hershey cocoa, unsweetened
½ cup sugar
½ cup whole milk or whipping cream (your choice)

1. **Bring the above ingredients to a boil.**
2. **Lower to simmer and frequently stir for 3 minutes.**
3. **Cool to warm stage before serving.**

The following breakfast dish can be prepared easily in a minimalist kitchen. Though we consume this infrequently, we don't feel quite so guilty using this recipe because of the orange juice utilized rather than milk. I have no excuse for the consumption of the Italian bread and the maple syrup. Once in awhile, I figure you are allowed to spoil yourself. It is very important to use butter in this recipe, not margarine. Otherwise, you will end up throwing the pans away. Yes, that once happened to me when entertaining friends in our home—ugh!

FRENCH TOAST
Pain Perdue

½ cup butter (not margarine)
¼ cup honey
2 t. cinnamon
6 eggs
1 cup orange juice
¼ c. sugar
½ t. salt
½ t. cinnamon
16 slices French or Italian bread, sliced and left out for 8 hours or overnight, turned once, if possible.

1. In a small bowl, combine butter, honey, and 2 t. cinnamon. Mix well. If warmed in the microwave for a few seconds, it will pour more easily.
2. Pour mixture evenly into 2 non-greased 15x10x1" baking pans.
3. In medium bowl, slightly beat eggs, orange juice, sugar, salt, and ½ t. cinnamon; mix well.
4. Dip bread in egg mixture.
5. Place on butter mixture in pan. Pour any remaining egg mixture over the bread.
6. Bake @ 400 degrees for 20 minutes, turning halfway through baking.
7. Serve with warmed maple syrup.

This recipe can easily be cut in half.

Margie, my sister-in-law, introduced us to this breakfast casserole, and members of our family now prepare it, especially when preparing for several guests.

BREAKFAST CASSEROLE

12 slices of bread, without crusts and cut into bite-size pieces
1½ cups cubed ham (or cooked sausage or crisply-fried bacon)
1 cup red or green pepper
1/3 cup onion
¾ cup Monterey Jack cheese, shredded
7 eggs
salt to taste
½ t. mustard powder
3 cups whole milk

Camping and Cruising in the United States | 13

1. Grease a 13x9x2" baking dish and place bread pieces in the bottom.
2. Combine chopped ham, chopped green or red pepper, chopped onion, and cheese. Scatter evenly on top of bread.
3. Mix eggs, salt, mustard, and milk. Pour over top. Cover with foil and place in refrigerator overnight.
4. Bake @ 325 degrees for 1 hour to 1 hour, 10 minutes.

(Serves 10 to 12.)

The following breakfast dish is another tasty way to start the morning, especially when serving several. The advantage of this one over the above recipe is that it can be ready for the table more quickly. You can get some of the ingredients ready the night before, and it will take less time in the a.m. to prepare the dish for the oven.

My advice to cooks, not just beginning ones, is to complete as much as possible prior to the guests' arrival. It provides peace of mind and, also, more time to enjoy your company. I once experienced an evening spent visiting with the host and Hal while the hostess prepared dinner in the kitchen. I noticed that she was starting with an uncooked chicken so you can imagine how long she was away from the evening's conversation. She preferred being sequestered in her kitchen and not being disturbed.

EGG CASSEROLE

2 cups seasoned croutons
1½ cups (6 ounces) Cheddar cheese, shredded
6 eggs
2 cups milk (whole, 2%, 1%--your choice)
1/8 t. pepper
½ t. salt
½ t. dry mustard
1/8 t. onion powder

1. Place croutons in greased, baking dish (9x13 or 8x8). For the larger dish, I used 1½ recipes.
2. Sprinkle cheese over croutons.
3. Combine next 6 ingredients. Beat lightly and pour over cheese and croutons.
4. Bake @ 350 degrees for 30 minutes.

(Serves 6 to 8.)

The following Scandinavian dish is a meat loaf wrapped in pastry. The pastry is homemade and takes time. I recommend it for a holiday dinner, maybe the night before Thanksgiving. It's the kind of meal that I would serve to friends visiting over the weekend. It shows that you really care about your dinner and have gone that extra mile. You can prepare much of the dish ahead of time, then put it together prior to baking.

MEAT LOAF IN SOUR CREAM PASTRY
Liihamurekepiiras

Pastry:
2¼ cups flour
1 t. salt
12 T. chilled, unsalted butter, cut into ¼-inch bits
1 egg
¼ cup sour cream (+ additional sour cream for a side dish when serving the meat loaf)
1 T. soft butter

Meat filling:
4 T. butter
¼ c. finely-chopped mushrooms (about ¼ pound fresh mushrooms) or 6.5-ounce can mushrooms, chopped
3 pounds finely ground meat (beef, pork, ham, lamb, or veal or a combination of any of these (approximately 4 cups ground meat)
1/3 cup onion, chopped
¼ cup parsley, finely chopped
1 (10 ¾ ounce) can cream of mushroom soup
¼ cup oatmeal
2 eggs, beaten
1 cup Cheddar cheese or Swiss cheese, grated
½ cup milk
1 egg combined with 2 T. milk

Pastry:
1. Mix the flour and salt together in a large, chilled bowl.
2. Drop the ¼-inch bits of butter into the bowl. Work quickly, using your fingertips to rub the flour and butter together until they have the appearance of flakes of coarse meal.
3. In a separate bowl, mix together the egg and sour cream. Stir the flour into this, then work with your fingers until you can gather the dough into a soft, pliable ball. Make certain that the pastry is smooth and well mixed. Wrap it in wax paper or plastic wrap and refrigerate 1 hour.
4. Cut the chilled dough in half. Placing the dough in a microwave for a few seconds will make it easier to handle. Roll out each half to rectangles of 6x14-inches each, setting aside any scraps. It helps if the pastry for the top half is slightly larger than the bottom.
5. Butter the bottom of a baking sheet with 1 T. soft butter. Lift one sheet of the pastry over the rolling pin, lift it up and unfold it into the pan.

Meat filling:
1. Melt the 4 T. butter in a 10x12-inch skillet. When the foam subsides, add the chopped mushrooms, (drained if using canned) and cook them over moderate heat, stirring frequently for 6 to 8 minutes, or until they are slightly colored. Add meat to the skillet and cook, stirring occasionally, for another 8 to 10 minutes, or until the meat loses its red color and any accumulated liquid in the pan cooks completely away. Drain off

any liquid remaining. Place the meat mixture into a large mixing bowl. Stir in the chopped onions, parsley, mushroom soup, oatmeal, 2 eggs, cheese, and milk.
2. Gather the meat mixture into a ball and place it in the center of the dough in the pan. With your hands, pat the meat into a narrow loaf extending across the center of the dough from one end to the other.
3. Lift the second sheet of pastry over the meat mixture and gently drape it on top. Press the edges of the 2 sheets together.
4. Dip a pastry brush into the combined egg and milk mixture and moisten the edges of the dough. Press down on the edges all around the loaf with the back of a fork. Prick the top of the loaf in several places with a fork to allow steam to escape.
5. Roll out the pastry scraps and cut into interesting shapes such as leaves; brush the leaves, also.
6. Bake @ 375 degrees for 45 minutes or until the loaf has turned a golden brown.
7. Serve thick slices of the hot meat loaf, accompanied by a bowl of cold sour cream.

(Serves 12.)

Our dear friends, Doc and Reube Moorehead from our home neighborhood in Pennsylvania, were called back from New Mexico to run a family restaurant which they managed for 25 years, ending their main careers--he, a veterinarian; she, a nurse. One of their contributions to our gatherings was the following Mexican chili con queso.

CHILI CON QUESO

1 pound ground beef
¼ cup green onions
1 cup tomato sauce
4 ounces green chilies, chopped
1 t. Worcestershire sauce
16 ounces processed American cheese
garlic powder, dash

1. Brown beef; drain.
2. Add chopped green onions; cook over low heat till tender; do not brown.
3. Add tomato sauce, chilies, Worcestershire sauce, and cheese.
4. Cook until cheese melts.
5. Serve in chafing dish or slow cooker over low heat with tortilla chips on the side.

From the Young family, I obtained one of my favorite cookie recipes. My mother-in-law would often put a container of these into our car as we headed across country. I have not come across anything similar to these cookies and they have a flavor all their own. They stay chewy on the inside and crisp on the outside for a long time. I cannot have just one. Before eating, I like zapping them in the microwave for a few seconds;

makes them even more yummy.

You must use shortening. I tried using margarine once and the result was a failure, one of my "ughs:"

COCONUT COOKIES

1 cup flour
½ t. salt
½ t. baking soda
½ cup shortening (not margarine)
1 cup sugar
1 egg
1 t. vanilla extract
1 cup quick oats
1 cup coconut
½ cup nuts, optional

1. Mix flour, salt, and baking soda.
2. Cream the shortening and sugar together. Add to flour mixture.
3. Add 1 beaten egg and the vanilla extract.
4. Stir in the quick oats, coconut, and chopped nuts. I use one hand as dough is thick.
5. Drop by teaspoons on greased and floured baking sheet.
6. Bake @ 350 degrees for 12 to 15 minutes.
7. Remove from sheet at once.

(Makes 36.)

Margie spent a good many months of the year camping and, therefore, is very competent at preparing food at the campground, as well as in her own home. She and Lynn raised five sons. Even after the boys had moved out of the house, they continued to come around for mom's good cooking. They would bring their wives and children and friends so the number around the dinner table had grown from five to many more. One evening when we were visiting them, a son and his family stopped by around 9 p.m. They had not eaten so Margie proceeded to charcoal them steaks. This openness continues to this day, though it is not quite so frequent as in years back. Still, at Thanksgiving the granddaughters say they like Grandma's noodles or Grandma's broccoli dish and every other dish she prepares, and they ask to stay home and not go to a restaurant.

Margie's tasty marinade is always our preferred choice for barbecuing steak. Without sounding too opinionated, I prefer using a high-quality steak, such as Porterhouse, T-bone, or New York Strip. We have pretty much given up on ordering steak when in France. Occasionally, we have been known to break down and give their steak another try. Even when dining in a top-rated restaurant where President Mitterand was known to have visited during summers, the steak was too tough to enjoy. Every other item served in restaurants is usually topnotch, quite exceptional, but the steak continues to be a disappointment. We must have tried steak at least on ten occasions to be able to make this declaration. A friend of ours who ordered steak in a nice Paris restaurant when six of us were dining together said that the steak should be chewy. Go figure.

MARINADE FOR GRILLED STEAK

¼ cup soy sauce
1/8 t. garlic powder
¼ cup water
1/8 t. black pepper
1 T. salad oil
1 t. hot sauce
1 T. brown sugar

1 T. lemon juice

1. Place all ingredients and steak in a closable plastic bag; mix well; refrigerate for at least 30 minutes.
2. Turn the steaks over, at least once.

(Quantity is enough for 4 to 6 medium-size steaks.)

Keep it Simple – Some foods require little addition to them. For example, vegetables are often more tasty if just a tad of butter or margarine and some salt are added. Lobster would be another food that takes little in the way of spices or sauces, just butter and salt. In my opinion, fresh vegetables and certain seafood do not require much in the way of additional ingredients.

However, there are times when you wish to make your vegetable a bit more exciting. One favorite dish of mine can be made ahead and is especially appreciated when one is at the campsite about to light the grill for a barbecue. This is a good accompaniment. A comparable recipe is served at the village church when folks from the surrounding neighborhood gather for a potluck dinner.

LIMA BEANS IN TOMATO SAUCE

4 strips bacon
2 medium onions
1 green pepper
1½ cups canned tomatoes
2 cups cooked lima beans
1 T. sugar
½ t. salt

1. Fry bacon in a skillet; remove bacon, cut into bite-size pieces. Set aside. Return 2 T. bacon fat to skillet.
2. Slice onions and green pepper thinly and cook in bacon fat or vegetable spray until onion is transparent.
3. Add chopped tomatoes and simmer 5 minutes.
4. Add lima beans, bacon, sugar, and salt; cook on low heat for 20 minutes.

(Serves 4.)

In many of my recipes, I substitute turkey bacon. If you do, spray the skillet with vegetable spray as little fat is produced when frying turkey bacon.

Another vegetable that we eat often, usually just salted with a tiny bit of butter, is Brussels sprouts. I prepare most of my vegetables in the microwave using a dish especially made for vegetables. However, I occasionally give this vegetable some added attention.

The recipe can be halved and will make three large servings.

BRUSSELS SPROUTS WITH ONION AND BACON

6 cups Brussels sprouts
6 bacon strips
1 medium-size onion or leek
salt and pepper, to taste
2 T. olive oil
1 garlic clove, crushed
1 T. red wine vinegar
2 T. dried parsley

1. Remove ends of Brussels sprouts and cut sprouts in half. Place sprouts and onion slices in microwave dish that holds water in the bottom. Microwave until tender, around 8 to10 minutes. Check for the amount of tenderness that you want. Drain well.
2. Fry bacon or microwave bacon between paper towels until crisp. Cut bacon into bite-size pieces. Set aside.
3. In a skillet, brown Brussels sprouts, onion slices, and garlic in olive oil or a combination of oil and a bit of bacon fat until heated through and somewhat brown. Add salt and pepper to taste but little salt will be needed because of the vinegar. Remove from skillet.
4. Add bacon pieces, vinegar, and parsley.

(Serves 4.)

II

Building Our First Boat in England: Cruising in England and on the Continent

The classroom has been left behind.
Now, my work calls for more muscle.
Sanding and painting require less from my mind.
But more get up and go—hustle, hustle.

BOAT NO. 1 PENNSYLVANIA YANKEE

Home is where you hang your hat. My home for most months of the last thirty years has been afloat on a boat. We did purchase a small camping tent on wheels in England and utilized it as both a camper and a flat trailer on which to carry boat supplies. Since we spend part of each year in the U.S. and part of it in Europe, it is difficult to pin us down. In fact, I find it confusing at times myself to separate the two lives. Over the years, our time in Europe has been variable. When we are into building a boat, we have remained for longer periods of time, returning to the U.S. for a few weeks twice each year to see family and to schedule medical appointments. During other years, we have often visited in Europe from three-to-five months, then, spent the rest of the year somewhere in the U.S.

While first traveling in England back in the early 80's, we visited some 30 boatyards to see where we would be able to complete a steel shell of a narrowboat. We traveled in a friend's French Citroen Ami 6. We were on a very limited budget at the time and were staying four weeks in a Bed and Breakfast in Stratford-upon-Avon. We were given a hearty English breakfast (sausage or bacon, eggs, baked tomato, fried mushrooms, etc.), had a simple snack for our lunch, and cooked the evening meal in our automobile. Our funds were limited because we were helping to support daughters Diana and Sarah through university.

Knowing that we would be staying in England on a limited budget, we brought along with us an adaptation of a gas swing stove that we had used when sailing in the U.S.

Hal built a holder for this stove so that it would rest on the floor of the car. There was ample room to set the stove between the two front seats. Thus, we were able to purchase our evening meal ingredients, thereby eating for a lot less than had we needed to dine in restaurants. We would find an interesting spot in the country and/or looking out on a body of water, watch the sun set, and dine in comfort. Though we weren't supposed to bring food into the bed–and-breakfast room, we managed to put a bit of washing-up items into a bag and washed a few dishes in the lavatory sink, without causing any conflict with the manager. We eventually became good friends with the owner and his family and were invited to share Boxing Day (the day after Christmas) with them. We were treated to a roast beef and Yorkshire pudding meal, then, taken out to the country to observe an English foxhunt. We felt very lucky to have participated in a true representation of an English holiday, though in recent years foxhunts have been banned.

This is one of our favorite dishes that we prepared in the car. We continue to prepare this dish wherever we are and have served it frequently to our guests, when we needed to produce a simple meal. It's great for cooking at the campsite. Our friend, Doc, was served this on an RV trip we took with him and Reube to Arizona from Pennsylvania, and he not only raved about it once but continued to repeat how tasty a dish it was. He probably just appreciated being away from the restaurant and having someone else prepare the meal. We gave it the name of *Soul Food*, which stuck over the years; and its meaning is basically that of a real down-to-earth, one-skillet dish.

ROAST BEEF HASH
Soul Food

3 T. butter and oil combination
1 (12-ounce) can corned beef
3 cups of potatoes, cooked and diced
1 medium onion, chopped
1/8 t. pepper

1. **Fry cooked potatoes and onions together in butter and oil until crispy.**
2. **Add the corned beef just long enough for it to be heated. The corned beef will replace any need for salt.**

(Serves 4 to 6.)

<u>Grandma's Tip:</u> If you are in a hurry and do not have cooked potatoes in the refrigerator, you can cook them in their skins in the microwave, then, finish them in the skillet. Or, you can slice the raw potatoes thinly and fry them prior to moving forward with the recipe.

In order to introduce a popular English favorite to our friends and family who have not been to England, I have occasionally put together Cornish pasties. I remember from 1981 our first taste of these when we were traveling by automobile through the southwest part of England, Cornwall to be exact. We had a week or two of free time on our hands before our order for a boat shell would be ready and chose to see parts of England we would not be able to see from the inland waterways. We stopped at a small factory near Polperro that was making these pasties that also had a carry-out business. We went in and placed an order for two. They smelled so good that we got into them before departing from the factory parking lot. They went down so well and tasted so good that we had to go back in and order more.

I have put together the following recipe based on what we remembered from that experience plus listening to my English friends. Some cooks include shredded carrots in the pasties but that is not how we remembered them.

Centuries back, mine workers in England would carry these pasties in their lunch boxes. I've been told that sometimes the pasties included the meat pie ingredients at one end and sweet ingredients, like apples, at the other.

PORTABLE MEAT PIES
Cornish Pasties

Pastry:
2 1/2 cups flour
1/4 t. salt
1 t. baking powder
1/2 cup butter
1/2 cup water

Filling:
1 1/2 cups lean beef, bite-size pieces
1 1/2 cups of red potatoes, diced
3/4 cup turnips, diced
3/4 cup onions, chopped
½ t. salt
1 t. pepper
1 t. marjoram, dried
1 t. thyme. dried
1 t. parsley, dried
2 T. butter
1 egg

1. Mix flour, salt, and baking powder. Rub in butter until coarse crumbs.
2. Stir in water. Divide pastry into 10 balls.
3. Roll pastry into 6-inch rounds.
4. Mix first 9 filling ingredients.
5. Heap ¼ cup of filling in each center. Dot top with ½ t. butter.
6. Brush edges with warm water and fold pasty over filling to make half-moon shapes. Press seams by hand, then, with fork to seal. Cut a small slit in the top of each.
7. Brush with beaten egg.
8. On ungreased baking sheet, bake @ 400 degrees for 10 minutes. Reduce to 350 degrees for 20 to 30 minutes.
9. Cool on rack 5 minutes.

(Makes 10.)

Not always were my attempts at serving foreign dishes to family totally appreciated. I remember a nephew after having a bite of my *country pate* saying that it tasted like meat loaf. In a way I suppose he was right but I had certainly gone to more trouble to prepare the appetizer. I never bothered to fix it again. *Country pate* is something we like to purchase or order in a restaurant occasionally when traveling in France.

But, I am getting ahead of myself. Where we begin is you find Hal and me saying goodbye to immediate family members, relatives and friends. Hal retired at age 49 ½ and I resigned at age 43. His rationale for such an early retirement was based upon observing fellow employees in the education field who would work until age 65 and beyond. Unfortunately, several of his fellow workers became terminally ill and were never able to enjoy their retirement years. He participated in a retirement seminar and concluded that, given careful control of living expenses, we could manage. It was a difficult choice for me at the time, but it did not take long for me to switch gears and participate fully in our endeavors.

In 1980, our initial departure from the U.S. brought us back within the week. We had spent months preparing to sail Sea Quester to Europe. Regarding food, we organized meals from cans and stored some 57 meals. After three days at sea, we held a staff meeting and decided to turn back.

Our second departure from the U.S. in November, 1980 took us to England by air. Our destination is a small community called Evesham. The largest city from our marina is Worcester, the home of Worcestershire china and its well-known sauce. I often wonder what percentage of homes in this world has a bottle of the Worcestershire sauce in their cupboards.

The happy captain sitting in the shell

We have located a boatyard where we will begin a mammoth project. We are taking an order for a canal boat, a 7-foot wide and 46-foot-long steel shell. The width is limited to 7 feet because of the narrow locks in central England; the length can be as much as 72 feet. There are large holes in the steel designating the windows, the doors, and the engine area and lockers. Hal had given the boat builder the dimensions for windows and doorways, designating both port and starboard and left and right, but when the steel shell was delivered, the window locations had been reversed. The information had not been carefully followed. But that has absolutely nothing to do with food; it's just an interesting situation that caused Hal some rethinking and designing. After all, you cannot send the steel shell back for redoing—at least that would not be an easy option. This half of the pair is just slightly involved in the design details but will be sharing the work responsibilities. We're over the moon with excitement, the beginning of another stage in our lives.

Our first 2 nights in Evesham were spent staying in a local hotel because the boatyard owner who runs a hireboat company did not have an empty rental boat in which we could temporarily live. I must backtrack just a bit. Our explorations are now over and the Original Boat Company is where we'll be hanging our hat this summer. The owners are Roger and Tere Davis. He is English and has spent most of his working life on boats; Tere was a teacher of English from Buenos Aires.

She had married into the situation; it does happen. Most people when they decide to become a couple end up adapting to a somewhat-changed lifestyle—some of us perhaps more than others. They met while Roger was working in the Falkland Islands and she was teaching there. They were most welcoming from the beginning so we will be able to stay on task but at the same time, save money. We will move our luggage and portable typewriter from one unoccupied hireboat to another but all kitchen necessities and bedding come with the hireboats, so it is similar to moving into a different self-catering accommodation each week. Notice that it was not a notepad or laptop that we were moving but a typewriter. Settling down in this case is a relative term, as each week we needed to move. This we did until our shell was livable. That, too, is a relative term.

At the same time, we enjoy the sounds and sights of living by the water. The boatyard is on the shore of the Avon River. Later I learn that this Avon is one of three in England. This is the one which runs from its southern tip in the city of Tewkesbury and north to Stratford-upon-Avon where many Americans vacation as it was Shakespeare's home. The Shakespeare Theater draws many visitors each season.

In the evenings after a long day's work, we are able to watch the swans attempt their flights over the weir next to the lock house, listen to the ripples of the water against our hull, awaken to rain on the roof—all delightful sounds that mooring on the water can provide. Yes, it does rain in England, on occasion. The green pastures, so noticeable the first time I arrived in England, need a lot of watering to develop.

This May, 1981, however, finds us able to work most days in good weather. The puffy white clouds appearing against the bright blue, watercolor sky make us feel even more cheerful. And, our first day of work sees us putting bank gravel into the bed of the boat. That's our ballast to make us ride on the water with stability. Having been on many boats, we knew that some craft could be tipsy while others hardly moved when you stepped aboard. The correct amount of ballast is important. Hal is wheel-barrowing the stone to the edge of the river and shoveling it through a window hole and I am spreading it about the floor of the boat, trying to make it as even as possible. The real test of our labors will come one day when six or so adults can stand on one side of the deck and the engineer declares the angle of movement meets a certain standard. Keep shoveling.

In order to use the tools of the trade and avoid huge expenditures, we helped the yard owners turn their boats around each week. Government regulations do not allow us to be paid in monetary funds for our labors, as it is necessary to keep the English citizens employed. As a result, we were given access to the boatyard tools in place of English pounds. I helped by making certain that all inventory was in good form and accounted for when folks returned in their hire-boats. Hal assisted with guiding the new arrivals, acclimating them to the workings of a canal boat. Sometimes Hal found that it was necessary to explain that the pointy end was at the front. Many rental people, however, had some knowledge of how to run a boat and took to it immediately. Hal enjoyed this part of his assignment, teaching and getting to know the people. One other task was emptying the refuse hold of the boat. As he said, somebody had to do it. There were thirteen boats in the fleet, half departing on Saturday and half, on Sunday but usually one or two were not rented. After moving our belongings to another boat and seeing that all jobs were finished, around 9 p.m. on most sunny-and-warm Saturdays and Sundays you could find the owners and us sitting outside by the river having a barbecue. It doesn't get dark until around 10 p.m. These outdoor dinners occurred most every weekend. Rain was not falling on us much that Spring.

Barbecues with Roger and Tere lasted for several hours and included the basic meat course, along with several vegetables. There was always a sweet as the English refer to desserts and the evening began and ended with good wine. Sometimes we bought New York or California wines from the local wine shop and often, the Davis's served their favorite Argentinean wine. A relative of theirs owned a line of freighters and did business between Argentina and England. The captain would deliver wine to the boatyard with his car boot full of wine cases. (I like to throw an English word or two out occasionally just to emphasize that differences in our English do exist and, also, to keep you alert.)

Now I am not a huge fan of lamb for two reasons. I think that there is insufficient meat on the lamb chop to make it worthwhile preparing and eating and secondly, I don't like to recall how the young animal was treated and butchered. This is not a subject that I wish to pursue as my arguments are not sufficiently strong enough to keep me from eating fish and chicken and other animals. The good news is that Roger couldn't get enough of the lamb so he graciously traded me his "bangers" for my lamb. Bangers in England are between a sausage and an American hot dog and usually include both pork and beef. I liked them as much as Roger liked his lamb and I can still recall the gorgeous flavor. Gorgeous as a word to describe food came from our English friend, Muriel Gealer.

One of the vegetable dishes that I contributed to the barbecues came from an English newspaper. It was different from anything we had eaten back in the U.S. and everyone seemed to enjoy it. I continue to make this recipe, sometimes as a side dish but very often as a main course.

BAKED CAULIFLOWER

1 large head cauliflower
¼ t. nutmeg
½ cup breadcrumbs, fresh
½ t. salt
2¾ cups Swiss cheese, shredded
1½ cups half-half
3 egg yolks
¼ cup melted butter

1. Wash cauliflower; break into flowerets. Cook 10 minutes in small amounts of boiling water.
2. **Place cauliflower in greased, shallow baking dish.**
3. **Combine remaining ingredients except butter; pour over cauliflower.**
4. **Drizzle butter over top.**
5. **Bake @ 350 degrees for 15-20 minutes.**

(Serves 6.)

When living on the Falkland Islands, Tere Davis found eggs were hard to come by so this dessert was a popular choice. However, we think it's good anywhere and who said that an egg was necessary to make a cake-like dessert. Serve this warm with some pouring cream or ice cream—after you've completed your jogging.

During the baking, the cake mixture rises to the top and the chocolate sauce settles to the bottom. Invert a serving square of pudding onto dessert plates. Dip sauce from pan over each.

HOT FUDGE PUDDING

1 cup flour
2 t. baking powder
¼ t. salt
¾ cup sugar
2 T. Hershey cocoa powder
½ cup milk
2 T. melted shortening
1 cup nuts, chopped

1 cup light brown sugar
4 T. Hershey cocoa powder
1¾ cups hot water

1. **Mix the flour, baking powder, salt, sugar and 2 T. cocoa.**
2. **Stir in ½ cup milk and 2 T. melted shortening.**

3. Blend in 1 cup nuts.
4. Spread into 9" square baking pan.
5. Sprinkle with brown sugar and 4 T. cocoa
6. Pour the hot water over the entire batter.
7. Bake @ 350 degrees for 45 minutes.
8. Serve warm with whipped cream or vanilla ice cream.

(Serves 8.)

So, the summer work proceeded as planned. We met lots of interesting people in the region, kept to our rigorous workday, and were occasionally invited for a meal to people's homes. We learned to shop for supplies in all kinds of stores and basically became familiar with the culture and ways of a typical town in middle England. Usually Hal needed to stay on task so part of my responsibilities was running errands for boat supplies and the groceries. That sounded easy enough, especially since we spoke the same language. At least I thought I did until I began exchanging words with the local ironmonger (hardware) clerk. I was embarrassed to have to ask him to repeat his comments until I understood. He was probably having the same reaction. I once sat next to a woman in a laundry in Dudley near Birmingham, and I could not understand any of her comments, seriously, not one. I often nodded and used nonverbal gestures, hoping I was agreeing to the right thing. People often told me about their trips to Florida and New York City, and Pennsylvania was where?

Dining at a restaurant during this early part of our retirement was not a part of our budget. I recall going to a pizza restaurant when we were visiting the many boatyards in central England. We were in Stratford-upon-Avon at the time. We ordered pizza topped with chicken and eggs. We had not come upon this kind of topping before; since then we often see pizza served with eggs in France, as well. The pizza was served to us just lukewarm. Since it was the only meal out for a very long time and we were celebrating my earning a graduate degree, we called for the waiter and asked that the pizza be returned for additional heating. It was important to me to enjoy the meal to the fullest and I dislike food that is not heated properly. After all, we would not be enjoying another restaurant meal for months.

In 1981, we were proud in every way to be an American. It became a bit different in more recent times when Americans traveling in Europe were warned to be watchful and alert to possible trouble. Our image had changed, people reacted differently, questions were posed about our country's leadership but here again, I am getting off the subject and into another topic. Hopefully, in time, we will be considered a friendlier nation, and we will feel comfortable flying the American flag again. That's another story.

Hal has the practical ability to design and build and repair. He attended Baltimore Polytechnic Institute high school in Maryland where he learned some basic engineering skills, and he also picked up pointers from his father and maternal grandfather. He is often asked where he got his skills, especially when they learn that his career was a primary school headmaster, (principal). In our boat building, he is the one who plans the layout along with my minor suggestions; he is the one in charge of planning for the plumbing and heating; he is the one who selects the type of engine and how it will be installed, with assistance now and then from the professionals. And, I might add with assistance from the first mate. One cannot easily hold up a 4 by 8-foot sheet of plywood by himself while at the same time nailing it in place. In fact, there are many jobs that require an extra hand when dealing with window fitting, electrical wiring, plumbing, etc. For another fact, I'm wondering how I fitted in my other responsibilities. An "extra or hired hand" was what my father called a man who worked on the farm. First mate sounds more professional. I didn't arrive at this point in my life without some building skills. I had helped build a modular vacation home that sat on a sloping river's edge, and I applied most of the cedar roof shingles as well. I also worked alongside Hal as we built our small house in Pennsylvania on another slope, this time looking out at the Allegheny mountain ridge. Now, I have moved from land to water and I'm in charge of painting the boat inside and out, varnishing, and minor carpentry tasks.

After some instruction, I can handle certain rather sophisticated wood-working equipment and boat-building tasks. One of my first assignments was to measure, cut to fit, and glue sheets of Styrofoam wall insulation. The sheets were around 1-inch thick and in some places on the boat, the insulation needed to be as thick as 4 inches. This keeps the boat warm in the cool months and cool in the warm months. In all four other boats we have built, the insulation was sprayed on by a professional. What took me three weeks in 1981 can be done these days in one-half day. The insulation makes a huge difference which reminds me of another story. It's not that I did a poor job of insulating the first boat, (of course, not) but the professional system of spraying covers more efficiently. When visiting a city in France in our second boat, we noticed how much less we heard the noisy lorry (truck) traffic crossing overhead than we had heard during our previous visit in boat number one.

Hal first learned about narrowboats from an article in National Geographic magazine, a copy his mother had passed on to him knowing of his interest in cruising. He had also been involved in walking the canals of Washington, D.C. with a group from the American Canal Society who volunteered to keep the towpaths clear of debris. We brought with us his experience as a sea scout, our individual cruising experiences plus the past few years in which we had cruised together on the Intracoastal Waterway in the U.S. from Maine to Florida.

We named our new boat Pennsylvania Yankee, pulling from a well-known seaman, Irving Johnson, who had sailed the world aboard Yankee and written books about the canals of Europe. We had heard this gentleman lecture about his travels on the canals and rivers, and it was added encouragement for us to find out what it entailed. Hal was eager to get started on his retirement years, so much so that when I met him, six years before he ended his career, he was carrying a paper in his jacket pocket, similar to a grocery tape, that listed the months and years to retirement. I found out how quickly six years can pass. I was, also, learning how organized Hal was in planning for retirement years.

When it did rain in Evesham, we used that time to run the many errands necessary to keep our project going. And, when the weather was good we progressed on the exterior work. Very near the beginning of my painting of the exterior, Roger came by Pennsylvania Yankee. He didn't think that I was painting at an acceptable rate so he climbed upon the roof where I was adding a bright orange color. Our narrowboat was painted in an English traditional way. We liked the hire-boat color scheme so much that we followed it. Roger took my paint bucket, tipped some paint from it onto the roof. From that moment on I don't recall what was said or how I reacted. However, we remain very good friends to this day and often laugh about the incident.

Painting the exterior of a boat was new to me. The spectacular finish on some narrowboats is unbelievable. The paint used at the OBC yard was a coach paint and was put on using a very high-quality, sable brush. When you compared the brushed finish with boats that were spray-painted, you could hardly tell the difference. Before the dark blue finish on the sides of the boat was declared done, I had added seven coats, starting with primer and sanding and filling after the first coats and sanding after each coat. I had three "experts" on whom I called for advice. There was Hal, of course,

Pennsylvania Yankee at Worcester

and Roger, and a third party, the carpenter. The carpenter was working in the boatyard during the day but specialized in furniture making—which later became his full-time work. He had first-class expectations for anything he tackled. If I was questioning whether or not to begin the enamel coats or to redo another coat of primer, he was the one who would say, "I think you better give it one more round." Roger would say that I should proceed on to the next coat and Hal, with his advice, was somewhere in the middle. I will brag a bit by saying that when Pennsylvania Yankee approached another boatyard later in her cruising, I was offered a job painting boats. Since then, I have gotten less particular about the painting of hulls and the carpenter is not around to encourage better results. But, here again, I'm ahead of my story. Before I leave the carpenter, though, I must report that he went on to build replicas of antique furniture, fabricating 4-poster beds for clients in London, returned to earn a college education, and taught at an institution of higher learning.

Along with the painting and the fitting of insulation, I learned to fabricate curtain hangers out of mahogany, using a band saw. Hal showed me how to make the first one and, then it was up to me to make a dozen or more. Once we got the windows in place, I fitted the rubber seal around them, not a difficult task but one that helped to move the production line forward. Just this simple task was a break from the sanding and painting.

It was always a joy to take a few hours' leave from our long workday. On one occasion, we invited the carpenter and his wife to a pub half-way between their home and our boat. We had a pub lunch followed by a very tasty dessert. This is very English and very sweet and don't bother to figure the possible number of calories. My mother had seen to it that her family had many opportunities to partake at the dessert table and, as a result, desserts continue to be appreciated.

STICKY TOFFEE PUDDING

8 ounces dates, finely chopped (1¼ cups packed)
1 cup boiling water
½ cup unsalted butter, room temperature
1 cup light brown sugar
4 eggs
1¾ cups self-rising flour
2 T. instant coffee granules
1 t. baking soda
powdered sugar
whipping cream
caramel sauce (See below.)

1. Butter a 9" spring-form pan. Line with wax paper and butter the paper.
2. Placed chopped dates in small bowl. Pour boiling water over dates and let cool, about one hour. Set aside.
3. Using a mixer, beat butter and sugar in large bowl.
4. Add 2 eggs, one at a time.
5. Add half of flour and beat to blend
6. Add remaining 2 eggs, one at a time.
7. Add remaining flour and beat until blended.
8. Combine coffee and baking soda in small bowl. Pour into date mixture, stirring to dissolve coffee.
9. Add date mixture to cake mixture and beat to blend.
10. Pour into prepared pan.
11. Bake @ 350 degrees about 1 hour or until knife comes out clean.
12. Cool until warm. Unmold. Sprinkle with sugar. Cut into wedges.
13. Serve with caramel sauce and whipped cream.

Caramel Sauce:
2 cups whipping cream
1 cup dark brown sugar
¼ cup unsalted butter

1. Stir all sauce ingredients frequently while bringing to a boil. Then, simmer about 15 minutes.
2. Cover and refrigerate; re-warm to use.

(Serves 10 to 12.)

We both knew how to put in a good day's work and one afternoon, while I was standing on the narrow deck of the boat sanding the side, a gentleman approached and asked, "Do the two of you ever take any time off?" He was a local man and he and his wife and two young children lived nearby; they had their own private boat in the marina. He asked if we would like to come to dinner at their house. In the end, we borrowed an Austin Mini pickup truck from Roger and headed out into the Cotswold area. As we followed the map of directions, we soon realized that we were not going to a typical home. We approached a long lane leading up a hill on which stood a small chateau. We learned later that Prince Charles had been looking at

Loading up for our first guests

property in this same vicinity. The family was very welcoming and we were given the royal treatment. Unfortunately, no notes were taken of the evening and memory does not serve me well. I do recall that the fireplace was larger than any I had ever seen in someone's home. The children were put to bed before we gathered at the dining table. When the evening was over, we returned to our little truck. It would not start so the husband helped push us away from the castle; he must have gotten some insight and had a few chuckles, as well, about the lives of others.

Our months flew by quickly that first summer in England. By October, the plan was to welcome our first American guests, fellow boaters from Maryland. The night before their arrival, we had our first harsh words since beginning the project. The boat was in chaos but a bit of persuasiveness (Hal would call it nagging.) produced fantastic rewards. Cushions were borrowed from the Davis's inventory and tools and pieces of our own inventory of goods were stored temporarily off the boat. By the time our friends arrived, Pennsylvania Yankee was looking presentable.

Our friends also appreciate good food, and they enjoyed our visit to the local market. I remember they were eager to taste the tongue that they saw in the shop window. Neither Hal nor I had ever eaten tongue, but we joined by including it in our lunch menu. You will not find tongue as an ingredient in any of the recipes in this book. It has always been my proclamation, however, that one should taste new foods and have a positive attitude about trying something different. That spurs me on to experience what other people in different countries eat and enjoy.

My introduction to the following dish came aboard Roger and Tere's narrowboat. Tere put this dish together for the arrival of Hal's mother and aunt who had come to visit us for a couple of weeks. Hal's mother was 78 and his aunt, 87; his aunt had never had a passport before.

Buying pumpkins in England, at least back in the early 80's, was difficult. The only place we could find one was at a garden center of a large city. This lovely dish comes to the table inside a warmed pumpkin shell. It makes such a beautiful statement while at the same time delivers a good combination of many flavors. This is definitely a winner for that October weekend when autumn is knocking at the door.

BEEF STEW IN A PUMPKIN
Carbonada

dab of butter and oil combination
2 onions, chopped
2 tomatoes, chopped
1 green pepper, chopped
3 corn-on-the-cob or 1 medium-sized can of corn
2 potatoes, diced
2 sweet potatoes, diced
pieces of pumpkin, taken from inside a medium-size pumpkin with a cut-out at the top (The amount is dependent upon how much you can remove easily from the pumpkin's interior. The quantity is flexible. You want enough to add the pumpkin flavor and, also, bulk to your dish.)
3 small pears, ripe, but firm, cut into bite-size pieces
3 fresh peaches, cut into bite-size pieces
paprika, to taste
salt, to taste
sugar, to taste
1 pound beef, cubed
enough stock to cover
2 T. flour or cornstarch

1. Fry in butter-oil combination, the chopped onions, tomatoes, and green pepper. Cook until tender.
2. Add all the other ingredients except the beef. Season with paprika, salt, and sugar.
3. Add the meat and cover with stock.
4. Cook for 1 hour or until beef is tender.
5. Before serving, add 2 T. of flour or cornstarch to thicken. To avoid lumps, take a cup of the liquid from the pan and stir in the flour, then, return this to the rest of the pan.
6. Clear interior of pumpkin leaving at least a wall thick enough to keep the pumpkin sturdy. Place pumpkin shell in oven to warm, just a few minutes being careful not to leave it in too long—just long enough to warm the interior of the pumpkin, about 5 minutes.
7. Add mixture to inside of pumpkin shell and bring to the table.

(Serves 6.)

One of the reasons for traveling is to learn about the likenesses and differences among people from other regions. Food is a huge part of our lives and in all my years since the beginning 80's, I have reaped much pleasure not only in visiting with foreign people but also by observing people's lifestyles and experiencing their serving of meals. Take the word tea, as an example. In England, we were invited to a home of friends; they said we should come for tea. We were to arrive after the husband had returned from work. We weren't sure what that meant; it could be that we would be served a cup of tea with biscuits (cookies) or we could be joining them for an early evening meal. Depending where you were, we found that tea meant different things to different people. We still aren't definite on the meaning including the use of the term, proper tea.

We were so excited about our new boat that we chose to remain in England for that first winter. While it turned out to be a super time, very early in the season we found ourselves all wrapped in white and frozen in along the canal near Birmingham, England's second largest city. It was written in the newspaper that England was experiencing its worst winter in one-hundred years. We ended up moored in the suburban area, Sandwell, which we got to know quite well. We were stopped in this one place for three weeks over Christmas and New Year's. Hal rewired Christmas lights for our 12-volt system, and we put up a small, artificial tree. I prepared a traditional English Christmas cake which gets a marzipan topping. Hal removed the handles from our pressure cooker so I could bake the cake in the oven. We had the usual holiday dinner including English bread pudding.

The good news is that there was a coal yard next door as well as a factory. We burned coal in a small stove for our heat. One morning around 8:30 a gentleman knocked on our door. Hal was still in bed. The gentleman asked if we would like to come to the company's Christmas party. He worked across the way at a steel company that also had a plant in New Jersey. They had noticed us and our situation and probably, also, noticed the American flag. I said that I would discuss the invitation with my husband and get back to him. Well, come the day of the event, we dressed in our best and off we went. We guessed that we would be attending a party with everyone in the plant, probably around punch bowls and other holiday nibbles. Wrong. We were guided into a dining room where a white tablecloth covered one large table. The chairman of the company sat at the head of the table; he rang for service from his seat. There were some eight or ten executives seated with us. Most of the conversation centered around our cruising in England. At the conclusion of the meal, we were presented with Christmas gifts. We couldn't believe how wonderful they had been to us.

This English, sit-down dinner served at this industrial company consisted of the following:

Sangria
Turkey with gravy and dressing
Mashed potatoes, Corn, and Cranberry Sauce
Cranberry Jello
Homemade Mince Pies
Wine

We were iced-in for three weeks plus ten additional days down the cut (canal) later on in Banbury, and we made the best of both situations. On the second unplanned stop, we were moored very near a large supermarket, so we didn't have to trudge through much snow to shop. I spent part of those days typing recipes on a portable typewriter. We have photos to remind us that we were able to walk on the canal.

But, let me take you back to the Evesham boatyard. I want you, the reader, to remember the name Roger Davis. The following carrot cake recipe was a very popular cake on the scene in the U.S. during the 60's and 70's. A very dear workmate of mine gave me the recipe, and I would have no idea how many times I have baked the cake. Years ago, I tried to communicate to her but had no success. I wanted her to know how popular her recipe became. Often I found time in the late afternoon to do some of the food preparations after I had finished my inventory tasks. Hal and Roger were showing newcomers how to run the rental boats and how to properly work the locks, and Tere was busy with the book work. I would prepare a vegetable dish and perhaps a dessert to add to the dinner that always included the meat portions. Carrot cake was served more than once. Over the years of our travels, this recipe got a good workout. It is easy to prepare when living and cooking in tight quarters. If oven space is limited, then, one large baking dish can replace the usual three layers.

This carrot cake has received the greatest reception of any kind of food we have served in the several countries we have visited. A few of our good friends will now ask if they can expect to have carrot cake when they visit. Two of the friends who are most adamant live in Argentina and France, but I'm not naming names. Others have requested it for their birthdays. A prospective bride in France announced to us that she was soon to wed and asked if we would be in the area at the time of her wedding. Though we could not attend, she said that she would have liked to have a carrot cake to serve to the guests.

One gentleman acquaintance from Poland who worked alongside us while harvesting grapes commented as follows: "It's my 55th birthday. It's the best cake I have eaten in several years. My father was a baker from Poland and sent cakes to France on a daily basis."

Just this one cake serves many people, 15 or more. We have often had friends to the boat and served every crumb—sometimes two pieces for the men.

Over the years, carrot cake has sometimes become a carry-out item. We've been known to transport a full meal by train to a guest list of ten adults and two children. The menu included pork barbecue sandwiches, a green salad with blue cheese dressing, and carrot cake. On another occasion, we again hopped the train in London to join our boatyard-owner friends in Evesham. They had invited many of their friends and included us and, oh yes, a carrot cake would be lovely. Once it was carried up a mountain as we and friends hiked to the top for a picnic. A young man and woman were working next to us, doing the same thing to their sailing yacht. We shared a meal or two and would visit some during the working day. One evening we were having dinner aboard a Dutch barge; there were five or six of us. The young man with the sailboat was a chef on oil rigs off of Saudi Arabia. He prepared a lemon cheesecake which was delicious. I asked him for the recipe and he said: "I am a professional chef and I do not share my recipes."

A couple of nights later we were on the barge for dinner again, and I made a carrot cake for dessert. Everyone including the chef raved about the dessert and the chef asked for the recipe. He said the men on the oil rigs were mostly from the U.S. and enjoyed American food. I told him that it was a secret recipe. He immediately asked for a piece of paper and gave me his recipe.

CARROT CAKE AND ICING

2 cups flour
2 cups sugar
2 t. cinnamon
½ t. baking powder
2 t. baking soda
1½ cups corn oil
4 eggs, beaten
1 t. vanilla extract
3 cups carrots, grated very finely

1. Mix all dry ingredients. Add oil, eggs, and vanilla extract.
2. Blend well using electric mixer.
3. Stir in the grated carrots.
4. Prepare pan(s) with wax paper lightly buttered and dusted with flour.
5. Bake in (3) 8-inch pans or (1) 9 x 13-inch baking dish @ 350 degrees for approximately 45 minutes or until a knife comes out clean from the middle.

Icing:
8 ounces cream cheese, softened
¼ pound butter, softened
1 pound powdered sugar
1 t. vanilla extract
1 cup pecans, chopped or 1 cup almond flakes

1. Mix the cream cheese and butter with electric mixer.
2. Add sugar and vanilla and blend well. If icing appears too thick, you can add a teaspoon or two of milk; if too thin, add more sugar.
3. Spread 2 layers with the mixture.
4. Add the nuts and cover the entire cake.

Grandma's Tip: If you do not have a food processor available, you will want to buy a hand Mouli chopper. It's very inexpensive and grinds the carrots swiftly and finely. I have found the Mouli in kitchen shops in Europe, England, and the U.S. There are moulis for grinding coffee and nuts and they are very small. For the carrots, you want to buy the larger mouli; its cutting discs are approximately five-inches in diameter. The Mouli works so efficiently and quickly that I often choose to utilize it rather than getting out the food processor.

In the early 80's in England, we had to forget about our Tex-Mex cravings. Now, Mexican restaurants are everywhere. Back then, we could not locate a Mexican restaurant in London. I believe we did check out one of the popular chains but it had been closed—probably due to lack of interest at that time. Recently, we found ourselves choosing a Mexican restaurant in Paris and at the time, feeling a bit guilty. When in France, one naturally wants to visit French restaurants, however, the restaurant was across from the marina where we were living for the winter and its location was just too inviting. The food was great and three musicians provided the ambience to make it a pleasant evening of dining and entertainment.

The following appetizer is a family favorite from Mary Jane and represents one way that I can easily take general produce wherever I am and add the flavors of Mexico to the beginning of an evening meal.

BLACK BEAN APPETIZER

2 (15 ounce) cans black beans, rinsed and drained
1 (17 ounce) can whole kernel corn, drained
2 large tomatoes, seeded and chopped
1 large avocado, peeled and chopped
1 medium-sized purple onion, chopped
¼ cup chopped, fresh cilantro
3 to 4 T. olive oil
1 T. red wine vinegar
1 t. salt
½ t. pepper

1. **Combine all 10 ingredients in a large bowl. Cover and chill.**
2. **Serve with tortilla chips on the side.**

(Makes 6 cups.)

Probably the following is one of my most used vegetable dishes, as it accompanies most meat dishes nicely. I created this recipe because of the availability of inexpensive, fresh vegetables during the summer growing season. Evesham is one of two market garden regions in England.

If serving crusty bread with the meal, for example, one can eliminate the fresh breadcrumbs and merely use the cheese or avoid the cheese entirely. The combination of the zucchini and the tomatoes and onions plus the spices will suffice. As you will notice in the recipe, the herb marjoram in dried form is used and it gives the dish a special taste. Are fresh herbs necessary to

Geraniums on Oasis

enhance good flavor? I found when living on a boat that I utilized fresh basil and parsley quite often—sufficiently so to make growing them in a planter worthwhile. I would add other herbs to the planter just to make it look nice but seldom used them in cooking. In Pennsylvania and Georgia, I rely solely on dried herbs. Again, I think we have to harken back to the elderly folks in Europe who are in the habit of growing herb gardens. And, everywhere I have traveled I observe the younger generation is following suit. Were I living in one place, I, too, would join them. But, given my situation, I cannot handle winter weather and traveling in campers and boats; it gets too complicated. So what appears in my two large boat planters? Along my way seeing flowers decorating houses and boats and town bridges, I fell in love with hanging geraniums.

TOMATO ZUCCHINI GRILL

1 medium onion
1 pound zucchini
¼ cup butter
5 fresh tomatoes, large bite-size pieces
1 t. dried marjoram
salt and pepper to taste
½ cup sharp Cheddar cheese
3 T. fresh breadcrumbs

1. **Slice onions. Wash zucchini and trim ends; do not peel. Cut into ¼-inch slices.**
2. **Melt butter, add onion, zucchini, tomatoes, marjoram, and salt and pepper.**
3. **Simmer until zucchini is crisp tender or reaches your desired tenderness, around 10 minutes, stirring occasionally.**
4. **Drain some of the liquid and place vegetables in dish suitable for grilling.**
5. **Mix cheese and breadcrumbs and place on top.**
6. **Grill until cheese is melted.**

(Serves 4 to 6.)

I sometimes omit the cheese and breadcrumbs.

Troubling times on the canal were rare. On one occasion, however, we came to a complete stop to find that a sheet of plastic half the size of our boat had gotten wrapped around the propeller. This required the captain to get into the water along with the borrowed bread knife from the galley. I figure I can include this experience in a recipe book since the bread knife from the galley played a part. And, troubles along the way are not always something that deals directly with the boat. One day Diana and the three Kraft grandchildren could not pass by little ducklings in distress. The babies were caught behind a grill and mother duck was unable to reach them. Hal and I took the boat on, continuing to climb a hill of locks while our family stayed behind until the ducklings were freed and able to join their mother.

In the early days, Hal and I were eager to set a pace for ourselves that kept us well ahead of the other boats. In England in most canal locks the boat crews are required to work the locks. I would run ahead and start setting the lock, then come back to where Hal was maneuvering the boat through a lock. Then, it was on to the next lock to open the gates before heading off down the hill to another one. I recall we were on the heels of a younger couple and they wondered how our system was beating them. At the end of the day, we could pat ourselves on the back and feel proud that we had worked 32 locks that day. We usually traded jobs during the day so that 50 percent of the time you were the captain. That sharing of the lock work and being captain half of the time has held throughout our cruising. Though we no longer try to maintain that kind of pace, in France we still catch ourselves watching the clock in the mornings so that we will be the first boat at the lock when it opens.

Our cruising parameters were extended to the Continent after having seen most of England's waterways. We transported our canal boat across the English Channel and, thereby, opened up another huge set of waterways to explore. In most cases, locks are managed by lockkeepers and boat crews can choose to assist.

In our favorite marina in Auxerre, France we were sprucing up the looks of Pennsylvania Yankee early in the season while the boat was still on the hard, before having it placed in the water. We expected the sanding and repainting and general maintenance to take at least a week. For anyone who has spent any time on the hard in their boat while working on it, you know that it is not the most pleasant time. Not far from where we were working was a large Dutch barge moored on the bank of the Yonne river. There was a woman on board with whom we had some conversation. She was planning to be away for a week or so and suggested that we move onto her barge while working on our own. I mention this because we did move, we experienced the use of a large refrigerator, the use of a bathtub, a fireplace, and a living-dining area as large as a small apartment. What luxury! Little did we realize that this week would have an impact on us some twenty years later. Stay tuned.

The boating community is a friendly one and you just never know when an experience will crop up that will be so much fun and so memorable. We were sitting on the bank one evening enjoying the end of the day and relaxing with a glass of wine. A small hotel barge was moored behind us. The couple running the boat could receive six to eight passengers. The barge was one of the prettiest on the French canals with flowers everywhere and the whole boat glistened. The chef and her husband had no guests on board at the time. Later in the evening as we sat visiting, she asked if we would care to join them for a meal. In a very short time, out she came with excellent food prepared the way it seems to come naturally to the French. But, she isn't French. She and her husband are English. Never mind, the meal was memorable, especially the dessert.

Up to that time, we had never had *Tarte Tatin* and somehow she managed to prepare and serve it up quickly. Since then, I have tried this version of apple pie in several restaurants and have not found one that tasted any better. I have about six French cookbooks and have been tempted on occasion to try my hand at this different kind of apple pie. I tried it once and it did not turn out as well as I thought it should. In fact, the restaurants don't always get it right either. I usually end up returning to my old favorite, the Dutch Apple Pie recipe.

One weekend just south of Auxerre, we were cruising what became our most-often visited canal, the Canal du Nivernais, a picturesque waterway some hundred miles southeast of Paris. We were sharing the use of the locks with another boat. Two couples, one from Scotland and one, from England, were traveling on a rental boat. The couple from Scotland, Anne and Robin Stevenson, are referred to later as they became good boating friends. While the water level changes in locks, there is time for crews to visit. By the end of a long day, we had become quite friendly with our fellow travelers. We had made it down the flight of 16 locks to a mooring near Sardy. Before any thought of preparing a meal, nibbles and bubbly and more conversation were enjoyed as the six of us sat on the canal bank resting from the day's lock work.

The following day it was decided that we and our new friends would remain moored and give ourselves a day of rest and relaxation. Toward mid-afternoon, we all took a walk to where we thought there was a small restaurant as no one was much in the mood to cook, especially having consumed some more of the red that afternoon. Once we reached the restaurant, we found that it was just a bar serving drinks. Naturally, we had to have more wine to quench our thirst before the hike back to the boats. Though we had experienced a good promenade and had a fun day, there were six people who were starting to feel the need for some sustenance. Just as the three women were wondering what magic we could come up with, a French delivery van drove toward us on the towpath selling pizzas. Our luck had come through.

When we first participated in the *vendange* (grape harvest) in the heart of the champagne region, I was in pretty fair physical condition so picking grapes in a crouched position all day was not so difficult. Unfortunately, today I would not be able to hold that position and move along the rows for very long, probably not at all if I'm being very truthful. It was a delightful experience, however, one that combined my liking for the outdoors, observing French cooking, and getting to meet the locals. There was one gentleman who came from Poland each year to help with the harvest. It was rumored that he could leave his homeland because the immigration officials knew that he would return home because of his family. The owners of the vineyard were an American, Al Ricciuti and his French wife, Paulette. They had met during WWII and 18 years afterward, had married. Hal had met the husband as a part of his National Guard experience in Baltimore, MD. We would ride our bikes uphill two miles each day to get to the vineyard. Describing the whole experience would take pages and doesn't really connect to food except to say that I learned a few things from the wife and co-owner. Each day she and her sister-in-law prepared two meals for consumption in the vineyard and the evening meal was served back in their small chateau. Some of the pickers were housed there but we stayed on our boat, thankfully, a two-mile bicycle ride downhill to the canal.

Paulette showed me how she made her French salad with dressing. In France, this salad is usually served after the main course, the idea being that it helps with the digestive process. The salad takes on an even better flavor if you can prepare the dressing a few minutes ahead of time and allow the tomatoes to rest in the dressing. The recipe can be used wherever a vinaigrette is needed.

TOMATO SALAD WITH HOMEMADE FRENCH DRESSING

fresh tomatoes, sufficient quantity for number of persons being served
lettuce greens, sufficient quantity for number of persons being served
French dressing, being careful not to overdo

Dressing:
4 T. olive oil
1 T. red wine vinegar
½ t. French mustard
1 garlic clove, mashed
salt and pepper, to taste

1. **Pour the above ingredients into a jar with lid.**
2. **Shake and add to salad, prior to serving.**
3. **If time is available, marinate the tomatoes in the dressing for a few minutes prior to serving.**
4. **Combine the lettuce greens, tomatoes, and dressing and serve. In France, this is served after the main course.**

To vary the salad, eliminate the lettuce greens. Variation in this salad is dependent upon your ingenuity.

1. **Layer the chopped tomatoes on a serving platter. Cover lightly with French dressing.**
2. **Add hard-boiled eggs atop the tomatoes. Onion in optional.**

You have to serve both salad versions with French bread.

At the conclusion of the *vendange* and after all the workers have ridden through the nearby towns in a truck or wagon announcing the end of their year's harvest, they are treated to an evening banquet. Everyone comes in nice clothes, and there is much singing and celebration during the enjoyment of many dinner courses. Everyone participates, some with talent; some, with less. Hal and I were brave enough to sing "Side by Side," which has become our theme song over the years. We enjoyed the entire process, especially the friendship with those involved, so much so that we returned on two more occasions when we were near the champagne region. Everyone looks forward to the dessert as it is spectacular. It requires much time and attention and I do not make it frequently.

Hard meringue is readily available in Europe from bakeries, food stores, and *patisseries,* and its availability makes the preparation of this cake much easier over there. I was unable to prepare this specialty except in my home kitchen for lack of freezer space. And, it's discouraging that I cannot locate hard meringue locally. Back in the 1940's and 1950's, my mother could purchase hard meringue nests from a bakery in Lancaster, Ohio. She served them filled with vanilla ice cream and fresh strawberries. If hard meringue is available to you, I highly recommend the following *Vacherin*. You can prepare your own hard meringue, but the cake loses its simplicity at that point. I'm certain that my European friends will enjoy this form of ice cream cake.

I caution anyone who wants to make this cake that they should be careful when using raw egg yolks. My solution over the years has been to lightly poach the yolks, hoping that would be an ample solution to consuming them raw and be susceptible to food poisoning.

ICE CREAM CAKE WITH HARD MERINGUE
Vacherin

4 eggs, separated
2 ounces sugar
8 ounces whipping cream
1 t. vanilla extract
2 ounces powdered sugar
5 hard meringues
½ gallon vanilla ice cream
½ gallon strawberry ice cream
1 purchased pound cake

1. Work the yolks of the eggs with the sugar. Add the whipped cream and vanilla.
2. In a separate, large bowl beat the egg whites and add the powdered sugar.
3. Mix the two preparations together.
4. Pour half of this egg mixture in a large mold or bowl.
5. Mash the meringues; place half of them into the mold.
6. Add half of vanilla ice cream, slightly softened into the mold.
7. Place half of the strawberry ice cream over the vanilla.
8. Place half of the cake atop the ice creams.
9. Add the remaining half of the cream mixture.
10. Add remaining half of the meringues.
11. Repeat the ice creams, the cake, and additional meringue, if available. Freeze.

Topping:
1 package frozen raspberries, sweetened

1. **Thaw the raspberries, strain them, and add the sweetener.**

2. **Place in a serving pitcher and serve with vacherin.**

(Serves 12 to 15.)

When living on a boat with a small refrigerator, it is necessary to plan for guests with a bit more preciseness. Boat and camper refrigerators can be quite tiny. Though the steps are the same as in a house, one has to be cognizant of what items must be stored in the freezer and cold sections of the refrigerator. Another factor to consider is approximately how many days you will need to plan for, if food stores are not going to be available. Initially, you plan the menu for the number of days and include breakfast, lunch, and dinner. Secondly, you itemize the items from each meal that must be refrigerated. On the very small refrigerators that we had on all our boats but one, the tiny freezer's main task was to make ice. There was little room for anything else. With a somewhat increased capacity, one could include a package of ground beef or enough fresh salmon to make a meal. I always begin my planning wherever I am, including at home, with a menu. Then, I prepare a grocery list, marking those items that require cold storage. A large refrigerator does not guarantee that you will have sufficient space, especially when guests bring with them an item or two to contribute. Back in Pennsylvania, I have even had to make space for a week's supply of dog food.

When cruising, I always have several meals in the plan that require zero cold stuff. I find canned salmon very serviceable, as well as canned ham for evening meals and, of course, tuna for lunch sandwiches.

This is an easy supper if you have a can of salmon and a package of butter crackers in your cupboard. I used to be content with just the salmon cakes until I spent time in England and became familiar with mango chutney. For me, the chutney just adds the final touch to the taste of salmon. One pays dearly for a jar of mango chutney in the U.S. and I often talk myself out of buying it, but it's something I crave. No longer will I serve the cakes without the chutney or a commercial sweet-and-sour sauce on the side.

An aside to these cakes—when we were residing on a boat at the boatyard in Evesham, England, Roger and Tere's Scottish terrier who would have nothing to do with us for several months became our best friend after he was given a taste of a salmon cake.

SALMON PATTIES WITH MANGO CHUTNEY

1 medium-size can of salmon, not drained
1 egg, beaten
butter crackers, one package (approximately 30 crackers)
mango chutney or a commercial sweet and sour sauce, on the side
olive oil--slight amount to dampen skillet and keep patties from sticking to the bottom

1. **Empty salmon into medium-size bowl. Crush crackers by hand and add to salmon. Add egg and mix well.**
2. **Make into patties and fry on medium heat until both sides are nicely brown.**
3. **Serve chutney on the side.**

(Makes 6 patties, 3 1/2-inch diameter.)

When cruising in countries outside of England, our traditional English narrowboat received lots of attention. On one occasion in Belgium, we were greeted eagerly by a gentleman from across the canal. It happened that he was in charge of a fete (festival) being held in his town and he was unbelievably knowledgeable about narrowboats. He asked if we would participate in the boat parade, which we agreed to do, and take a few folks along on our boat. The following morning we met several people who were attending the festival. One of the women aboard introduced herself as the English representative to the European Union in Brussels. As was normal, Pennsylvania Yankee was always in tiptop shape—hull shining and windows sparkling and back in those days, brass shining as well. I don't do brass any longer. It's in the same category as silver. During the course of our guest's time with us and probably because of the condition of our boat, she extended to us an invitation to stay in her apartment in London for the year. Well, I was blown away by the offer and living in a large city was always a desire, so I was eager to let Hal hear of this. You can guess his reaction. Why go live in an apartment when we have our own right here on the boat? I soon got over any disappointment but have always thought it a real nice gesture on her part. It isn't the only time we have been extended similar invitations which just goes to show you that there are friendly, generous, nice people all over the world. The favorite appetizers given in this book were served during the parade, and they never fail to make a hit. Carrot cake ended our feast.

It was not the one and only time that we participated in boat festivals. We were once made honorary guests in the city of San Quentin, France, and were presented with gifts and made to feel like celebrities.

Sometimes the situation arises when you meet other boaters and immediately start up a friendship which doesn't end that day but lasts for a long time. One couple from the Isle of Wight was staying at the Paris Marina and we spent an evening together. We arranged to meet again in the countryside. Before we arrived, the couple had walked into town and purchased from a *charcuterie* a large platter of lasagna. Most towns in France have these shops where prepared foods can be bought. It's important to visit them early in the day as the locals are buying early in the morning. These kinds of prepared food stalls are available throughout all countries I have visited and in the U.S., but the French seem to partake of this service in greater numbers. We met with our friends again and again after that, including one visit to their home. She was in the process of making orange marmalade in large quantities—something I had not observed before. From them, we have adopted their boat's drink and often serve it to our other friends. If you like gin and tonic, this will go down well. They called it the Madge Wildfire Ship's Drink.

SHIP'S DRINK

Gin
Vermouth
1 lemon slice
tonic water

1. **Add ice to glass.**
2. **Add 1 shot of gin and 1 shot of vermouth.**
3. **Top with tonic water and a slice of lemon.**

By the time we had cruised several years in Pennsylvania Yankee, Roger and Tere has sold their Evesham boatyard and moved to Buenos Aires. They extended an invitation to us to come visit with them. We made a lengthy travel plan. This story is about how we traveled in South America. We flew to Lima, Peru, then boarded buses and trains south to Buenos Aires. Unlike most Americans who travel from one country to another, we chose land transportation, thus, being able to see more of the country and the people. We had extra-ordinary experiences doing it our way. We were often the only foreigners on the bus. Sometimes, we were the only middle-age people sharing the bus with college-age kids. They were lovely to visit with and even shared their candy with us. Pit stops were provided along desert roads and one went searching for a secluded spot behind a sand dune. Buses were filled to the brim with locals boarding after the bus left the city station. Their only seat was finding space on the floor. Sometimes the only way to get off the bus at night for a stop was to walk out using the seats' arm rests.

We carried with us a portable kitchen. Our major concern was that we did not want to start out the journey having any stomach problems, especially since we would be "on the go" every day. To begin the month or so of travel, we wanted to watch carefully everything we ate and drank. We consumed fruit that could be peeled. We boiled enough water each night for the next day. We, also, bought bottles of Coca

Cola along the way. When the bus would stop in the middle of the night to provide passengers with a hot meal, the propane lights would come on and everyone would vacate the bus, stand around the temporary tent, and consume the food that was being served. We would not partake but would rely on bananas and packaged breads such as Pannetone which we learned to like very much.. It wasn't until we joined our friends in Argentina where we were staying for one month over the holidays that we began to eat the local diet. And, we managed to make the entire round trip free of stomach bugs except for one instance. In Santiago, Chile on our return, we came across a restaurant specializing in yogurt and fresh fruits. Anyone who has traveled in South America knows how wonderful tasting are its fruits. The buffet breakfasts in hotels offer fresh fruit unlike any I have ever tasted—except for fresh pineapple in Hawaii. Well, maybe that's a bit of an exaggeration as peaches and strawberries from Ohio and Pennsylvania can't be beat and fresh apricots in my backyard in California were scrumptious. I thought canned apricots were representative of the fruit until I tasted them fresh from the tree. My travels haven't taken me everywhere so you probably know more places where you can taste excellent fruit. My examples are just that, mine.

Our luggage was limited to two backpacks, not the very large size. We had three changes of clothes and the rest of the space was devoted to our kitchen. The portable kitchen included:

A one-burner camp stove that could be started without matches
A small skillet
A spatula and serving spoon
A paring knife
2 serving plates
2 bowls to hold soup
2 sets of eating utensils

When we reached Lima, one of the first things that we shopped for was small propane canisters, as we could not carry propane on the airplane.

We had one very nice outfit that we needed for party-going in Buenos Aires. Otherwise, we wore casual clothes that could be washed by hand and left to dry overnight. Our black piece of luggage could be carried in the normal way or placed on our backs when walking a longer distance. That's nothing to do with food but thought you might find it of interest.

This was my first, real introduction to observing people who live in very poor conditions. It was nothing in comparison to anything I had seen in large U.S. cities. We took a bus trip through the city of Lima, Peru and sometimes, it was hard to look. One lunch time, we decided to sit outside at a sidewalk café and that was the first and last time. Mothers with children would come up to the table begging for food. It was terribly hard to want to eat in those situations. Restaurant owners would tell them to leave, a pitiful situation. We would often see people bartering for food in the downtown area. These squalid conditions were seen in Brazil, Bolivia, and Argentina, as well.

III

Building a Sailing Yacht and Cruising in the Western European Waters

So, you say, you want to travel the sea.
Well, it will take something different from Pa. Yankee.
We have a plan and we both agree.
If it's built well, it will take us to another country.

BOAT NUMBER 2 – K*I*S*S (Keep it Simple, Sailor.)

Cruising the inland waterways provides you with your own "stuff" about you, it is an extremely peaceful, relaxing way of life, and you are enjoying your own cooking and not spending more than you want to on restaurant meals. You are not frequently packing and unpacking; all your needs are in one compact place. And, the waterways take you off the beaten track and closer to the country's culture. For those of you who travel in recreational vehicles, you will relate to how comfortable it is traveling with all your basic needs about you.

Having covered all of England and most of France, Belgium, and the Netherlands in our narrowboat, we decided it would be nice if we could cruise from country to country without relying on someone else for transporting the boat. So, in the summer of 1987, we decided to sell our narrowboat and build a motorsailer. We had spent one entire day cruising in company with another narrowboat. At dark that evening Hal and I had gone inside. It was raining and we had decided to watch a movie. There was a knock on the roof and it was the English couple with whom we had traveled that day. They yelled, "We want to have your boat."

*K*I*S*S on the Crinan Canal*

Sometime during our conversations at locks we had mentioned that we planned to sell. Our boat looked so good from the outside and they had, also, noticed that it was much more stable in the water than theirs. But, their decision to buy had been made without examining the interior, which by the way was quite lovely.

If one maintains a boat by such simple means as keeping it scrubbed and having shiny windows and shiny brass, then we have found that selling it is not difficult. Naturally, it has to be pleasing to the eye, well built, and maintained in good order. I can't begin to count the number of "thumbs up" we have gotten along our travels. I often waxed the boat's exterior. Just a good washing would bring out the praise.

We began our work on K*I*S*S at a boat building company. We made ourselves a comfortable spot in one corner of the plant's property and rented a 6½-foot by 13-foot camping caravan from a friend of a friend. We were so happy to be back in Worcester. Since our good friends from Evesham knew us well, they did not mind coming to an industrial site to see us. We picked blackberries around the periphery of the industrial site with John and Muriel, the camping friends who traveled with us across the U.S. The berries were huge in size and our friends took many pints home with them to make jam. We ate blackberries often that summer—atop our cereal and pancakes, over ice cream, and occasionally in a pie.

BLACKBERRY APPLE PIE

double crust 9-inch pie shell
1½ cups sugar
¼ cup flour
1/8 t. salt
¼ t. nutmeg
½ t. cinnamon
2 cups fresh blackberries, washed and well drained
2 cups cooking apples, peeled and sliced (I prefer Granny Smiths.)
2 T. butter or margarine

1. **In a mixing bowl, combine sugar, flour, salt, nutmeg, and cinnamon. Add blackberries and apples and mix well.**
2. **Place the above in bottom of pie shell; dot with butter.**
3. **Cover the pie with a lattice-top or a full sheet of pastry. If using a full sheet of pastry, brush top with water or egg white and a light sprinkle of sugar.**
4. **Bake @ 425 degrees for 10 minutes.**
5. **Reduce heat to 350 degrees for 40 minutes longer or until apples are tender.**

The boat-building staff welded together a 31-foot Bruce Roberts' Spray and Hal designed a pilothouse to be welded on top. We had admired a Fisher sailboat in the waters of England and, also, when sharing locks with a couple who owned this beautiful craft, but we could only admire as it was too costly. The Spray was a good alternative and once the shell was finished, we could do the completion ourselves.

Work on this sailing boat was in many ways more involved and required more time. After all, we were installing all the rigging for sailing, quite a change from a typical canal boat. But, the tasks held their same interest and we enjoyed the people around us. Within fifteen minutes, I could bicycle to the city center for supplies, passing the Worcester Cathedral on my way and soaking in all the historical significance of this medieval town. There remains part of a Roman wall nearby and where we often enjoyed our Friday night fish and chips were houses built before North America was discovered. These houses remain standing and no one, over the years, tore them down to build high-rise apartments. We can dine on English pasties bought at the bakery or choose to eat the very popular cuisine from India, or have Chinese take-away. Mostly, our meals were prepared in the tiny camping caravan. I once entertained the staff at the boatyard to a typical American lunch—our pork barbecue sandwiches, potato salad, and cc, you know, the cake. Well, one man who was often at the yard but not directly related to boat building often joined everyone for morning or afternoon tea. He was usually very quiet, especially with me. After the day of the lunch and his taste of the cake, he always had something nice to say as he walked by the boat where I was working. That's what life is all about for us, making friends and enjoying their company. Later on, this man has a big impact on our boat building. Stay tuned.

Another couple from the U.S. via Ireland where they spent their summers joined us for a weekend though they had to stay in a Bed and Breakfast. The couple worked in the same school district as we had. The man had been born and reared in Ireland and had lived there for some twenty years before coming to the U.S. As long as you serve a nice meal and enjoy each other's conversation, it doesn't seem to matter that you're eating in a less-than-desirable setting. Later, they joined us on board for a weekend's cruise. And, another friend from Evesham, Mike Tittensor, who worked in Worcester, joined us most every Wednesday for lunch.

The one negative about living here was that there was no shower facility. I had scrubbed one of the restrooms in the plant and made it our own. We borrowed a plastic baby bath from the Tittensor's and could take a sit-down bath in that. And, on Saturdays we would drive to Evesham which was some 20 miles away. There we could have a proper bath or shower. We were quite close with both the Tittensors and the Gealers, so we would alternate where we slept overnight. They would prepare the main course one week and I would contribute the dessert. On the following week, we would reverse it and carry the main course to their house. Sometimes, we six came together for the evening meal. Also, we were included in festive gatherings, dining in local pubs and restaurants. Since we were all amateur radio operators, we became honorary members of the local club and attended their holiday parties. Amateur radio continued to open doors to new friends. Some have come to stay with us on our boats and some have come to the U.S. for lengthy visits.

The treat on Friday is to have fish, chips, and ice cream.
Tomorrow we wind down and put down our tools.
The week has been long; the boat is improving it seems.
Life is fun, boat's looking good; working as a team is cool.

K*IS*S was completed in June, 1989. When looking back over five boats, I think this sailing yacht gave us the most highlights of our cruising. We had been warned of how treacherous it was to leave Worcester, England and sail south on the Bristol Channel. This channel has the second highest tide in the world, over 40 feet. I'm told that the highest is in Canada. From our experience, people often make the prospect of an experience sound much worse than it really is, so we pretty much filtered the information given to us and chose to depart via the channel. After all, we were on a sailing boat and if we were careful, all should go fine. We built the boat so that we could raise and lower the mast ourselves which we did up against a walkway in Gloucester. We needed to be careful as near the walkway was an all-glass front to a restaurant. We had no problems and were soon on our way Ireland-bound. Ireland was having its worst drought in years and the Barrow river depth was 11 inches lower than normal. Hal walked out into the middle of the river trying to find a clear passage so that we could get to Dublin but had no success. In the meantime, I was fighting horse flies along the bank while holding a line to the boat. Not every day is a pleasure on a pleasure boat. That has nothing to do with food but was such an experience that it had to be mentioned. As a result of this low water, we were forced to forego reaching the Grand Canal and had to raise the mast again and go out to sea skirting the eastern coast of Ireland.

After an interesting visit in Ireland, we sailed on to Scotland, Denmark, Norway, and Sweden. Every country was exciting to visit. No one had written about the Telemark Canal in Norway for the magazine, <u>Waterways World</u>. Hal had been authorized to write of our experiences so that was our destination for the summer. The canal was a spectacular one, cut out of rock for some of its locks. Even though it was July, we could see the white caps of snow on the mountains. People were so very friendly and all in all, the difficulty of finding enough good sailing days was far overcome by the joy of visiting these different countries.

We had no overnight guests during our sailing on open waters. Perhaps some folks did not wish to travel on the sea. It wasn't until we returned to cruising on rivers and canals again that friends began to join us.

However, it wasn't totally impossible to meet and to be with other people. We attended an Amateur Radio Club meeting in Scotland and were warmly received. When staying in a marina, we often spent time with other boaters, mostly people who were on their vessels for the weekend. Seldom did we come across other live-aboards in these northern waters during the colder months.

One evening while sitting in a marina in northern Scotland, a fisherman came by and offered us a bucket of brown crabs. An order had not been picked up by a customer of his so he thought we might appreciate them, as we did. This was a nice gesture by a complete stranger. We ate the crabs as we had learned to do back in the Chesapeake Bay for a couple meals, then resorted to our favorite crab cake recipe for another day.

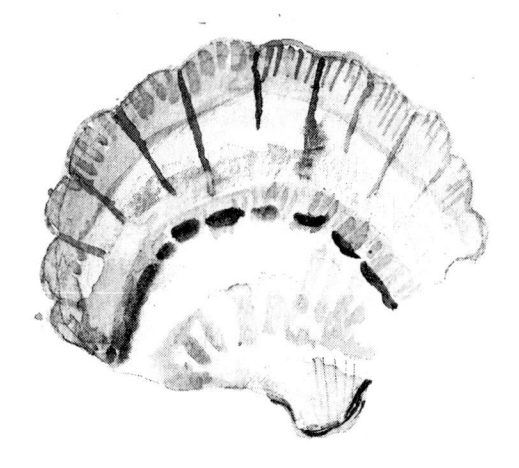

CRAB CAKES

4 (7-ounce) cans crabmeat or the equivalent in fresh crab
1 slice of bread, cut into fresh breadcrumbs
1 large egg
½ cup mayonnaise +/- to suit-enough to moisten but no more
1 t. Worcestershire sauce
½ t. salt, ½ t. pepper
1 t. dry mustard
½ cup onion, finely chopped
½ cup green bell pepper, finely chopped
½ cup celery, finely chopped
½ cup dry breadcrumbs

1. **Drain crabmeat well.**
2. **Beat egg. Add fresh breadcrumbs, egg, mayonnaise, Worcestershire sauce, s&p, and mustard to crab.**
3. **Chop onion, pepper, and celery, finely; add to mixture.**
4. **Make into patties and coat with dry breadcrumbs.**
5. **Fry in oil/butter mixture over medium heat until brown.**

(Makes 8 patties, 3-inch diameter, ½-inch thick.)

This is a different version of the delicious crab cakes served in Maryland restaurants. I have included the green pepper, onion, and celery to suit our tastes. Hope you like them.

Our friends from Scotland, Anne and Robin Stevenson, whom we had met in France lived not too far from one of our chosen watering holes. The mooring basin was a small indentation and one had to maneuver between tall rocks to get into the anchorage.

As you approached, you could not really spot the opening until you were just a few feet from it. And, we and our guests who came to meet us had to use a very long ladder built into the stone wall. In other words, they had to work for their supper. We returned with them to their home for a lovely weekend visit and saw much of their community, including their favorite local restaurant. Though it has been years ago, I can still remember enjoying a delicious walnut cream cake.

Since we had been away from supermarkets for quite some time, I put together the following main course for their evening meal with us.

This is one of the dishes that Hal prepared when living alone. It is now included at Easter time and other holiday dinners. Nothing gets my mouth watering more than combining this ham with my favorite casserole of scalloped oysters.

GLAZED BAKED HAM WITH ORANGE SAUCE
Jambon a la Orange

cooked, canned ham (2, 3, 5, or more pounds) Quantities given here are for 3 pounds
1 orange
½ cup orange marmalade
½ cup light brown sugar
2 T. prepared mustard
25 to 30 whole cloves

1. Remove ham from can and remove all the gelatin that adheres to it.
2. Place ham on baking pan.
3. Make short, diagonal knife cuts, across the top of the ham; cuts should be about 1-inch apart and about ½-inch deep.
4. Make the same kind of cuts in the other direction so that you form diamonds.
5. Place one clove in the center of each diamond.
6. Wash the orange, cut it in half, then slice one of the halves into 3 or 4 slices.
7. Place the slices on top of the ham.
8. Squeeze the juice of the other half into a small bowl.
9. Add the marmalade, sugar, and mustard. Mix well and spread about half of it over the top of the ham and orange slices.
10. Bake @ 350 degrees for 1 hour.
11. Occasionally during the hour, dribble some more of the glaze mix over the top of the ham and let it run down the sides.
12. If whole cloves do nothing for you, they can be omitted and it's no big loss but do make slits in the top of the ham to allow marinade to seep down into the roast.

(A 3-pound ham serves approximately 10 to 12.)

It was Hal's role as captain to plan sailing destinations taking into consideration the weather forecast and the amount of wind and tide. It was somewhat stressful and he did have some heart concerns to consider. After five sailing and cruising years, we chose to make plans for another boat. Prior to the commencement of boat number 3 and having returned to inland waterways, we enjoyed inland cruising in the Netherlands, Belgium, France, and a small section of Germany. The motorsailer's draft was 4 feet so we could easily navigate the canals with no problem. As soon as we returned from the open seas, Hal's heart problems decreased dramatically.

One afternoon while stopped along the canal bank, I was in the process of making English breakfast scones. A woman walked by, spotted our American flag, and stopped to inquire about us. She was traveling on a hotel barge nearby. It turned out that she was the food editor for the Pittsburgh Gazette. She was amazed that in our very small galley I was baking scones. Before she left, she made plans to visit us in our home when we returned to Pennsylvania. She wrote an article for her paper about our cruising in France and included three or four recipes from my list of favorites. Here is our best attempt at making scones that were comparable to those we liked so much, obtained in the gourmet section of one of England's major department stores. Many department stores in England and Europe have a floor, usually the lower one, which sells food.

TEA SCONES

2 cups flour
4 T. sugar, divided
2½ t. baking powder
½ t. salt
2 eggs (Save whites from one egg.)
1/3 cup milk
1/3 cup shortening
handful of raisins
1 T. sugar

1. Mix flour, 3 T. sugar, baking powder, and salt.
2. Mix eggs and milk.
3. Cut shortening into dry ingredients.
4. Add raisins, then, eggs and milk all at once.
5. Mix with fork, then with hands, make dough into 10-12 rounds.
6. Place on greased baking sheet.
7. Cover with egg white, slightly beaten, and sprinkle sugar over all the scones.
8. Bake @ 450 degrees for 12 minutes.

(Makes 10-12.)

This is a tasty dish that can be served as a main course. For the warmer months, the Summer Pasta Salad is, also, an excellent vegetarian dish. (It is listed in the Index under Pastas.) During our travels, we have made some long-lasting friends. Peter Mastenbroek, a Dutchman who resides in France on a barge, has caught up with us in most every country we have visited as well as back home in Pennsylvania. He found us in England, in Belgium, and very often, throughout France. We would find him waiting outside our galley window on a morning, waiting until he saw that we had been up for awhile and had finished our breakfast. He's thoughtful in that way. He is a vegetarian so I have gotten lots of practice preparing tasty dishes that suit. I remember one time I failed to remember that tuna wasn't an acceptable food. He took one bite and, well, you can imagine the rest.

He might be around for lunch or dinner so I always had possibilities in store. One holiday, we invited him and another man who was alone on another boat to join us for dinner. I prepared the Coquille St. Jacques for the three of us and Peter had the pasta dish with Brie. I am confident that you will enjoy the warm, melting Brie.

SUMMER PASTA WITH MELTING BRIE

10 ounces dried pasta
9 ounces fresh green beans
8 ounces Brie cheese
1 garlic clove
9 ounces fresh, ripe tomatoes
juice of ½ lemon
3 T. olive oil
salt and pepper, to taste

1. **Cook pasta in boiling, salted water for 10 minutes. Half way through, add beans. While pasta is cooking, chop tomatoes and brie into quite small pieces.**
2. **Mix with garlic, lemon juice, olive oil. Season with salt and pepper.**
3. **Drain pasta and beans. Mix everything over a low heat until Brie starts to melt.**

(Serves 4.)

English people we met one afternoon were traveling in their car in France and they stopped to chat with us, as our boat was moored at the canal bank. This happens frequently because English people are happy to find folks who speak their language and secondly, our boat and flag captured their attention. They invited us to ride with them to a restaurant in the country for an evening meal. We did and I still remember the potato dish that was served family-style. As is often the case in French, country restaurants, the exterior may not look inviting and in this particular case, we were one of two tables being served. Maybe it was early in the evening, as most restaurants get busy after 8 p.m. Once I returned home, I checked out recipes for this potato dish and learned that it included large amounts of cream and cheese but it was oh, so delightful. It's called *Gratin Dauphinois* in case you would like to investigate how it is prepared. It contains potatoes baked in cream and can be made with milk, eggs, and cheese.

The French know how to make a potato sing. I often turn away from the recipes knowing that it is definitely not healthy. The question you must ask yourself is, "How often can I afford to consume or should I just forget it?" So far, I have chosen not to include these over-the-top potato recipes in my collection, but I do serve the following. The use of yogurt makes it a bit healthier.

CHEESY POTATOES

6 medium potatoes, cut coarsely
2 cups Cheddar cheese, shredded
¼ cup butter
1½ cups sour cream or yogurt or combination of the two
1/3 cup green onions, (approx. 3 small bunches)
salt and pepper, to taste
2 T. butter

1. Cook potatoes in skins until tender. Cool. Peel and cut.
2. In a large pan, combine cheese and ¼ cup butter over heat. Remove from heat and blend in sour cream/yogurt, chopped green onions, and s&p.
3. Fold in the potatoes, turn into greased 9x13" baking dish. Dot with 2 T. butter.
4. Bake @350 degrees for 25 to 30 minutes.

(Serves 8.)

To our guests who have come back again and again, we have a reputation for finding a good source for *croissant aumonde*, (croissants filled with almond paste and topped with almonds.) We have managed to find decent-tasting ones in Connecticut and Maryland, as well. Paris got us started in this search in 1983 and we have continued to research all of France for the best ones. We once found a bakery inside a supermarket at Auxerre as our number two choice, but the store was renovated and the bakery is no more. One morning we were climbing the locks on the Nivernais Canal to the summit when we received a telephone call from our friends, John and Sheila Nye. Upon our arrival at the top around 11 a.m., our friends were sitting along the dock waiting for us. They had brought us a treat, *croissant aumonde*. What good friends! At the last count, we have their source plus 3 of our own which turns out to be about the right number for a stretch of canal that runs some 100 miles and through 100+ locks. Though we exercise by riding our bikes and walking the towpath, too many croissants could defeat our purpose.

Shopping in France creates a dilemma that does not exist in the U.S. Why did it take me so long to realize that the food stores or the banks or the other shops were not open when I had expected them to be? Perhaps it was because I utilized my lunch hour for food shopping back in my career days. Back then I refused to step inside a store on a Saturday if at all possible. The French way is to take a long lunch and the commercial business closes for two to three hours each day. I soon learned and resorted to making notes for future visits to the village as not all businesses are the same. This, in part, explains why the French cherish their noon meal and are not so much in the habit of grabbing a sandwich from a fast-food establishment. In fact, some businesses give a stipend to workers toward their noon-time meal. I once observed workers in a Paris hospital taking large dinner plates outside to enjoy their noontime meal, thinking that this was probably one of their fringe benefits.

Perhaps one of the biggest impacts from our many travels on my food preparation has been the experience of shopping, especially in France. I no longer consider purchasing certain fresh fruits out of season. For example, back home in wintry Pennsylvania I am so often disappointed when I cut open a pear or a peach to find the flavor is not there. They appear enticing on the outside, but inside the juice and flavor are lacking. French shoppers visit a market and then decide what to buy. Their shopping cart choices are made more on what month it is than on what may appear at first glance to be a good choice.

So, peaches are enjoyed during the summer months when they are at their peak and not during mid-winter when they have been picked in some far-off country and have landed on store shelves pretty on the outside but blah on the inside. Seasonal peaches are just so very appetizing sliced and put into an ice cream sundae or a pie, but here is another way that I found was a great finish to one of those summer barbecues.

PEACHES IN SHERRY

6 medium fresh peaches
2 T. light brown sugar
½ cup almond flakes
½ cup medium sherry
whipped cream or ice cream

1. **Dip peaches in and quickly out of boiling water, 30 seconds.**
2. **Peel peaches and halve them.**
3. **Arrange in casserole and sprinkle with sugar, almond flakes, and sherry.**
4. **Cover and bake @ 350 degrees for 20 minutes.**
5. **Serve at room temperature with whipped cream or ice cream.**

(Serves 4 to 6.)

Whole villages come out to celebrate certain local delicacies all over the world but I have never seen it as common as it is among country folk in France. My introduction to Andoulette, a white sausage, was a total disaster. Remember, eating out is not something we do every week so when the occasion arises, I try to order something special. A very dear friend of ours who stayed with us some eleven times on our boats was a retired Air Force Colonel. He had knocked on our door after seeing the American flag. On that first occasion, he visited for a time, took us to a friend's home for a meal, and, also, offered to take me to the laundry—one of the most helpful things a person can do for someone living on a boat. He is no longer with us and we miss him. But back to Andoulette. Our friend was taking us out for dinner and I ordered it from the menu of a very nice restaurant, one that we had visited times before. And, I could not chew and swallow the sausage; it was that tough. I have since tried it again and it was very tender and tasty. We recently visited one of our favorite towns in Burgundy, Clamecy, and most everyone in that town and surrounding area came to a festival that was totally geared to dining on this sausage. We had eaten away that particular day so could not participate, but if we get back there for another festival, we will make an effort to give the dish another try.

On occasion when moving throughout France, I was sometimes asked directions and was always surprised that I was thought to be a resident. I figure it may have been because I was pulling a grocery cart, called a granny cart by some. Once I was taken to be German by a French lockkeeper. That is a bit more understanding since my forefathers came from Germany. When scanning some of my world cookbooks, it peaked my interest to note that dishes served in my home growing up in Ohio were popular, regional dishes of Germany. For example, my mother often served this vegetable dish, and I have never been served it by anyone else.

PEAS AND POTATOES

6 to 8 medium-size potatoes
1 (10-ounce package) frozen peas
2 T. flour
2 T. butter
salt and pepper, to taste
1 cup light cream or half/half

1. In a large pan, cook potatoes; drain and add peas.
2. In a small pan, prepare a roux of 2 T. flour and 2 T. butter by melting butter in pan over low heat.
3. **Add flour off of the heat. Return to heat and pour in 1 cup of cream or half/half, stirring constantly. If the roux is too thick, add milk or cream to reach desired consistency. Season with salt and pepper.**
4. **Back in the large pan using a low-to-medium heat setting, combine the roux, the peas and potatoes. Stir occasionally and serve when completely warm.**

(Serves 6 to 8.)

Most everyone has a sweet tooth that kicks in from time to time which brings to mind our friend, Sheila, who does not usually have a dessert. The only one of my desserts that she will eat is a small piece of carrot cake. Other than fresh fruit, she usually declines.

For most, however, the following which is a different take on the brownie is well received.

TRI-LEVEL BROWNIES

1 cup quick oats
½ cup flour
½ cup light brown sugar
¼ t. baking soda
½ c. butter, melted
1 egg
¾ cup sugar
2/3 cup flour
¼ cup milk
¼ cup butter or margarine
1 ounce unsweetened chocolate
1 t. vanilla extract
¼ t. baking powder
½ cup walnuts, chopped
1 ounce unsweetened chocolate
2 T. butter or margarine
½ t. vanilla extract
powdered sugar
1 to 2 T. hot water

1. **Combine oats and next 4 ingredients. Place in greased 13x9-inch baking dish or pan; bake @ 350 degrees for 10 minutes.**
2. **Stir together egg, sugar, flour, milk, melted butter or margarine, melted chocolate, vanilla, and baking powder. Fold in chopped walnuts. Spread over first layer. Bake 25 minutes. Cool.**
3. **Heat and stir 1 ounce melted chocolate and 2 T. butter until melted; add vanilla and enough powdered sugar to make it close to an icing consistency. Add 1 to 2 T. hot water to make it almost pouring consistency. Spread over brownies.**

(Makes 30.)

It is a bit more difficult to find frozen vegetables in the right quantity to serve two to four people when living in England or France, at least not as easy to acquire as back home. So, one relies more on fresh vegetables. These glazed carrots are yummy served along side a main course. Remember, too, freezer space is limited so fresh is the answer.

GLAZED CARROTS

10-12 medium carrots, cut in 2-inch shapes
1½ cups beef or chicken stock
4 T. butter
2 T. sugar
2 T. parsley
½ t. salt, ½ t. pepper

1. In a skillet, bring carrots, stock, butter, sugar, parsley, and salt and pepper to a boil.
2. Cover and simmer over low heat, stirring occasionally.
3. In 20 to 30 minutes, carrots should be tender.
4. Remove carrots and boil syrup on high heat to a brown, syrupy glaze.
5. Return carrots and simmer an additional minute or two to assure they are heated well.

(Serves 4 to 6.)

Corn on the cob may appear on a French restaurant's menu when it is nowhere to be found on the grocery shelves. Twenty some years later it is now available in food stores, usually in packaged form. It does not compare to the farm-fresh sweet corn of Midwestern U.S.A. In my travels, I have never come across sweet corn being sold at street markets.

There are many forms of corn pudding served in the U.S.; it varies about as much as do family recipes for potato salad or turkey dressing. Below is another version which uses a prepared, packaged item. It's fortunate, also, that this recipe can be prepared using canned corn.

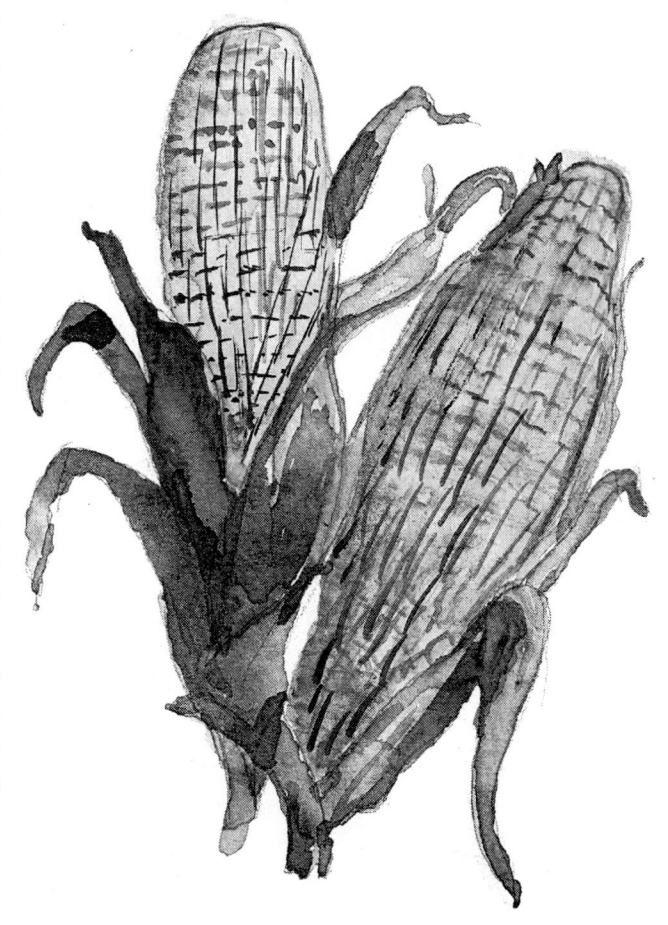

CORN CASSEROLE

2 medium-size cans corn (1 cream-style, 1 regular)
2 eggs
8 ounces sour cream
1 box corn muffin mix, 8.5 ounces
4 ounces butter, room temperature

1. **Drain the regular can of corn. Combine all ingredients and mix well.**
2. **Place mixture in greased, baking dish**
3. **Bake @ 350 degrees for 1 hour.**

(Serves 6 to 8.)

There is another version of the vegetable.

SCALLOPED CORN

(Serves 4.)

1 onion, small
2 T. butter
2 T. flour
1 t. salt
¼ t. nutmeg
1 medium-size can cream-style corn
1 t. baking powder
1 egg
½ cup butter crackers, crushed
Dot of butter on top

1. **Chop onion and cook in butter; add flour, salt, and nutmeg. Mix well.**
2. **Stir in corn, baking powder, and beaten egg.**
3. **Pour into buttered baking dish; cover with cracker crumbs and dot with bits of butter.**
4. **Bake @ 350 degrees for 30 minutes.**

When you can make a certain dish almost blindfolded, it demonstrates how frequently you resort to an old favorite of Mom's. *Maman's* (a French mother) or *Grandmere's* (a French grandmother) recipes often lack that exactness, too. In my earlier years, I would follow a recipe from a cookbook carefully, especially the first time—now, not necessarily so. Now, I often add ingredients to a casserole just because I want to and/or the item is in the cupboard. As in so many of my favorites, I have taken the original recipe and adapted it to my personal taste. Mom's scalloped potatoes are so often prepared in an unmeasured manner but what follows is my best estimate.

SCALLOPED POTATOES

6-8 medium-sized potatoes
½ cup flour, divided
salt
¼ cup butter, divided
whole milk
butter crackers

1. Peel and slice potatoes thinly.
2. Grease a 2-quart baking dish.
3. Layer the following: sliced potatoes, flour to lightly cover, sprinkling of salt and butter pieces.
4. Repeat three layers.
5. Add milk to cover 2/3 of potatoes.
6. Mash crackers and cover as topping. Bake at 350 degrees.
7. Once the topping is browned, cover lightly with foil to finish the baking process. The total baking time takes approximately 1¼ to 1½ hours. Test for doneness by placing knife in middle of casserole.

(Serves 6 to 8.)

We were staying with friends in France while Hal and I and the host were working on the repair of a French car. We were in the process of changing the engine. The task took place outside in a garage that had no doors and in very cold temperatures. It, also, took much longer than anticipated. Though it's too long of a story for now, I'll just say that it took two or three tries to get the correct parts and everyone was beginning to grow a bit weary. Since the work was being done over our Thanksgiving Day, we decided to prepare a meal for the family with whom we were spending several days. We did not stay with them at night but still, we wanted to do something to merit our time with them. Hal and I walked to the nearby village and bought ingredients, as close as we could to a typical turkey dinner. Chicken was substituted for turkey but included were candied sweet potatoes, dressing, gravy, a vegetable, and dessert. By the time we had finished our meal, the hostess remarked that Americans prepare more items that are sweet. For example, she would not prepare a sweet potato with a sugar covering. After thinking about it, I'm sure she is right.

When I think of sweet potatoes, I often relate them to Thanksgiving, though we eat baked sweet potatoes with a pat of butter throughout the year. This recipe comes close to what my mother served, though as I recall she used the canned sweet potatoes; I prefer the fresh. Be careful not to overcook them as you may wish to put them back into the oven just before serving time.

SWEET POTATOES, CANDIED

6 sweet potatoes, cooked
1 cup light brown sugar
¼ cup water
¼ c. butter
½ t. salt

1. Grease a 2-quart baking dish.
2. Combine sugar, water, butter, and salt; bring to a boil, then, simmer for 3 or more minutes until syrup becomes thick.
3. Peel sweet potatoes that have been cooked with skins on; cut into smaller pieces.
4. Add potatoes to dish and top with syrup.
5. Bake @ 350 degrees for 45 minutes.

(Serves 8.)

After baking if you want the syrup to be thicker, you can remove the potatoes and cook the sauce in a small pan for an additional time. From sometime in his past, Hal had fond memories of eating marshmallows atop sweet potatoes. We had this rendition in the past year during two of our holidays and now, it's a keeper. I chose to place the mashed sweet potatoes in a buttered, individual serving dish. I made a split down the middle, inserted some of the topping, and placed more of that mixture on top.

SWEET POTATOES WITH PECAN AND MARSHMALLOW STREUSEL

3 ½ pounds of fresh sweet potatoes (approx. 6 large potatoes)
¼ cup light brown sugar
¼ cup evaporated milk or heavy cream
2 T. butter, room temperature
2 T. orange juice
1 t. vanilla extract
½ t. salt
½ t. cinnamon
¼ t. nutmeg
¼ t. ground cloves
½ cup pecans, chopped and sautéed in a small amount of butter
2 cups miniature marshmallows

1. Cook potatoes covered in water until completely done. Cool. Remove skin and mash.
2. Combine potatoes (around 4 cups), sugar, milk, butter, orange juice, vanilla extract, salt, cinnamon, nutmeg, and cloves and beat until smooth.
3. Spoon into lightly-greased, individual ramekins or 1 baking dish.
4. Saute pecans in a bit of butter until lightly toasted.
5. Insert half of pecans in the middle of ramekins or baking dish.
6. Place remaining pecans on top.
7. Bake @ 350 degrees for 30 minutes.
8. Place 2 cups of marshmallows on top and broil until marshmallows are slightly brown, being very watchful as they brown quickly.

(Serves 10 to 12. Half of this recipe serves 6.)

Here is another version:

STUFFED SWEET POTATOES
WITH PECAN AND MARSHMALLOW STREUSEL

12 large sweet potatoes
¾ cup (1½ sticks) unsalted butter, at room temperature
¾ cup light brown sugar
¾ cup flour
¼ t. cinnamon
¼ t. salt
1 cup pecan pieces sautéed in small amount of butter
1 cup miniature marshmallows

1. Wash sweet potatoes and prick them, then place on a baking sheet.
2. Bake between 30 and 45 minutes or until knife inserted in center comes out clean.
3. In a large bowl, mix butter, brown sugar, and flour until it is crumbly.
4. Add cinnamon, salt, toasted pecans, and marshmallows.
5. Mix the streusel topping.
6. Slice sweet potatoes lengthwise down the center and push end towards the middle so it opens up.
7. Stuff sweet potatoes generously with the topping and return to the oven.
8. Bake for an additional 15 to 20 minutes or until topping is brown.

(Serves 12.)

We have often driven from France to England to visit with our friends and/or to collect supplies for the boat-building projects. We would sometimes stay with our friends in Evesham. I have not included herein all the lovely desserts that were served to us. Sometimes, I have difficulty making them using U.S. measurements. In order for us to share our recipes, I have translated any European recipe included in this book by using the standard American 8-ounce measuring cup. The British cup is 10 ounces. Another plus about eating with our friends is that they served multiple vegetables with meals. They also warm the dinner plates and some use a warming tray when serving a meal.

I thought you might be interested to see what Barbara Tittensor served during an entire week's visit. Not every lunch or dinner was eaten at their home but the following represents some of the foods Barbara prepared. Wine was always served with the evening meals and cocktails before dinner for those who wished.

Now this is definitely not a complete list of everything brought to the dining table, but it gives you an idea of the selections. Though it was served to us in England, it could very well be a menu from any of the countries we have visited, including the U.S. The Tittensors have done quite a lot of traveling since his retirement and, like I do, Barbara picks up ideas from the many hotels and restaurants they have visited throughout Europe.

Some of the Week's Menus

1. A quiche, a salad with prawns, and an apple tart.
2. Chicken Tarragon with potatoes and vegetables and a dessert of ice cream, strawberries and hard meringue.
3. Smoked Haddock with side dishes and Chocolate Cake.
4. A pork and pasta dish along with potatoes and peas.
5. Stuffed mushrooms, Fresh Salmon, Asparagus, and for dessert, Rhubarb Custard and ice cream, two different desserts.
6. Jambalaya as a main course with other side dishes and dessert.

We were cruising near Milton Keynes in England where another Ham Radio friend and his wife resided. We invited them and a couple of other amateurs to our boat for afternoon tea and cake. When dining with our friends, we were served the following dinner, another example of a typical English meal.

Leg of lamb with mint sauce (very English), potatoes, cauliflower, carrots, and for dessert, apricot-apple pie.

The above menus were served in English homes. The following are two meals served by friends who invited us into their French homes.

Collin, a mild fish (served chilled with aioli (mayonnaise mixture)
Green Beans
Steak
Cheese Course
Gateau (cake), a fancy cake purchased at a *patisserie,* a shop selling breads and desserts
Two wines plus champagne

An informal dinner was served to us by Paulette, the owner of the champagne vineyard. She's a competent cook no matter the circumstances.

Crab soup
French bread
Trout with almonds
Salad
Strawberries and ice cream
with raspberry liqueur

Granddaughters Becky and Colleen enjoyed this dish on one of their stays on our boat in France. Back in Connecticut, they often asked their mother to prepare it and now that they are older, they prepare it for themselves.

TOMATO HALVES WITH HERBS

4 large, firm, ripe tomatoes
salt, to taste
¾ t. sugar
2 cups fresh breadcrumbs, finely grated
4 T. butter
1 garlic clove
2 green onions
1 t. dried oregano
½ t. pepper

1. Cut tomatoes in half. Salt each half lightly and sprinkle with a pinch of sugar
2. Combine breadcrumbs, melted butter, crushed garlic, chopped green onions, oregano, and pepper.
3. Mound the mixture on top of tomato halves.
4. Bake at 325 degrees for 15 to 20 minutes.
5. If necessary at the end of the baking, grill for a couple of minutes to reach desired golden top.

(Makes 8 servings. Can easily be halved.)

While the main reason for residing at a boatyard or a marina is often to have work done on the boat, it seems that quite often it becomes a coterie of folks, as well. One summer we were residing at a boatyard for several weeks while Hal was told to rest after a mild heart incident. Several English folks pulling trailers loaded with canoes arrived. They used the yard as their jumping-off place and either paddled away for the day or stayed near and took us and others for short rides around the village. A picnic for them by the yard owners and the marina boat crews was planned and everyone participated in the preparation. Hal and I spent most of one day making several large bowls of potato salad. It's difficult to specify the amount of ingredients exactly, but here is my best estimate. The dish is based on what my mother's salad tasted like, but she never had any quantities for it.

POTATO SALAD

6 to 8 medium sized potatoes, cooked to tender stage but not soft
celery, 3 or 4 stalks
onion, small
pimientos, half of a small 4-ounce jar, drained
salt and pepper, to taste
½ t. celery salt
mayonnaise, enough to cover potatoes to your liking
prepared mustard, enough to color mayo to your liking
cider vinegar, 1 to 2 T

1. Cook potatoes to tender stage but not soft; cool and dice.
2. Chop celery, onion, and pimientos; add salt and pepper and celery salt; combine with potatoes.
3. In a large bowl, mix mayonnaise, mustard, and vinegar.
4. Combine both mixtures and chill in refrigerator for 2 to 3 hours.

(Serves 8.)

One salad stood out that day and it's a winner. Don't be put off by the unusual ingredients; after it sets in the refrigerator for a couple of hours or more, the salad blends nicely.

Here, too, I never obtained the quantities for the ingredients but have made a good stab at it.

BROWN RICE SALAD

1 cup brown rice
1 can medium-size corn, drained
½ cup green olives, halved
½ cup black olives, halved
½ cup salted peanuts
1 large banana, sliced
French dressing (same as given for tomato salad)

1. Cook rice according to package directions; cool.
2. Mix corn, olives, and peanuts.
3. Add dressing (enough to moisten rice) over all ingredients.
4. Chill at least an hour before serving.
5. Add sliced banana prior to serving.

(Serves 8-10.)

Just before serving, you may want to add a bit more dressing for added moistness.

Several friends gathered by the canal bank in France to share an afternoon with us. One couple had driven down from Belgium; another was an American who was cruising on his own barge. I decided to prepare the following recipe which comes from the Burgundy region.

CHICKEN WITH WINE FROM BURGUNDY
(Coq au Vin de Bourgogne)

4 ounces of bacon
2 ounces butter, divided
4 pounds chicken pieces
12 shallots (could substitute onion, about 2/3 cup)
6 to 8 T. brandy
3 garlic cloves, crushed
1 bouquet garni
1 bay leaf
4 ounces button mushrooms, chopped
2 T. flour
1 bottle red Burgundy wine

1. Lightly brown the bacon. Remove from pan.
2. Melt half the butter; add chicken, and fry until browned. Remove from pan.
3. Drain off excess fat. Add shallots and sauté 2 to 3 minutes.
4. In a large pot, add wine, brandy, garlic, bouquet garni, bay leaf, salt and pepper. Place shallots, chicken and bacon in pot.
5. Bring to boil; cover and simmer 1 hour.
6. Add mushrooms and cook 15 minutes.
7. Blend remaining butter with flour, remove approximately 1 cup of sauce from pan and mix with butter and flour; return this to pan and stir well. This mixture may need adapting for the mixture to meet your satisfaction.
8. Remove bouquet garni and bay leaf.

(Serves 6.)

When we return to areas that we have visited previously, we are able to cook and visit with old acquaintances. Auxerre, France remains one of those places. The managers of this marina say that we are their oldest customers. Now that can be taken two ways and probably, we come close to meeting both criteria. Regardless, it's much like coming home when we arrive in Auxerre. Often other boat crews are also beginning or ending their summer's cruise, so it becomes a real reunion of friends. What's especially convenient for the cook is that we are in a large city with great seafood markets, supermarkets, *charcuteries* (delicatessen), and *patisseries*—all in the proximity of the marina. Like most French cities and towns, there is a weekly market. I often shop daily and select fresh fish or salmon from the fishmonger. Here are three of my favorite seafood main courses:

SALMON WITH TARRAGON-LEEK SAUCE

8 T. butter, divided
4 large leeks (4 cups of ¼" sliced white and pale green parts only)
1¼ cups dry Vermouth
1¼ cups whipping cream
¼ cup parsley
1 t. tarragon
salt and pepper to taste
8 (6-ounce) salmon fillets

1. Melt 4 T. butter in skillet over medium-low heat. Add leeks to butter and sauté until soft and transparent, around 15 minutes.
2. Add Vermouth and boil over high heat until liquid is reduced to 2 T., around 5 minutes.
3. Add cream, boil until thickened, around 2 minutes.
4. Stir in parsley and tarragon, salt and pepper. Keep warm on low heat.
5. Sprinkle salmon with salt and pepper. Dust lightly with flour.
6. Melt 2 T. butter in 2 skillets over medium heat. Cook salmon 3 minutes per side.
7. Serve leek sauce over salmon.

(Serves 8.)

This makes a pretty serving plate and is quite tasty.

TERIYAKI SALMON

4 or 6 salmon fillets, about 6 ounces each
dab of butter/olive oil combination
2/3 cup Teriyaki Marinade and Sauce
mixed salad greens, enough to partially cover the individual serving plates
½ c. sliced almonds, browned in butter
Dressing:
¼ cup Teriyaki marinade and sauce
2 T. pineapple juice
2 T. canola oil
1 T. honey

1. Prepare dressing in a container. Set aside.
2. Marinade salmon in teriyaki sauce for 30 minutes or longer.
3. Fry salmon 3 to 4 minutes on each side. In order to reach doneness but not overcook, I cut one piece in half to check. Near the end of frying, I add a couple T. of the marinade. Fry an additional minute or two and it gives the salmon a lightly- browned effect.
4. Spread greens on serving plates.
5. Top with almonds.
6. Place dressing in microwave to reach warmth. Be careful not to heat it too long as it will quickly boil over.
7. Add salmon to serving plate and drizzle with dressing. Serve remaining dressing in a small pitcher.

(Serves 4 to 6.)

Next is a fine dish I prepare after a long day at work and it is also elegant enough to serve to guests. I like to begin this dinner with Shrimp Avocado salad. I think the fish is better when prepared in the microwave as it allows the fish to remain moist.

FILLET OF FISH WITH ALMONDS IN MICROWAVE

¼ cup slivered or flake almonds
¼ cup butter
4 pieces of mild, white fish
¼ t. dill seasoning
1 t. dried parsley + some for garnish
1 T. lemon juice
Dash of paprika

1. In a 10-inch pie plate or comparable microwave dish, heat the butter in the MW until melted, just a few seconds. Mix in the almonds making sure they all come in contact with the butter. Cook the almonds in butter for 5 minutes on High with no cover.
2. Remove almonds. Place fish in dish, turning to coat both sides in butter.
3. Sprinkle with dill, parsley, and lemon juice.
4. Cover and cook 4 to 8 minutes on High. The timing will depend upon the size of the microwave and the thickness of the fish. Check for doneness after 4 minutes. Then, check at 2-minute intervals. A thin filet can cook in approximately 4 minutes.
5. Uncover, top with almonds and cook an additional 1 minute.
6. Sprinkle with paprika and bits of parsley. Serve the fish with a bit of the lemon-butter sauce on top.

(Serves 4.)

A favorite ending to these get-togethers using fresh summer fruits is a cobbler or shortcake. I make this often during the summer months. It's quite easy to find juicy, fresh peaches during the summer, and it's hard to prepare a dessert any tastier than this. It's scrumptious. Add some pouring cream or vanilla ice cream to the warmed cobbler and wait for the oohs and aahs.

BLUEBERRY-PEACH COBBLER

1 T. cornstarch
¼ c. light brown sugar
½ cup cold water
2 cups ripe, fresh peaches
1 cup fresh blueberries
1 T. lemon juice

½ cup milk
1 T. butter, softened
1 cup flour
½ cup sugar
1½ t. baking powder
½ t. salt

¼ cup butter, softened
sugar, dash
nutmeg, dash

1. Mix cornstarch, brown sugar, and cold water.
2. Add peeled and sliced peaches and blueberries; cook over low heat until thickened.
3. Add lemon juice and pour the mixture into a baking dish.
4. Add milk and butter to dry ingredients all at once. Beat until smooth. Layer by spoonfuls over fruit.
5. Sprinkle with a dash of sugar, add the ¼ cup of soft butter, and a dash of nutmeg.
6. Bake @ 350 degrees for 30 minutes.

(Serves 8.)

We have our favorite rural villages that we enjoy visiting over and over again. The canals lend themselves to the quiet, slow-paced lifestyle. Often the canal is lined with trees providing beautiful landscapes, as well as much-needed shade on warm, summer days.

Summer is an especially wonderful time to cruise the countryside, whatever country you're visiting whether spending the entire summer or just a week or two. Meals are often decided by what is available along the way. The idea for a meal will come not from the cookbook but from the market's stalls or the lockkeeper's garden or orchard. It is our custom to buy from lockkeepers in order to provide them additional income and to benefit from the freshness of the produce. They will ordinarily place a sign by the lock or a box containing the kinds of items being offered. Occasionally, the lockkeeper will have baked a pie or produced some cheese that he or she is eager to sell. Some lockkeepers are friendlier than others, which is no surprise. Often we can be greeted like old friends and a visit will ensue. We have even shared our lunch with a lockkeeper on occasion. The keepers and their houses are an important element of the whole canal scene, giving the day's journey a stopping place and adding to the waterway's personality.

I prepare the following during any time of the year but would most likely serve it in the cooler months. You can always have canned pineapple and the other ingredients in your cupboard. It became a staple dessert on our boat, especially when fresh fruit was unattainable.

Hal calls it like it is:

PINEAPPLE DOWNSIDE-UP CAKE

Cake:
1½ cups cake flour
2 t. baking powder
½ t. salt
2/3 cup sugar
½ cup vegetable oil
½ c. milk, room temperature
1 egg, room temperature
1 t. vanilla extract

Topping:
6 T. butter or margarine
2/3 cup light brown sugar
1 medium-size can sliced pineapple, drained
8 maraschino cherries, rinsed and drained
½ cup pecans, chopped

Cake:
1. Mix flour, baking powder, salt, and sugar.
2. Add oil and milk; blend.
3. Beat for 2 minutes.
4. Add egg and vanilla; blend.
5. Beat 2 more minutes. Set aside.

Topping:
1. Melt butter in 8x8-inch baking pan and sprinkle with brown sugar.
2. Place sliced pineapple over sugar mixture.
3. Add cherries and pecans over the pineapple.
4. Cover with cake batter.
5. Bake @ 350 degrees for 40 to 50 minutes.
6. Cool for 5 minutes before turning onto a plate.
7. Serve warm with whipped cream.

(Serves 9.)

In the years following our initial two-day get-together on the French canals, we have met with Anne and Robin on several occasions. Eight years lapsed between one of our meetings. We wondered if we would recognize them as they approached us at the train station. Our concerns were not a problem and within a short time, we were again enjoying each other's company. The first evening on one of their visits they asked if they could have carrot cake. We told them that if they went out in the morning and bought the ingredients before our departure, we would bake them a cake. Early the next morning, they left shopping bags in hand. One summer we joined them on their hire-boat for an evening meal. They served a very popular dish in their country, Shepherd's Pie. I have adapted it to mesh with U.S. ingredients.

BEEF PIE WITH MASHED POTATO TOPPING
Shepherd's Pie

2 T. onion, minced
2 T. butter or margarine
1½ cups ground beef, cooked and drained
½ cup cooked carrots, diced
1 (10 ¾-ounce can) condensed tomato soup
¼ t. hot sauce
½ t. salt
dash of pepper
1 cup mashed potatoes, hot
paprika

1. Saute onion in butter until golden brown. Remove onion; brown beef and drain.
2. Add carrots, soup, hot sauce, salt, and pepper.
3. Mix and place in a greased 9-inch pie plate.
4. Cover with a thin layer of mashed potatoes.
5. Swirl potatoes to make a design; dust with paprika.
6. Bake @ 400 degrees for 20 minutes or until potatoes are golden brown.

(Serves 4.)

There were several times throughout our cruising that we went into the Bastille Marina in Paris for a few weeks' visit, in fact, over 25 times. We have often heard of the Cordon Bleu Cooking School, in Paris, but my having grown up in a little town in Ohio certainly did not provide me any opportunity to delve into their cuisine methodology. My friend, Gwenda who was staying at the marina on her boat and I decided to check out their summer program. We were lucky enough to be able to select any morning or afternoon sessions that interested us. We went to some of the same programs and, also, chose some different ones for personal reasons. I attended four days and during that time, I observed top chefs preparing their gourmet food. There were some 25 prospective chefs in the audience and some ten of us who were there just out of interest. At the conclusion of each session, everyone had the opportunity to taste what had been prepared. There was no opportunity for hands-on at these particular lessons. One has to sign up for more extensive programs to be able to practice the culinary skills.

I brought back with me tips on how to make the sauce that accompanies the Pork Chops with French Mustard. (See Index.) I had ordered from a restaurant a dish that was to my liking, *Lapin a la Moutarde,* rabbit in a mustard cream sauce. Since rabbit is not easily found in the U.S., I substitute pork or chicken. *Cordon Bleu* translates, for me, as an approach to cooking that starts with the basic, fresh food item and uses top-quality herbs and spices in their right combination. For example, when preparing *Lapin a la Moutarde* the chef began with a whole, fresh rabbit.

I, also, came back one day from lessons with a recipe for pear-almond pie that had been demonstrated. A few days later this pie was prepared as a special treat for Karen, our granddaughter, who had arrived in Paris for a three-week visit when she was 11 years of age. Though the pie was enjoyed, it did not make the favorite list.

One evening while sitting in a marina in Sweden, we met an American couple who had crossed the ocean in their own yacht. Recognizing our American flag, they stopped at our boat to chat. We were about to have a pizza so we invited them to join us. He was of Italian extraction and upon reflection, either I was very naïve or very brave to serve Italian pizza to them. Since that first meeting, we became good friends. They followed us along the coast of Sweden and Denmark before setting off for their homeport. Back in the U.S., we were invited to come to their home in Osterville, Massachusetts. Naturally, I often remember the meals that I am served in someone else's home and her dinner was easy to recall. She came home from a full day of teaching, put together a pastry and its stuffing, and we all made our own calzones. We were impressed. I have since used the same idea with our visitors; it's fun and guests seem to enjoy joining in the preparation. So, here follows my recipes for pizza and Louisa Guzzitti's recipe for calzones. Calzones are an Italian wrap-around, portable sandwich.

There are many variations in many countries that use some form of flat pastry. We are most familiar with the French crepe, the Mexican tortilla, the Spanish tapas, or the Chinese egg roll but if you think of any country, they probably have a similar pastry that they use to wrap around food, sometimes making it portable. Dining in an Ethiopian restaurant, we enjoyed eating a pastry placed in the center of the table from which you tore away some for yourself, then placed a filling within it.

As I have mentioned previously, during our early days of cruising we were on a very limited budget so going out, even for a pizza, was not an option. I would begin early in the day preparing the crust and the sauce. The lockkeepers often commented about the good smells coming from our boat. By evening, it was easy to put the ingredients together. Pizza was an every-Friday-night occurrence, and it continues to this day. Not many Friday nights go by without our having pizza. Making your own is easy assuming that you have the time. It is more rewarding to make it yourself as well as more economical. And, it's a nice feeling to know that the sauce and crust are waiting in the refrigerator or freezer. I have not made it recently and Hal commented that it had been some time since I had put a homemade pizza on the table. Soon, dear, soon. I'll get to it.

CHEESE PIZZA

Crust:
1 1/3 cups warm water (105 to 115 degrees)
1 package active dry yeast
Salad oil
2 t. salt
4½ cups flour

Sauce:
¼ cup salad or olive oil
1 cup onion, chopped
1 garlic clove, minced
1 large-size can Italian tomatoes, undrained
16 ounces tomato sauce
1 T. sugar
1½ t. salt
½ t. dried oregano leaves
½ t. dried basil leaves
¼ t. pepper

Topping:
1 pound mozzarella cheese, grated
1 large green bell pepper, thinly sliced
1 large red bell pepper, thinly sliced
You can stop with the above
or add additional topping
to your liking.

Crust:
I used hot water from the tap and it always worked well but, if possible, you may want to check the temperature.

1. Sprinkle yeast over warm-to-hot water in large bowl, stirring until dissolved. Add salt and flour.
2. Turn out onto lightly floured work surface. Knead in flour until smooth—takes about 10 minutes.
3. Place in medium bowl; brush very lightly with salad oil. Cover with towel; let rise in warm place (85 degrees) free from drafts until double in bulk—about 2 hours. I warm the oven slightly, turn it off, and place bowl in oven for this rising procedure. Or, in the summer on the boat I set the bowl by a window in the sun.
4. Divide the dough among pizza pans or freeze excess for another time. Lightly grease the pizza pan, then spread dough with your hands. Number of pizzas will depend upon your preferred thickness of crust.

Sauce:
1. In hot oil in large pan, sauté onion and garlic until golden brown—about 5 minutes.
2. Add the remaining sauce ingredients and simmer for an hour, stirring occasionally.

Toppings:
1. Bake the crust for 5 to 8 minutes @ 425 degrees. Remove from oven. Add sauce and toppings. We most often stuck to just the peppers, thinking we were keeping it vegetarian and less fattening.
2. Continue baking until suitably brown around the edges, approximately 12 to 15 more minutes. We like a thin crust so the amount of baking time is less than for a thicker crust.

(Makes 2 or 3 – 9 x 15-inch pans.)

CALZONE

Crust:
1 package active dry yeast
1¼ cups tepid water
3 cups flour
1 t. salt
1 T. sugar
2 T. olive oil

Filling:
4 sweet Italian sausages
1 medium onion, sliced
4 Italian plum tomatoes, sliced
¼ pound Monterey Jack cheese, sliced thinly
1 green bell pepper
½ cup fresh basil and parsley, chopped
½ cup olive oil
salt and pepper, to taste
cornmeal for the baking sheet

Crust:
1. **Sprinkle yeast over 1¼ cups tepid water in a bowl. Let it stand for 5 minutes to proof.**
2. **Add flour, salt, and sugar and the olive oil and stir.**
3. **Add a little more water or flour as needed to make a soft dough that holds together.**
4. **Turn it out onto a floured board and knead until smooth and pliable.**
5. **Put in lightly oiled bowl and turn to coat it with oil.**
6. **Cover and leave an hour. Punch it down, divide into quarters and shape each into a ball. Set them on the counter loosely covered with cloth. (Have a glass of good, Italian wine.)**

Filling:
1. Slit the sausage casing, crumble the meat and brown it in small skillet along with the onion until no pink shows.
2. Remove meat and onion from skillet; drain.
3. Roll out pastry making 8 serving rounds. Add to the sausage/onion mixture the tomatoes, cheese, green pepper, basil, and parsley. Place filling on half of each round and fold over into half-moon shapes. With fork dipped in water, press edges of calzones to seal. The size of the rounds are to your liking. I usually make them approximately 6 inches in diameter.
4. Bake @ 450 degrees for 18 to 20 minutes.
5. When baked, brush top with olive oil.

(Makes 8 portions.)

This pizza is very different from the usual and offers one a nice alternative. It gives pizza a Mediterranean flavor.

PIZZA WITH FETA AND SHRIMP

1 (12-inch diameter) baked pizza crust
8 ounces mozzarella cheese, grated, about 2 cups packed
1 pound plum tomatoes, thinly sliced
8 ounces feta cheese, crumbled
16 black olives, pitted
½ cup green onions, chopped + additional for garnish
2 T. fresh oregano leaves or 2 t. dried oregano
½ pound shrimp, cooked, peeled, and deveined

1. Bake crust @ 425 degrees for 10 minutes, remove.
2. Sprinkle mozzarella over. Arrange tomatoes atop mozzarella.
3. Sprinkle feta over tomatoes.
4. Sprinkle olives, ½ cup green onions, and oregano over pizza.
5. Bake 10 minutes.
6. Arrange shrimp atop pizza; continue baking until crust is golden and cheese melts, about 4 minutes longer.
7. Cool pizza in pan 5 minutes. Sprinkle the additional onion over pizza.
8. Cut into wedges and serve.

(Makes 1 large pizza.)

IV

Building a Second Narrowboat and Continuing to Cruise in England and on the Continent

You have sailed to eight different lands.
And, it has been all you hoped it would be.
The stress, however, is a bit out of hand.
So, we're returning inland and rejecting the sea.

ALLEGHENY, BOAT NO. 3

While we were most pleased with our adventures on K*I*S*S, we had managed to do some very complex navigation and rough sailing. Years ago we had dealt with handling strong currents and following ranges when sailing Sea Quester along the Carolina coasts in the U.S. Therefore, we felt prepared to deal with the rushing waters at sea in Europe. I remember following another boat that was also planning to enter the Kiel Canal in Germany. He missed the entrance by a lot because he had not compensated for the amount of current that was pushing us sideways. That first summer on K*I*S*S was probably our most interesting and challenging summer on the water and possibly, the most memorable.

Because of the degree of attention that sailing required of us, we decided after seven years that we would sell our motorsailer and build another narrowboat. We knew that the rivers and canals provided a more peaceful cruising ground. We had returned from Norway and traveled along the inland waterways throughout Europe. We spent a couple seasons in the Netherlands enjoying their lovely waterways. We became good friends with Carla and Bolle Verweij who owned a marina in Aalsmeer. We were invited to their home for a weekend now and then. Bolle and Carla are known among their friends for their preparation of an Indonesian rice table. We have enjoyed these meals more than once. They frequently visit us on the boat and once, they brought a chicken satay meal all the way from their home to France.

It was not difficult to find a buyer for the motorsailer. The designer of Sprays, Bruce

Roberts and Gwenda decided that they would like to own it, and we turned it over at the Aalsmeer boatyard. We packed our belongings into a small rental van and off we went, back to England. We chose to build this boat at the same boatyard in Worcester where we had built K*I*S*S, so it was as if we were going back home. Hal had spent much of the winter drawing the design on the computer in Pennsylvania, the steel shell was ordered, and Roger Apperley, the builder, had commenced building the shell for us.

We wanted our new boat to have inside steering. The solution—Hal would design a pilothouse based on what he knew from his years of research on the subject and from our years of cruising in Dutch barge country. The carpenter from the Evesham days now had his own shop some 30 miles from our location. With his guidance, we were able to construct a pilothouse, traveling by car to his work place for several weeks.

We were able to get back into visiting with our long-time friends from Evesham. We knew our way around when shopping for supplies, and life was great. We bought ourselves another used car and easily adapted to driving again on the left-hand side of the road.

One afternoon while having tea with the workers, Hal mentioned that he was getting a bit nervous regarding the vandalism that was occurring around us. I had watched a horse trailer leave the next-door establishment, not realizing that it was being stolen. Kids were climbing fences and making themselves a nuisance. One of the gentlemen sitting around the tea table was the person the yard hired when they needed to have a boat transported. Yes, he is the one whom I described earlier, the one who had seem reserved and not too talkative. He turned out to be a good friend. He said to Hal that we could bring our shell to his back garden to finish the work. He, also, said that we could reside in a vacant mobile home he had on the property. You mean leave this industrial site, move to a residence which had a big lawn, have a bathtub and a fireplace, and one of those old-fashioned clothes washers of days long ago. In my opinion having an old-style clothes washer and a drying line outside in lovely sunshine is far better than going to the public laundry. All those facilities were available to us and we couldn't refuse. So, Gil Harding who is in the boat-transport business with his son moved our unfinished shell to the village of Powick. If you have ever spent any time working and living in a boatyard, you will appreciate this opportunity.

We entertained our friends from close by as well as friends from Argentina, France, and the U.S. Our first grandchild was just 13 when she came to stay with us for three weeks. Since we were in the process of boat building, there was no major cruising planned during her stay. However, one day we rented a hire-boat and invited the Gealers and Tittensors to join us. Christina was in her glory as she had six adults who doted on her. She helped her Grandma prepare the meal that we enjoyed half way through our boat trip. Our menu included:

Roast Ham and Roast Turkey
Potato Salad and Brown Rice Salad
Bakery Rolls
Tri-level Brownies and Pouring Cream
Wine and Juice

The above side dishes are included in this book.

I mentioned earlier that painting our first boat was a real learning experience. I didn't realize that it could involve so many coats and one was expected to reach such perfection. When working with steel hulls, one spends long hours filling and sanding. I continued to be the "gofer", the cook, and the builder's assistant.

The whole time we are spending our days working, we are also thinking of where we may take short trips to see the sites or plan a dinner party. We often got together with the boat builder and his family or dined with the welder and his wife. It turned out that many of the friends whom we made over the years were not into cruising. It was we who introduced them to the waterways.

Another way that we end up meeting folks is by just working in the boatyard. Other boaters are interested in what you are doing and stop to talk. Often, they will visit with Hal as he is usually more willing and able to stop what he is doing. My excuse is that the paint must keep flowing. I was reminded of this during a trip I was taking with the Krafts. While Hal remained at a marina in England putting finishing touches on Allegheny, Diana, Christina, TJ and Karen and I drove to Ireland.

While we were away and Hal was on his own, he said that he often prepared a salad for his dinner and had so enjoyed a commercial, honey-mustard dressing. I have put together this easy dressing using the ingredients that are most always in the cupboard.

HONEY-MUSTARD SALAD DRESSING

3 T. honey
2 T. French mustard
¼ cup cider vinegar
½ cup olive oil

1. **Combine honey and mustard until smooth.**
2. **Add vinegar, whisk until blended.**
3. **Slowly add oil while beating with whisk.**
4. **Shake well before pouring onto salad greens.**

(Makes 1 cup.)

On our return from Ireland, we were staying the last night in Wales. We had planned to get a Bed and Breakfast but found all desirable B&B's had no vacancies. One B&B owner said that possibly we could stay at such and such a place. This "place" didn't usually rent rooms as they were more into housing for conferences but she gave us directions and we backtracked a few miles to investigate. We turned into a lane and came upon a guardhouse. It seemed to be closed so we continued along the lane. Around a bend in the lane, we came upon a small chateau. Our first instinct was to turn around but we soon talked ourselves out of that and drove up to the front entrance. The owners were gracious enough to offer us a place to stay for the night. They gave us directions of where we could dine in the next town, so everything was fantastic. We couldn't believe where we were staying, and the price had been within reason.

Our room in the chateau was huge. A mural of a battle scene which included swords, horses, and fighting men covered one entire wall. There was one bed against the mural and TJ who was 11 was not about to spend his night in that spot. We all slept in one large room except for one connected room where Christina slept. What a find. Now this chateau was close to a day's travel by car from where we had been building Allegheny. In the morning, a young girl who must have been three or four years of age came into our room as we were about to depart. She asked us where we were from and I told her that we lived on a Dutch-barge narrowboat near Worcester. She said, "I live on a BIG Dutch barge." When I went down to the kitchen to pay the bill, I remarked about the Dutch barge and the young man said, "Yes, I know your barge." He and his wife had been walking about the boatyard and had spoken with Hal; he said that I was busy painting. Hal and I returned to this chateau for a visit some months later as I wanted to show him this gorgeous "place," and we took with us a couple from Maryland who were visiting us and celebrating their anniversary. They are the same folks who were our first guests in boat number one, Pennsylvania Yankee.

Allegheny received an award at the National Waterways Festival so we were beginning to be known in the boating world. That award has nothing to do with food except for the party we held the day of the winning. We didn't expect to be in the running since we were U.S. citizens and Allegheny was not built in the traditional narrowboat design but was altogether different. However, it made a hit with the judges at this national rally, and we walked away with the trophy for the best amateur-built boat out of some 350 boats registered. Friends Bolle and Carla from the Netherlands were spending the week with us and our Evesham friends drove to the rally. They, along with the editor of <u>Waterways World</u> were treated to a lunch and what else—carrot cake.

Allegheny on the Nivernais Canal

I shall never forget the day in early September just before we were to ship Allegheny across the English Channel to France. It was a Sunday morning and we were about to go through a lock in Reading, England. I went up to the lock and as I introduced myself to the lockkeeper and told him that we would like to pass through, I commented that it was certainly a very sad day for the country. We had learned on the radio that morning that Princess Diana had died. The lockkeeper's comment was that he could care less about any royalty so I quickly removed myself from further conversation.

The following day we were placed upon a flatbed lorry (semi-truck) and were headed to France. We rode in the cab of the lorry and received the same hospitality on the ferry boat as other truckers. We ate meals on white tablecloths and drank wine. Isn't that how all truckers live?

Each boat that we have owned has spent summers throughout England and Western Europe. I probably concentrate my writing on experiences in France more than any other country. This is not to insinuate that other countries were less interesting or less capable of selling and preparing good food, but France just seems to have a bit of an edge regarding food, in general. Worth mentioning, however, are the Belgium patisseries that seem to be on a par with those in France.

I frequently ask myself, "What do my family and friends think that we are doing day in and day out?" Do they picture us relaxing, drinking cocktails, and leading a more carefree, retired life? Yes, we do all that. However, our friends who have visited us on our boat know that we do sometimes dig in and get dirty. I'm wondering if I don't feel a bit guilty at times because we do lead such a wonderful life. I have reflected on my years since 1980 and have admitted to myself that I have worked harder at times since 1980 than I ever worked for wages. Working at boat-building yards is certainly a big change from our careers in education. It has been quite different but rewarding. There is something to be said for working on a physical product, an accomplishment you can see at the end of the day. But, it has not been steady work and there are days when we are extremely lazy. That's the great thing about being retired—you have the option of declaring any day a holiday. Or, as we often say, "Every day is Saturday." Of the total thirty years so far, approximately 12 have been spent in boat building. Those 12 years were spread among five boats. So, you could say that in our retirement years, we have worked some and played some. During our 30 years, we have also maintained property, a house (sometimes two), a camping vehicle of some sort, etc. It was never difficult to find tasks to complete and to this day, there are always projects waiting.

During the boat-building phases, we lived in one place, became a part of a community, and had an opportunity to get acquainted with the locals. How pleasurable it was to communicate with local business people and do business with them on a weekly basis. To this day, we can enter a DIY store in Migennes, France, be greeted by the cashier as if we were just a local shopper, and feel good about the association we have developed.

We became good customers and received fair treatment. On one occasion I had worn out a sander. The local salesman whom we knew by first name graciously honored the warranty period, gave us a new sander but kidded me about the condition of the old one.

We probably eat healthier while living in one place. We can shop daily for fresh foods. We became familiar with the local customs and would look forward to shopping at the weekly markets. While cruising, we are not always near food stores and other commercial businesses, though we do have bicycles that allow us to go short distances.

When building, we find it necessary to have some form of vehicle but usually do not bother with a car once we begin cruising. We have never had any difficulty disposing of a used car. However, one time it was made easy for us. A crane operator lost control of his machine in the parking area and smashed our car into another car destroying ours totally. This was in the same boatyard where the straps on the crane broke and Allegheny was dropped along the dockside into the river. The insurance coverage and an enterprising young man who saw the wrecked boat on the Internet and bought it to restore left us with a nice amount in the bank. At this time, we were already into the beginning stages of building our fourth boat. People who heard the crash from a half-mile away came to the boatyard to see the damage. By that time, the boat had righted itself. The pilothouse had been removed in order that we could transport it across the English Channel; the entrance into the ferry was such that we did not fit without removing the pilothouse. Obviously, when our boat fell into the river, the water came into the interior from that large opening. Hal and I calmly proceeded to remove some of the dampened items. I put up a temporary clothesline in the boatyard in order to dry all the wet clothes. People remarked that we had remained so calm from the moment the accident occurred. I fall back on the thought that I have always held that items lost are merely material and most can be replaced. I was just thankful that no one was under the barge at the time.

V

Building a Wide-Beam Dutch Barge Replica and Cruising in England and on the Continent

Our narrowboat is just that—only seven-feet wide.
The thought of more living area strikes a deep chord.
We are building another boat; we cannot deny.
There's one thing for sure; we never get bored.

BOAT NUMBER IV – ALLEGHENY II

This was our ultimate boat for living aboard in luxury. We had 'lathered' for some time over the various barges we came across that had sizeable living areas in which four or more individuals could sit and have long visits in comfort. You must picture how we lived in the narrowboat. There were two comfortable lounging chairs. If we were entertaining that meant two others either sat at the dining table after dinner or made a space on the floor if wanting to watch a television broadcast. It didn't provide the best in comfort when more than two were aboard. Usually, the weather was pleasant and everyone could sit outside comfortably.

Hal had already designed the first Allegheny, so all that was needed was a different floor plan, a widening of the barge, and other details which he could develop using a computer-design program. We were excited with the new barge as it provided us with a dining/pilot house where we could seat six easily and be able to eat while

Allegheny II at Moret sur Loing

looking out on the scene around us. One misses so much when sitting down inside a sailboat and seeing on the outside only by standing up and looking out the windows. Also, our guests would have even more comfort with their own suite—what luxury!

So, we go to a different boatyard in England. Sirius Yachts in Stourport agreed to make us a shell according to Hal's design. It would be built in a large hangar, and we could live at the yard as soon as our part of the finishing commenced. We bought another used car and rented a small caravan (camping trailer) from the camping establishment next door. We were on cloud nine. We enrolled at the local community college for French classes. We started making ourselves familiar with the town of Stourport. We were not very far away from our familiar Worcester and, also, our friends in Evesham and elsewhere.

While I was occupied mostly in painting inside and out (Yes, my bit of steel siding and wall had grown.) I was reminded of how many coats would be needed to reach an acceptable level of coverage. When working with steel hulls, a great deal of filler and sanding is required. I just kept reminding myself that once we completed our task, the pleasure gained by residing in more living space would be worth it.

The construction of Allegheny II, though a larger craft, was made easier in some ways. The other boats had all been smaller and required built-in cupboards, drawers, and furniture. The wide-beam Dutch barge was sufficiently large, 13-feet by 49-feet, and, therefore, we were able to purchase cabinetry and chairs and sofas from stores. I was able to assemble the cabinets which came in flat-packs that were installed throughout the boat. Here again, Hal helped with the first one and I was able to complete the other five.

You may recall the nice woman who lived on a large Dutch barge, the woman who had invited us to stay on her barge while we were working on our boat out of the water. Well, her extending that invitation has, in part, brought us to where we are now—building a larger barge. In Allegheny II, there is considerably more living area, a large galley, a large refrigerator, and yes, space for a corner bathtub.

We take a break from our work over the Christmas holidays and fly to Ireland to visit with Bruce and Gwenda. They are renting a house right in the middle of Dublin. It's Christmas Day and Gwenda has prepared a mid-day dinner. We are called to the table and as we sat down just before starting to eat, we did the English tradition of pulling Christmas crackers. If you are unfamiliar with these, they are small cardboard tubes, the size smaller than a paper towel holder, that contain a small gift and you pull from one end as your dinner guest sitting next to you pulls from the other end. It's a fun idea and I remember I received a lipstick holder with a small mirror. Before beginning the meal, a radio announcer said over the air, "I would like to welcome Hal and Dorothy Stufft who are visiting us from England this Christmas. I hope your holidays are enjoyable." Well, we were both flabbergasted to hear our names being mentioned on Dublin Radio. Obviously, our host and hostess had made the request and timed it perfectly. It was a thoughtful and lovely surprise.

Back in Stourport, where we were putting the finishing touches on the barge, six of our family members, the Folignos's and Stuffts, were on board with us, three of them grandchildren. It was a wonderful time, especially for us.

At another time, we cruised with Ruth and brother-in-law, Jerry. They began their trip on the Kennett and Avon Canal in Bath, and there I was able to stock up for a week's cruise at a gourmet supermarket. We had gorgeous vegetables and fruit with which to make the Summer Pasta Salad, the cobbler, Mediterranean pizza, and other favorites.

At some point, we began to miss the French lifestyle so Allegheny II crossed the Channel with a pilot on board. This was called for by our insurance coverage, and it eased my mind to know there was another person on board in case of an emergency. It was great to be back in the world of *patisseries, charcuteries,* local markets, wider waterways, lockkeepers, and everything French. Often the canal is lined with plane trees providing beautiful landscapes, as well as much-needed shade on warm, sunny days.

We were even more eager to share our new boat with family and friends. We revisited many of our favorite towns. We had lunches at anchor under shade trees. During the extremely hot summer of 2003, we ate all our evening meals on deck, as it was just too stifling inside. And, we would not retire until around midnight when it began to get reasonably comfortable. Because of that one summer, we understand why the new owners have installed air conditioning. We have had only two summers in 30 when the heat has been that unbearable.

We entertained our friends and family as we visited in the Burgundy region. We received many compliments on the looks of our barge. We were both very proud of this barge and probably should have kept it for a longer time. This barge received an award for the best interior at the Canal du Nivernais rally of 2004.

However, we wanted to spend a winter in Paris and the stories from other boaters convinced us that probably it would not be feasible for Allegheny II to get a space. Now, we know that is not necessarily so. We should have pursued the idea ourselves rather than rely on word-of-mouth. Nevertheless, we decided to put Allegheny II on the market and to research the prospect of building a smaller boat in the design of a tug.

In the end we were able to live on the barge during a winter while working on the tugboat so that was quite comfortable—much nicer than living in a camping van. We continued to entertain on weekends while moored at a boatyard in Migennes. When Christina saw this yard, she said, "You're going to live here?" As boatyards go, they aren't usually the most appealing place to spend any length of time, but it met our needs.

The following is another easy dish to serve to guests. I could stand in the barge kitchen overlooking the living area while preparing the meal and yet not miss out on any of the conversation. It is so easy and quick that I could prepare it just before serving. You can put together all the ingredients ahead of time.

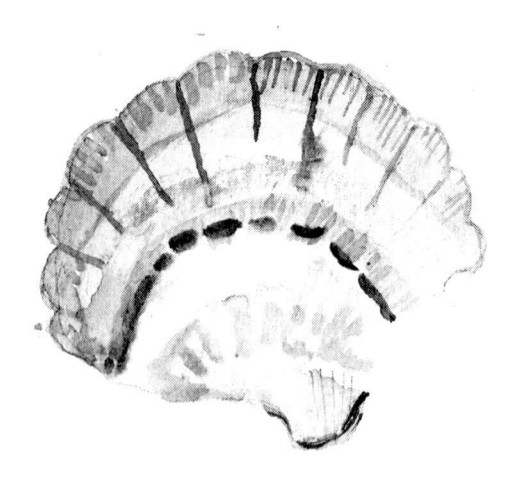

TERIYAKI-GLAZED CHICKEN

4 chicken breast halves, skinned, boneless, cut into strips
3 T. oil, divided
4 medium-sized carrots, julienne-style
1 medium-size onion, chopped
½ cup soy sauce
¼ cup light brown sugar
toasted sesame seeds, garnish
sliced green onions, garnish
rice, preferably brown

1. Cut chicken and vegetables prior to starting the frying.
2. Fry chicken strips in 2 T. oil for 6 to 8 minutes. Remove chicken.
3. In remaining 1 T. oil, fry the carrots and onions for 2 to 4 minutes.
4. Add soy sauce and brown sugar; bring to boil.
5. Return chicken to pan; fry 5 minutes.
6. Place a serving of rice on each plate.
7. Top rice with the chicken and vegetable mixture, garnish with sesame seeds and green onions.

To make the above more spicy, you can add a pinch of coriander and/or ground ginger.

The following recipe was spotted by Hal in a boating magazine in the middle 1970's and is another frequently-served dish for parties and dinner gatherings. Once Sarah and I drove to Old Saybrook, Connecticut to meet up with her dad and others who were cruising on his sailboat. We carried this dish with us to the gathering; the five folks on board reacted quite positively to our carry-in.

On board our own boat, we use special individual earthenware oven dishes for the baking and serving. Years ago when Hal was retiring from the school system, he wanted to entertain the teachers and fellow workers from the school by giving them a dinner party. We were able to find individual serving dishes that were oven proof but were a throw-away paper product. For that party, I recall taking off the day from work to put together 85+ individual servings. This dish is very special and surprisingly quite easy to make whether for four or for more. It has gotten better over the years as Hal always seems to appear when the mixture is cooking and after a taste, he often adds more wine.

A staff member of Waterways World and his wife joined us for a week on the Nivernais Canal. They had watched the building of the barge which was near their English home and were eager to experience French waterways and the positive qualities of the barge. They own a traditional English narrowboat. For them, it was both a business and pleasure trip, including an opportunity to celebrate a wedding anniversary. One of the dinners prepared in their honor included scallops as the main course.

If one wishes to raise this already-sophisticated dish to another level, they can substitute 1 pound of lobster and 1 pound of shrimp; the goal is a total of 3 pounds.

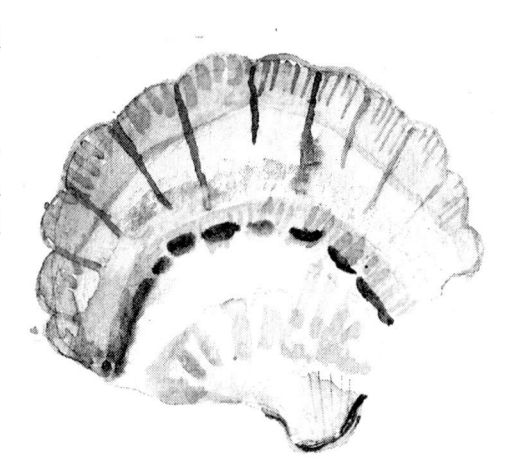

SCALLOPS IN WINE SAUCE
Coquille St. Jacques

4 T. butter
4 T. flour
¼ t. salt
2 cups light cream
2 pounds scallops
1 pound haddock or other mild, white fish
2 cans (4 ounces each) sliced mushrooms, drained
1 T. green onions, minced
2 T. brandy + 1 cup white wine, dry (You are on your own if you add more wine.)
few grains of cayenne
½ t. dry mustard
Parmesan cheese for topping

1. **Melt butter. Blend in flour and salt off the heat. Place back on burner.**
2. **On low to medium heat, slowly add cream without stopping, stirring all the time. If medium heat is too high, you will notice the mixture sticking to the bottom of the pan.**
3. **Simmer and stir for 5 minutes.**
4. **Add remaining ingredients and place in individual ramekins.**
5. **Bake @ 375 degrees for 30 minutes.**

(Serves 8.)

During one of our social gatherings with fellow boaters, I met a professional chef. During my conversation with her, she confirmed what I thought, too, about the preparation of scrambled eggs. In her words, "There is no better way to prepare moist servings of scrambled eggs than in a microwave." I remember the best scrambled eggs that I had ever been served. It was at a university gathering in the late 1960's and the eggs were prepared in large quantities. I don't know what they did to make them so moist, but this is my best attempt.

The following came from practice, as timing in the microwave is most important. You may need to prepare this more than one time to get the results you desire.

SCRAMBLED EGGS IN THE MICROWAVE

1 t. butter for 1 egg, s. & p.
1 T. water or milk for 1 egg

1. Melt the butter @ 100 Power, just a few seconds. Cover the butter lightly.
2. Add eggs and desired amount of liquid and beat until well blended.
3. Change power setting to 50. During the cooking, stop to stir occasionally to break apart the mixture. Let stand 1 minute until completely set.

1 egg	In 6-ounce cup	1 ½ minutes
2 eggs	In 10-ounce cup	2 ¾ minutes
4 eggs	8" round dish	5 ¼ minutes
6 eggs	8" round dish	6 minutes

The following was served to us in a Bed and Breakfast in Ireland. It seemed just a tad above the average scrambled eggs and one that I like serving to our guests.

SCRAMBLED EGGS WITH SMOKED SALMON AND CHIVES

8 large eggs
4 T. fresh chives, chopped, divided
3 T. milk
5 T. butter
1 large onion, chopped
6 ounces thinly sliced smoked salmon, cut into strips

1. Beat eggs, 2 T. chives, and milk in bowl to blend.
2. Melt butter in heavy, large skillet over medium heat.
3. Add onion and sauté until golden, about 15 minutes.
4. Add egg mixture. Cook until almost set, stirring occasionally,

about 4 minutes.
5. Mix in salmon. Cook until eggs are cooked through but still moist, about 1 minute longer.
6. Season with salt and pepper.
7. Transfer eggs to platter; sprinkle with remaining 2 T. chives.

(Serves 4.)

Sarah, Becky, and Colleen joined us on Allegheny II one July in France and we had a lovely, family cruise. Becky, in particular, liked the following vegetable side dish, and I hear that she makes it often.

SNOW PEAS AND CHERRY TOMATOES

1½ cups snow peas, trimmed
3 T. water
½ t. butter or stick margarine
¼ t. sugar
12 cherry tomatoes, halved
½ t. dark sesame oil
1/8 t. salt and pepper

1. Combine the first 4 ingredients in a large skillet.
2. Cook over medium heat 2 minutes or until the liquid mixture almost evaporates.
3. Add the tomatoes and cook for 2 minutes or until thoroughly heated.
4. Remove from heat; stir in remaining ingredients.

(Serves 2 of 1 cup each.)

Change quantities to suit.

VI

Downsizing by Building a Tugboat and Traveling Throughout France

We had the utopia; it received rave remarks.
But now we've chosen to start a new tug.
The barge is lovely, comfortable and smart.
Our friends think we're daft, that we're crazy as a bug.

The Dutch Barge is now history and we are starting the process of finishing a steel shell bought in the Netherlands and shipped to Migennes, France, where we will again put on our working clothes.

Our fondness for tugboats goes back to when we cruised the Intracoastal Waterway of the U.S. Back in 1983, we had written down all the names of tugboats that we saw during our passage. So now, we will have a tugboat of our own. It measures 33 feet in length and 11 feet in width. It is the first time we have chosen to build a boat outside of England. Jo Parfitt, whom we have known for 20-plus years, agreed to build the steel kit for us. If you wish to know more about the building of this tugboat kit, check out Hal's book, "Let's Build a Boat Together and Go for a Sail in Europe."

Oasis at Ecluse Bassou, River Yonne, France

In the early stages, welding of the shell was not moving as quickly as we had hoped so we decided to return home instead of watching nothing happen. We didn't tell Lynn and Margie about our return. Instead, we called the camping park in Florida where we knew that they would be spending the Christmas holidays. We reserved a site next to theirs and on December 24th of that year, we had our camping trailer parked, waiting for their arrival. We surprised them on Christmas Day while they were registering at the camp office. We shall never forget how much fun we had in planning the surprise. They thought that we were still in France. After all why should we be anywhere else? They had received a Christmas card sent to them from the place where we were building our boat. We found them in the registration office. I walked inside and sat down beside Margie. She looked at me twice, then screamed. Hal was standing behind Lynn at the desk. Besides the fact that Lynn said we almost gave him a heart attack, I think they were both glad to see us.

Building of this fifth boat went from slow to extremely slow. There were employee complications. One of the staff walked off the job. Jo was having difficulty finding a suitable welder. Once on the job, the welder suffered two accidents that took some recovery time. Then, when things did begin to move forward, we were always following in the footsteps of the welder getting in his way and vice versa. Fortunately, we got along splendidly with the welder so it did not create much of a problem.

I remember one late evening having just walked onto our barge from a day of sanding and painting the tugboat. It had been a cold, brisk day. There was a knock at the door and Jo and a friend were standing there holding a bottle of champagne. They knew somehow that it was my birthday and they came to help celebrate. All the tiredness quickly subsided and everyone relaxed and enjoyed the bubbly.

When spending all day working on a boat, I find it a relief to be able to prepare a microwave dinner, cutting back on the time element. Probably my favorite one is Chicken Parmesan. I often use it when I have some chicken in the refrigerator and less time to spend in the kitchen. Should there be any leftovers, they make a great sandwich.

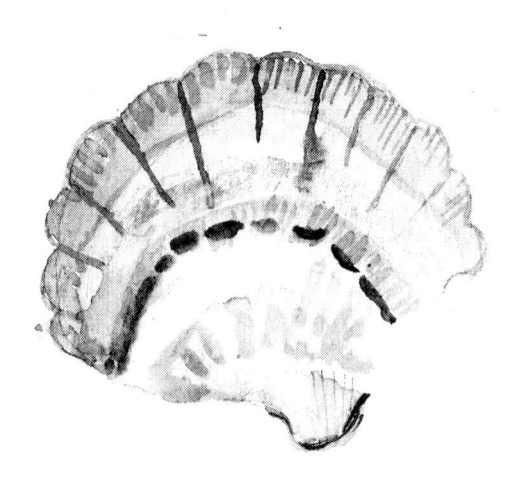

CHICKEN PARMESAN IN MICROWAVE

4 chicken breast halves, boned and cut into medium size pieces
¼ cup butter, melted
½ c. Parmesan
½ cup fresh bread crumbs
1 t. paprika
¼ to ½ t. garlic salt
1½ t. Italian seasoning (or ½ t. rosemary, oregano, and basil)

1. Score each piece cutting as much as half of the thickness. This enables faster and more even cooking.
2. Melt butter, then soak chicken well.
3. Secondly, coat chicken with a mixture of the remaining ingredients.
4. Microwave around 15 minutes at 5-minute intervals.

(Serves 4.)

Depending on the size of chicken pieces and power of microwave, the chicken could be ready to serve after 8 minutes. Check frequently; if overcooked, it becomes dry.

It is important not to extend the time in the microwave even 1 minute more than is needed as the chicken will dry out quickly. After the first 5 minutes, I suggest checking at 8 minutes. You may find the chicken is tender by then. Be sure to check that there is no pink left in the middle, as you need to cook the chicken fully.

I was a happy camper living on the big boat while building the little one. I was able to cook in a larger space and shop as often as I wanted. The markets in France are an institution. One does not normally go to the market with a list. Instead, one strolls among the stalls and chooses those items that catch the eye. Often you can tell if something is special by the long waiting line. Most often, it will be the first course (a "starter" in England and the entrée in France or the appetizer in the U.S.) or perhaps a delectable dessert which is popular. If Hal is along, he will often be guided by the aromas from the rotisserie stand, though similar products are available in many places these days. It is the stand selling fresh asparagus or ripened fruits, or other seasonal produce that may merit your attention. The choices are limitless and many times there will be two or more sellers competing for the same business. I would usually go to the stall with the longest line, thinking the locals knew something that I did not.

Though we served soup on occasion, it was nothing like what occurs in the typical French home. One of our French family friends had their main meal at noon, then had soup for the evening meal. Most everyone has at one time or another tried onion soup at restaurants. Hal has a long-time, fond memory of this soup he ordered in a restaurant which has since closed. But, he continues to search for a substitute. Over the years, he has been disappointed until just recently. He had an order at Outback Steakhouse which was the first time I heard him say it was as good as what he remembered. And, he also appreciated the onion soup from Applebee's. I continue to perfect my own recipe and the last report from my mate was that my soup was very good. I'll accept that and hope that those of you who try it will have the same response.

I think that Hal and I have enjoyed French Onion Soup more in the U.S. than in France. It continues to be one of Hal's favorite soups whether it is served to whet the appetite or as the main course.

When serving this soup for lunch or before a main course, I use one slice of bread. If the soup is the main course, then use more slices of bread per person and lots of cheese. For a meal, place 2 layers of toasted French bread, each layer buttered and sprinkled with grated cheese in the bowls. Pour heated soup into bowl, top with more cheese and a tiny bit of melted butter; place under broiler or in oven until cheese melts and starts to brown lightly.

FRENCH ONION SOUP

4 onions
1 quart beef or chicken stock or 4 (8-ounce) cups
½ cup butter, melted
salt
2 to 3 T. flour
8 slices French bread
Gruyere or Swiss cheese, shredded-- enough to cover toast plus additional on top to suit
1 cup white wine, dry—optional, to replace 1 cup of the stock

1. Slice onions. Add to butter and cook slowly until tender.
2. Add flour and blend well.
3. Add stock slowly, stirring constantly.
4. Season to taste.
5. Toast the bread, then butter and sprinkle with cheese.
6. Place prepared bread in the bottom of the serving bowl and add hot soup. Top with additional cheese.
7. Heat under broiler or in oven until cheese is melted slightly.

(Makes 8 small or 4 large servings.)

I halve the above quantities, and it makes 3 large bowls. I used 1½ T. of flour and it resulted in a nice consistency.

Wine has also taken a front seat in our approach to dining, having spent a long time in France. Perhaps it became a factor when we first arrived there and could purchase good-tasting wine for $1 a bottle. That fact alone made having wine at the table enticing. Now we are willing to go as high as $3 to $8 a bottle. Obviously, we are not experts in judging quality wine, though I know when I have tasted poor-quality. When served more expensive wines, we have not appreciated the difference. And, what's more, there isn't a big motivation to increase that knowledge since we seem quite content with the cheaper varieties. We were very intrigued watching the locals fill up their gallon containers at a pump, similar to a gas pump. And, we noticed them buying large quantities in red containers at the local markets. We became interested in the wine sold in boxes in the early 1980's when living in England. We have carried on this style of buying wine since then. For just the two of us, being able to have one glass is convenient. Boxed wine is prevalent now wherever we have traveled. When cooking, it is helpful to have boxed wine available thereby avoiding the opening of a bottle of wine for a small quantity. It was encouraging for us to see the Parisians pouring their wine from boxes as they monitored their stands at art fairs in Paris. However, we do not go so far as Walter Matthau who took a box of wine to his date, Sophia Loren, who was preparing an Italian supper for him in the movie *Grumpier Old Men*.

When entertaining friends, we serve wine from the bottle. And, we try to purchase wine that is not necessarily on the very low end of price. However, I make one exception. When I am planning to serve the popular drink called Kir, I buy a cheaper variety of white table wine. In my opinion, the strong liqueur tends to mask the taste of the wine. I realize that a specific French, white wine is recommended. I hope that my wine appreciation comments have not offended those who know much more than me on the subject. When we are in France, Kir is one favorite way of starting the evening. But, when we are back in the U.S., we seldom give it a thought.

KIR

To a glass of chilled white wine, add 2 teaspoons of *crème de cassis* (black current juice) liqueur. Some people like less liqueur; suit yourself. To make a **KIR ROYALE,** simply add chilled champagne in place of white wine. When dining at an outdoor, country restaurant, we were served a variation. The drink was made with a red Burgundy instead of white wine. It was a nice surprise. It actually tasted similarly to some Russian champagne that Bolle and Carla had often brought to the boat.

To illustrate the place of food in the French culture, I once tried to purchase a branch of celery and the store keeper didn't want to sell it to me, as he felt it was not of quality. Mind you, other countries are improving in their stocking of fine fruits and vegetables including the United States.

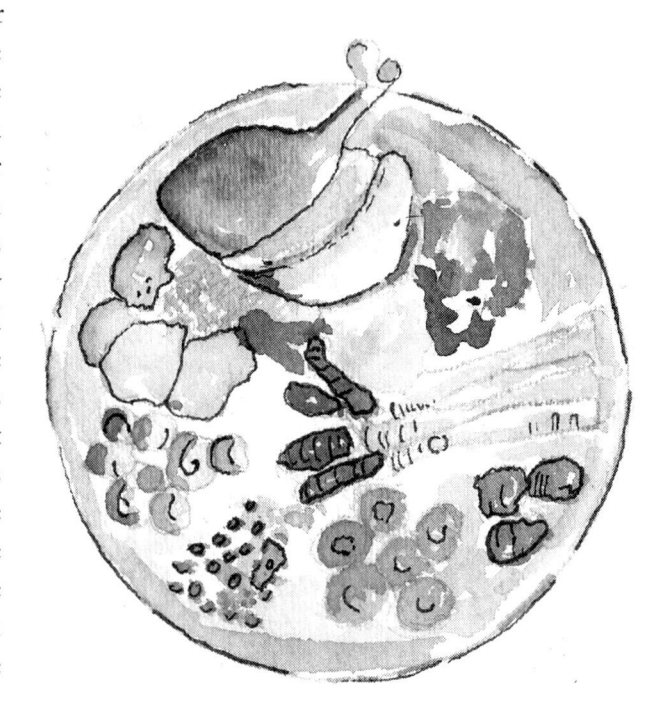

At meals when we are entertaining, it is not unusual for there to be several courses served prior to the main course. It is common to have our meat course along with potatoes or rice. In the summer months, tomatoes play a large role in the menu; they can be served stuffed or baked. They can be included in the quiche dish or prepared as a tart. The tart, which I now prepare wherever I am, is simply a pastry-covered shallow pan with some French mustard spread atop. The tomatoes are then added, followed by drops of olive oil, some herbs, sea salt and pepper. Twenty minutes in a hot oven and *viola,* there you have another entrée. The English, in particular, often serve two desserts whereas the French are more apt to have a course of cheese, then a dessert. What I especially admire about French eating customs is their serving simple foods one at a time rather than placing many different foods all together on one large plate. This French way would have been very foreign to my parents who lived in Ohio in the 1950's. But, once you have tried eating green beans served with toasted almonds and a dab of butter and a dash of salt alone without other tastes competing it just seems to bring out the greatness of the bean. I have no idea of how the majority of folks dine in their own homes but if you have not tried eating one or two foods separately, you should experiment. Recently, I read an extreme example of what I have developed in my own meals. A wealthy family living in the California vineyard area was entertaining friends and their method was to start serving the appetizer on the lawn of their home. Then, they moved to six different locations on their estate, serving a different course at each. Yes, that's extreme but it does follow my preference in dining.

In recent years, when Hal and I have been alone over the holidays, we have enjoyed our Thanksgiving or Christmas dinner in courses. We will begin during the early afternoon hours starting with the cranberry Jello; an hour later, a separate course, perhaps, the scalloped oysters will follow. We have some broccoli salad or cooked vegetable as a separate dish. Then, we will have a main course including turkey, dressing, and gravy with mashed potatoes. If sweet potatoes are on the menu, they would take the place of the mashed or could be served separately. The final course, a pie or cobbler, would end the meal sometime in the evening. Somewhere along the line, we would open a bottle of white wine and slowly enjoy a glass or two. Perhaps I should add that between courses we are watching a football game or the national dog show.

Take me out to lunch in France and very often, I will select the following salad from the menu. Before I ever selected this salad, I knew that I liked goat cheese. Though the salad varies from restaurant to restaurant, I have never been disappointed, and I give you my version. Once you have tasted it, you will probably agree that putting all the bits and pieces together is well worth the effort.

We consume a full-plate salad for an evening meal as often as twice a week. The ingredients vary. One salad is cooked chicken with greens and a blue cheese dressing. The dressing can be found in the Index, as it is also the topping for a hamburger sandwich. My favorite, favorite is the goat cheese, which gets my top salad rating.

GOAT CHEESE SALAD
Salade Chevre Chaud

11-ounce log of fresh goat cheese
½ cup dry breadcrumbs
salad greens
½ cup toasted walnuts (Fry walnuts in a dab of butter.)
¼ cup celery, chopped
French dressing of your choice

1. Cut cheese log into 8 rounds and place in refrigerator for 15 minutes to become firm.
2. **Coat cheese with breadcrumbs and place on baking sheet. Bake @ 350 degrees for 10 minutes; set aside.**
3. **Combine greens in a bowl along with walnuts and celery. Drizzle with French dressing. Place on individual salad plates and top each with 2 cheese rounds.**

(Serves 4.)

The three salads which follow give your meal a bit of sweetness. The Europeans would not choose these kinds of salad with their dinner. Nor do they usually serve a gelatin dessert. I have been told by good friends that the 24-hour salad which follows would not be something they would choose to include as a starter. However, it captures what I like and I would definitely include it at a summer picnic table.

My mother always served this salad on a salad plate at the left side of the dinner plate at our Thanksgiving dinners. My job in its preparation was seeding the grapes. Back then, I don't believe seedless grapes were available. This year my sister was preparing this same salad for her Thanksgiving table.

24-HOUR SALAD

1 large can chunk pineapple
1 small can crushed pineapple
1 pound of red grapes, seeded or seedless
1 large bottle maraschino cherries (drained and rinsed)
1 pound marshmallows (large ones cut in 4ths or miniatures)
3 T. powdered sugar
1 pound pecans or English walnuts

Dressing:
4 egg yolks
½ cup milk, with ¼ t. sugar added
½ t. salt
1½ pints whipping cream
juice of 1 lemon

1. **Saute nuts in a dab of butter. Set aside.**
2. **Drain chunk pineapple and crushed pineapple. Cut grapes and maraschino cherries in half. Add marshmallows and powdered sugar.**
3. **Prepare dressing by warming milk; add beaten egg yolks.**
4. **Cook over very low heat until thick, stirring constantly.**

5. Remove from heat and cool; add salt and lemon juice and lastly, add whipped cream. Mix with fruit.

6. Prior to serving on individual salad plates, add nuts.

(Serves 10 to 12.)

Hal's mother served this apricot salad and it hit the spot. One almost always has to have a second helping. Here again, there is a commercial product involved, but whipped cream could be substituted.

APRICOT SALAD

1 large package of apricot Jello
2 cups boiling water
1 cup cold water
1 large can of crushed pineapple (Save ½ cup of the juice for sauce.)
2 bananas
2 cups miniature marshmallows
¾ cup sugar
1 egg
2 T. flour
8 ounces cream cheese
Dream Whip envelope

1. Combine Jello, boiling and cold water; let this set in refrigerator for approximately 30 minutes.
2. Add drained, crushed pineapple, 2 sliced bananas, and the marshmallows. Place in a serving dish. Let it firm.
3. For the second layer, combine ¾ cup sugar, 1 beaten egg, flour, and ½ cup of the saved pineapple juice.
4. Cook until it thickens, then, add cream cheese and prepared envelope of Dream Whip according to package directions. Spread over first layer. Refrigerate for at least 2 hours.

(Serves 8.)

The following salad is so very simple. It appeared in a cookbook compiled by ladies living in a small village in Ohio, where I grew up. One knew practically everyone who contributed to this book and that made it all the more interesting.

The children might be interested to know that the woman who presented this recipe was the person who set my mother's hair each week. Beauty shops were not on every corner back in the 40's and 50's. My mother would wash her hair, then, drive to the woman's house. Her hair would be put in waves with clips and set with bobby pins. Mother would return home. Once her hair was dry, she would comb it out—quite a different lifestyle back then in the rural midwest.

PINEAPPLE CHEESE SALAD

1 large can pineapple chunks, drained well
½ pound Cheddar cheese, grated
½ pound miniature marshmallows
½ pint sweetened whipped cream

1. **Mix all ingredients; refrigerate until well chilled.**

(Serves 6 to 8.)

Mentioning my mother brings up another subject. When I was growing up, my mother on Saturday mornings would prepare a list of needed groceries and call in the order to the local store. In a couple of hours, all the groceries would be delivered. While visiting in Paris and in Buenos Aires, I noticed that a similar process was taking place in some of the food stores. What I didn't learn and needs following up is how the customers communicate their orders these days, perhaps via the Internet. I recently heard a local radio station advertising a delivery service, if the amount of groceries exceeded $10. So, just maybe, the service will grow as more people are employed and as more folks are living in their homes for a longer time.

We have christened five boats over the past thirty years and always have some kind of celebration inviting all the people who have been instrumental in the development or who have become friends. The party is our opportunity to share some American-style food. This had always called for carrot cake, the much sought-after dessert and champagne, of course.

Our largest launching party was for the fifth boat. We announced at the beginning of the day that a barbecue for six or so of us would be a nice way to end the day. Our day began at 5 a.m., adding bottom paint below the waterline where we couldn't get to earlier. The welding had held up some of the final painting to the very end. Hal, who usually liked getting out and doing jobs sometimes before eating breakfast, was maybe not quite alert at that early hour and had a bit of a fall. As a result, he was unable to do much the rest of the day except sit in a chair and visit with friends. Once the little bit of painting was done, I spent the remainder of the day preparing food. As the day wore on, the number of guests grew. Jo Parfitt was inviting his friends and family and we decided to include the welder's family and others from the boatyard and elsewhere. Before we knew it, some twenty were joining the evening barbecue. I had an emotional experience that afternoon shopping at the meat counter of the supermarket. I asked the clerk to start slicing from the large roast-size piece of steak, and I stopped him after he had made 11 or so large slices, leaving about 3 more on the end. He proceeded to wrap my order, and I noticed he had wrapped the remaining slices, as well. As I took my steaks from him, he gave me the remaining slices in a separate package, saying: "*Un cadeau pour vous.*" This translates: "A gift for you." I was and continue to be very struck by his gesture, I, a foreigner with limited language ability receiving this gracious gift.

The menu for the party included kabobs, steak, and sausages. And, this brings to mind another emotional event of the day. I asked Jo's son to be in charge of the barbecuing while I set the table and served the food. I had planned to borrow small grills from friends but began to realize that grill space would be tight. Later, that evening as it became time to light the charcoal, I noticed the son and the young welder approaching us carrying half a barrel. They had gone into the workshop, cut a barrel in half, and welded on a heavy-duty screen. *Voila*, a perfect grill on the spur of the moment. It's this kind of willingness to help out that is so much admired and appreciated. These two examples represent the kind of friendship and community involvement that comes from living and working in one place for a time.

Now, back to the barbecue. I made the mistake of asking Jo if there was anything else he would like to have on the table besides what I had planned. He said that he especially liked hard-boiled eggs. I was almost sorry I had asked as I had a lot to do already, but, hey, once you inquire, you have to be willing to follow-up. So, out came the cookbook for that one. Along with a fruit salad that was brought by a fellow boater, I prepared my favorite salads, including the cauliflower salad, the potato salad, and the broccoli salad, which are in this book. The final course--of course, the carrot cake again. Two of the guests sitting around the table that evening have long faces when anything else is served for dessert. The French bread was bought in large quantities and the wine and beer, brought by Jo and the guests, flowed throughout the event. It was a typical, warm summer evening and a good time seemed to be had by all. It turned out to be the largest boat launching party we had ever hosted.

This broccoli salad makes a welcome addition to any dinner. I often serve this separately before the main course. When back home in the U.S. I often substitute turkey bacon. We have more opportunities in the States to purchase turkey sausages and other products which help in the lessening of fat in our diets. It becomes the family's choice to alter recipes. What surprises me is how tasty these substitute foods can be.

BROCCOLI SALAD

2 large bunches broccoli
½ pound bacon slices, regular or turkey bacon
2 (8-ounce cups) sharp Cheddar cheese, shredded
1 small onion
lettuce in bite-size pieces, optional

Dressing:
1 cup mayonnaise
¼ cup sugar
2 T. cider vinegar

1. Wash broccoli, break into florets, and dry with towels.
2. Fry bacon to crisp stage and cut into pieces. Place in separate container until serving time.
3. Chop onion and mix with broccoli and cheese.
4. Prepare dressing and add to broccoli mixture.
5. Place covered broccoli salad in refrigerator.
6. To serve, top salad with bacon pieces and place on lettuce on serving plate or serve in a large salad bowl

(Serves 6 to 8.)

This is best when prepared a day ahead.

Not all dinner guests receive full-course meals. One of my favorite hamburger sandwiches is the following; it's a bit messy but oh, so delicious. Serve the sandwich with a fork. The dressing recipe is just that; it dresses the hamburger.

HAMBURGERS WITH BLUE CHEESE DRESSING

½ cup plain yogurt
½ cup mayonnaise
1 onion, small and chopped finely
1 T. red vinegar
1 t. sugar
salt and pepper, to taste
2 ounces blue cheese, cut into tiny bits
8 bacon slices
1 pound ground beef
4 sandwich buns

1. Combine onion with the combination of yogurt and mayonnaise.
2. Add vinegar, sugar, salt and pepper.
3. Mix all the above ingredients with blue cheese.

Sandwiches:
1. Fry bacon to crispness.
2. Fry hamburgers to desired doneness.
3. Warm sandwich buns; top hamburgers with dressing and bacon.

We finally reached the day when we were planning to depart from the boatyard. It was supposed to be a leisurely trip down the Canal du Nivernais to the boat rally that is held every two years. However, the welding and engine installation had been delayed and delayed again, so we didn't really know until 3 a.m. whether or not we could depart. We had moved all our belongings from the Dutch barge onto Oasis, though we had no time to put them into much order. It was just one big pile of stuff. Then, too, we were moving from a large barge into a much smaller craft. We wanted to entertain some special friends of ours while at the rally. Thank goodness, the weather cooperated and we were able to dine on the back deck. It's a lovely space and when the weather cooperates, it couldn't be better. Six of us enjoyed the broccoli salad followed by green beans and almonds and chicken casserole.

Because a couple from the States was also in attendance at the rally and they had shown interest in purchasing Allegheny II, we hurried back to the boatyard, some three-and-a- half days' travel including lots of locks in order to give our barge a good shining. We entertained them and Bruce and Gwenda for an afternoon anchored out under the shade of the trees with a multi-course lunch. It didn't really matter that they decided against buying another boat; it was just a fun afternoon being out of the boat-building regimen and relaxing with friends over food and drink.

That menu included salads (both the potato and the broccoli) plus French bread, a main course of crab quiche, and the cool, refreshing lemon pudding cake.

This cake is such a lovely item to serve to family and friends. It freezes well and one can remove servings, as needed. It can be warmed in the microwave and is delicious when served with vanilla ice cream or by itself. A small piece of this with your afternoon tea is "gorgeous," as they say in England.

LEMON PUDDING CAKE

2¼ cups flour, divided
½ cup powdered sugar
¼ t. salt
1 cup butter, chilled
4 eggs
2 cups sugar
1/3 cup fresh lemon juice
1½ t. grated lemon rind, optional
1 t. baking powder powdered sugar for dusting

1. Mix 2 cups of flour, ½ cup of powdered sugar, and salt. Using a pastry blender or 2 knives held close together, cut butter into flour mixture until mixture clings together and resembles coarse meal.
2. Press mixture evenly into 9x13-inch pan.
3. Bake @ 350 degrees for 20 minutes or until lightly browned. Cool 10-15 minutes.
4. In a large bowl, beat eggs until well blended and slowly beat in the sugar.

5. Blend lemon juice and rind into the egg mixture.
6. Mix remaining ¼ cup flour and baking powder and add to egg mixture.
7. Spread mixture evenly over baked, slightly cooled crust.
8. Return to oven for 25 minutes.
9. Cool in pan on rack, sprinkle with powdered sugar; cut into squares.

(Serves 12 to 16.)

I don't recommend freezing the whole cake though it can be successfully done. It requires a long thawing time.

We have since entertained numerous overnight guests aboard the tugboat. We always preface the invitation with the opportunity for them to stay at a nearby hotel and ride with us during the day. However, not one set of guests has chosen to go the hotel route, and some have returned for repeat visits.

Now you may recall that early in this book I asked you to remember the name, Roger Davis. Here it is years later, and he and Tere have flown from Argentina to England and are spending a couple days with us in Paris. I made a carrot cake prior to their arrival, never consciously thinking about the fondness that had developed over the cake back in Evesham some 25 years earlier. Well, Roger was on the boat a very short time before he said that he was looking forward to eating carrot cake. Was I ever glad that I had chosen to make it or I would have been relegated to the galley until it was produced.

Space is very limited in the galley region and I find it necessary to spill over (not literally) into the lounge seating. But, if guests remain topside enjoying themselves in the French summer afternoon or evening, I have no trouble serving four-course meals.

At another rally, we invited friends to dinner and they could not come on the night we had asked but we all agreed to move it to the next evening. That was fine, but when they left late on a Saturday night, I realized I needed to do some of the cooking for the next day's party for nine of us. Potatoes needed cooking for potato salad and other salads needed to be prepared and refrigerated. That preparation went on well into the night. I learned the hard way that I needed to schedule our entertainment more wisely. Here is the menu for a mid-day party on the lovely back deck of the Oasis.

Shrimp Roll with wheat crackers, Sparkling Wine
Broccoli Salad, Potato Salad
Brown Rice Salad with French bread
Chicken Casserole
Carrot Cake and Ice Cream
More Wine

When you see friends gathered, hear lots of laughter, and observe them obviously enjoying their meal, it makes all the effort worthwhile.

Having spent several years in France, it is always a good thing when one finds that there are some leftover, day-old baguettes. I find it is difficult to determine how much French bread will be consumed at any given dinner party. Sometimes, it goes quickly and at other times, one can end up with 1 or 2 baguettes leftover.

Again, this is easy and never fails to please.

BLUE CHEESE CRISPS

½ c. butter or margarine, softened
4 ounces blue cheese, softened
½ c. pecans or walnuts, finely chopped
French baguette, sliced

1. Bake the bread slices @ 350 degree for 3 to 5 minutes.
2. **Turn slices over and spread evenly with mixture of butter, blue cheese, and nuts.**
3. **Bake 5 additional minutes.**
4. **Serve immediately.**

(Makes 24 crisps.)

Grandma's Tip: Can easily be halved. Four crisps per person seems appropriate if no other appetizer is being served.

Let me set the scene as it does come almost to a performance. Diana and I are at a supermarket cashier's counter in Paris. My French is quite limited but even before I open my mouth, the French know that I am a stranger. It's our overall appearance that tells all. Though I never wore sneakers in the city, I usually wore slacks or Capri pants. The French female definitely dresses with more style, including her trips to the local food store. Their shoes are much more expensive and are more stylish, the scarves they wear set the tone, and they just seem to have a fashion sense that deserves notice. Both the men and women set a good example for everyone to follow. But back to the cashier's counter. A gentleman waiting in line behind us begins a conversation telling us that he owns a small restaurant nearby. He is planning to celebrate the upcoming 4th of July American holiday by offering hotdogs and beer to his customers. He extends an invitation for us to come by, saying that we would be most welcome. The cashier who has been handling our purchases picks up on the chat. She begins singing "America the Beautiful." As we departed, more of the customers and staff became interested in us strangers from the U.S.A. Diana asked if I always got such a warm greeting when shopping.

Though I could not speak a word of French when I first arrived in the country and according to my husband, my pronunciation needed some work, I jumped in with both feet. I practiced the language using audio tapes and books and I did eventually have the opportunity to enroll for one year in an evening, college-level course. I soon realized that I was not going to be able to accomplish much in the way of noun-verb agreement or even complete sentences for that matter. However, I always tried to use the French language and was able to get my thoughts across. The reception I received both in small villages and large cities, including Paris, warmed my heart and encouraged me to continue to speak, forgetting any shyness I might feel.

One encounter came just as we had entered into France for the first time on Pennsylvania Yankee. Hal and I had taken our boat off onto a side canal in order to avoid any boat traffic on the main canal. We had gone through one bridge before our mooring for the evening. The next morning when we returned to that bridge, there was no one handling bridge openings. So, what do we do? For some thoughtless moment, I suggested to Hal that I run down the nearby country road until I came to a house which was visible in the distance. He didn't bother to suggest that he would go, knowing that his French from high school would be a more positive approach. Back then, I liked to jog, and I am enjoying my morning exercise and not really thinking about how I would solve the bridge problem. I knocked on the door and a couple came to answer. I have no French words to call upon. The only word that I learned those first few days in our first port city was *perdue*. I remember going off to the laundry thinking that should I become lost, I could at least tell someone that I had lost my way. So, here I am standing at the door and now what? I pointed in the direction of the side canal, I made nonverbal gestures to show a bridge would not open, and *viola,* I received immediate action. The couple went to their telephone book, placed a call, and sent me on my way. Problem solved. Now, I cannot connect this story to food. But, I have a strong need to communicate to you that people have gone out of their way so many, many times in Europe, including France, to be helpful and friendly. Thirty years later with minimal language instruction, I can give in French a nice greeting following by a less than perfect set of words which gets my message across. And, never have I heard a response which used the French words for "get lost."

During a short visit on the German waterways, we were led by a German couple to marinas for the night. They would get there before us and be waiting to show us where to moor. Neither Hal nor I spoke German and we declined invitations to go to restaurants with them, knowing that they and we would be speaking via the dictionary—which makes for a long couple of hours. We have stood in the Paris train station studying our map when a gentleman has stopped to ask if we needed assistance. We have experienced a Belgium barge captain and his wife backing up their barge, throwing us a line, and pulling our tug from the mud bank. Likewise, a farmer who saw that our boat had come upon a high spot in the canal came to us with his tractor and pulled our boat to deeper water. We usually thanked such deeds with a bottle of our favorite wine or champagne—so I did get something about food into the story. It is important for me to tell of these good people and their good deeds.

Over the years, we stopped counting how many canal and river locks we had gone through or how many waterway miles we had covered, though the number of locks is probably surpassing 6,000. It was not our intention to accumulate any record number; however, we began our cruising with much eagerness. Mind you, cruising the inland waterways is always in the slow lane as canals are controlled, the speed often limited to six miles per hour. As I used to tell my father, a farmer in Ohio, the pace is similar to driving a tractor harvesting the crops.

We have continued to return to Paris and the Burgundy region for the last few summers. Both the Burgundy and Nivernais canals have lovely towpaths where we can get much-needed exercise. We're moving at a bit slower pace but continuing to enjoy the boating life.

Our boating life in Europe has come to a close. We have shipped our little tug to the States and hope to spend several years exploring the canals in New York and Canada.

I don't see another boat-building project in my future but, then again, I didn't see the other four coming. Instead, I envision watercolor paints and tiny brushes. I see continued travel of some sort, interest in new recipes, and the enjoyment of preparing my favorites for us, our family, and friends.

I hope that I have related to you the joy I have experienced from thirty years spent in campers and boats. It has been an unusual time, certainly not what I would have envisioned when I was a young person. I had no idea that travel and food would become so important in my life. For sure, I would have signed up for French classes rather than Latin. Oh, I just remembered, Latin was the only language course offered in my small high school. I am glad that my partner likes sharing this mobile life. Rubbing shoulders with people from other parts of the world has opened my eyes and ears to how we in the U.S. are the same and how we differ.

We have not only entertained our friends on our boats but we have also opened our home to them. Most of our close friends living in other countries have visited us in the home we were residing in at the time. We hope that they have enjoyed learning about the customs of the U.S., as well.

After 30 years of cooking, building, and cruising, I continue to get enthusiastic over good food. I continue to be curious about new recipes appearing on restaurant menus and on the tables of my family and friends. I taste a new dish and the desire to recreate it becomes a future goal. Most often, I have one or two recipes in my file, waiting for time to prepare them. I am continuously trying to utilize the microwave in certain steps and sometimes succeed in making the entire dish in the microwave.

Depending on where we visited, I was brought back in time to how my grandparents may have lived, as life in small European villages appeared closer to that time period than how we live presently in the U.S. I noted, also, that, in general, young adults in the U.S. enjoy more modern appliances and larger houses than the average person living in Europe, regardless of age. However, I have no wealth of research to back my opinions regarding the welfare of people in the countries we have visited. I have recently become more aware of the amount of wealth that was visible along the rivers and canals of Belgium and the Netherlands. But, mostly, I realize that we are all much the same and appreciate many of the same things—good friends, good food, and enough income in life to be comfortable. I saw more examples of people living with less but not less content or less pleased with their circumstances. Their kitchens were not equipped with every modern convenience. Clothes dryers and dishwashers have only become a common household item in the last decade.

We feel close to our family though we have not been near much of the time. Though we don't see them often because we are away, they, too, are involved in jobs and schooling. When we do meet up, we enjoy a warm and delightful togetherness. We have had opportunities to entertain our family members in England and France on more than one occasion. So, if you are considering retiring on a boat or in a camper of some sort and are concerned about your being away from loved ones, think about the opportunities you will have to share your exciting life. Also, communication has improved so unbelievably during our cruising years. I often reflect how nice it would have been to send and receive e-mails from my mother while we were in Europe back in the 1980's. By the time her letters and mine reached their destination using our amateur radio contacts with the Tittensors, the mail could be five or six weeks old. How great it is today to be able to communicate by e-mail or Skype wherever we are. Within a moment's notice one can be in touch. My brother and sister-in-law and my sister live near their children and I admit that being available to the family full-time has its merits. Making choices in life is a book waiting to be written.

In the last few weeks, I have learned that granddaughter number one, Christina, took two peanut butter and chocolate pies to her mate's family gathering over Thanksgiving. I learned, too, that granddaughter number four, Colleen, was planning to bake peanut butter and chocolate cookies for the holidays. I am hoping that in years to come they and the other grandkids will try more of my favorites as they become more involved in putting food on the table. I'm glad that I decided to write this book instead of writing recipe cards for just the family. I hope that you, the reader, will get pleasure in serving something from my favorites and, in turn, they will become your favorites, too.

I hope you have enjoyed reading some of my stories that frame my recipes. In the following chapters, I include more of my favorite recipes along with short clips about their origin. a bit of my nostalgia about the recipes, and *trucs,* helpful hints, that I have picked up over time, in their preparation.

Le Patio de Monet

VII

Additional Favorite Recipes Main Courses and Casseroles

Our neighbors to the south of us in the U.S. have left a very deep desire in me for Mexican foods. I spent three years in California in the 60's and liked the flavorful specialties of Tex-Mex cuisine.

The following recipes represent my attempt to offer a little bit of the southwest of our country. The enchiladas are on the mild side and are not a turnoff to someone who thinks they won't like spicy Mexican food.

CHICKEN ENCHILADAS

1 (4 ounce) can green chili peppers
1 T. olive oil
1 medium onion, finely chopped
1 garlic clove, crushed
3 medium tomatoes, peeled, seeded, and chopped
¼ t. oregano
salt to taste
1½ cups cooked chicken, shredded
4 oz. mild Cheddar cheese, shredded
1 cup unflavored, plain yogurt
12 flour tortillas

1. Drain and rinse chili peppers; remove seeds.
2. Chop tomatoes and peppers.
3. In skillet, add oil, onion, garlic, chili peppers, and tomatoes and sauté.
4. Add oregano and salt.
5. Simmer 30 minutes.
6. Place cooked chicken, cheese, and yogurt mixture in tortillas.
7. Top tortillas with tomato mixture.
8. Bake @ 350 degrees for 20 minutes.

(Makes 12 enchiladas.)

On one of our camping excursions to the southern region of the U.S., Hal promoted a party to surprise me on my 60th birthday, and the Kraft family agreed to organize it. We were on our way north from Florida and planned to spend a weekend in southern Maryland seeing the family.

When we arrived at the house, members of my family appeared from all corners. Because it was a Spring holiday, Sarah and her family could get away from Connecticut. Lynn and Margie were there from Ohio. He said that had it been warm and sunny, he would be working in the fields but since the weather was not cooperating with Spring planting, they were able to come. We had just departed from Ruth and Jerry's home in Virginia but somehow, they had managed to beat us to Maryland and were standing in the kitchen when we arrived. Bruce and Gwenda, then living in Annapolis, came over for the surprise. It was a lovely gathering, unusual for so many of the family to be together at the same time. And, the party was based on a Mexican theme: everything from the Black Bean Appetizer to especially-prepared tacos and enchiladas. They even had a piñata that blindfolded Grandma could not manage to hit and TJ had to come to her rescue.

CHEESE ENCHILADAS

2 cups Monterey Jack cheese shredded
1 cup Cheddar cheese, shredded
1 medium onion (1/2 cup), chopped
½ cup sour cream
2 T. parsley
¼ t. salt, ¼ t. pepper
15 ounces tomato sauce
2/3 cup water
1/3 cup green pepper, chopped
1 T. chili powder
½ t. oregano
¼ t. cumin
1 garlic clove
8 tortillas
¼ cup Cheddar cheese, shredded
Garnish of sour cream and green olives, optional

1. Mix Monterey Jack cheese, 1 cup Cheddar, chopped onion, sour cream, parsley, and salt and pepper. Set aside.
2. Heat tomato sauce, water, chopped green pepper, chili powder oregano, cumin, and crushed garlic to boiling; simmer 5 minutes.
3. Dip each tortilla into sauce to coat.
4. Spoon ¼ cup of cheese mixture onto each tortilla.
5. Roll & arrange in ungreased rectangular baking dish.
6. Pour remaining sauce over and sprinkle with the ¼ cup Cheddar cheese.
7. Bake @ 350 degrees uncovered for 20 minutes. Garnish with sour cream and sliced green olives.

(Makes 8 enchiladas.)

The freshness of this Mexican salad prepares the palate for your choice of main course. It's hard to imagine a more tempting beginning to the meal as we sit on the back deck of Oasis, enjoying the warm breeze with water all around us. You don't have to be serving a Mexican-theme dinner to include the salad; it's good with most everything.

MEXICAN FRUIT SALAD

2 ripe avocados
2 stalks celery
2 apples
1 banana
¼ cup raisins (preferably golden raisins)
¼ cup walnuts
lettuce leaves
Dressing:
½ cup vegetable oil
¼ cup lemon juice
2 t. sugar
¼ t. salt
¼ t. dry mustard
chili powder, dash

1. Place all dressing ingredients in a container with a lid and shake until well mixed.
2. Place a lettuce leaf on individual salad plates; add fruit mixture and nuts, then, a Tablespoon or 2 of dressing over the top.

(Serves 4.)

I have not met anyone except my brother who thought that chicken livers were a gourmet treat. Our mother used to freeze chicken livers from whole chickens that she prepared for Sunday dinner. She stored the livers until she had enough to satisfy my brother and me. I have to reflect for a bit here to describe my mother's cooking. She knew how to prepare food to make it so tasty. And, if necessary, she could start with the live chicken. If my father was busy in the fields, she could catch the hen, cut off its head, scald the chicken, remove the feathers, clean the bird, then serve her delectable fried chicken. We have come a long way since then but I often think of her as I search the poultry counter in the supermarket for the various pieces of chicken. During the harvest in the month of July, my mother would also tend to milking by hand the six or so cows so that my father didn't have to do that task after he would come in from the wheat fields around 9 p.m. And, this is the same mother who taught school in the village, always wore a dress and when teaching, wore heeled shoes. I am amazed at what she accomplished in her lifetime, but I'm rather glad that life has become easier for all women and mothers during the last couple of generations.

I am the only one in my immediate family who enjoys chicken livers. And, once or twice a year I just have to prepare them. Occasionally, I will select them from a restaurant menu. When at home Hal agrees to eat them, too, but he is only doing it to be nice. He would prefer that I add fried onions or anything to lessen the taste of the livers. But purists such as my brother and me like them plain, fried to a crisp. Add nothing; even the red-wine sauce is not necessary for my tastes.

SAUTEED CHICKEN LIVERS

1 pound chicken livers
salt and pepper
2 T. butter
1 T. oil
red wine, dry
whole wheat flour
cooked brown rice

1. Salt and pepper the livers and roll them in flour.
2. Heat butter and oil in a thick frying pan over medium heat until the foam on the butter subsides.
3. Add livers and sauté; turn until just browned.
4. Add wine to a depth of ¼". Reduce heat and simmer until the wine and flour form a sauce. Test the livers to see if they're done. May need more wine and flour. Simmer longer.
5. Serve with rice.

(Serves 4.)

Now this recipe begins to "ruin" the gorgeous flavor of liver but maybe it is more in line with what other people like.

CHICKEN LIVERS SUPREME

1 medium onion, thinly sliced
1 (2 ½-ounce) can sliced mushrooms, drained
2 T. butter or margarine, melted
½ pound chicken livers
1 (8-ounce) carton sour cream
1 t. paprika
1 t. salt and 1 t. pepper
hot, cooked noodles

1. Saute onion and mushrooms in butter in a large skillet until onion is tender.
2. Add chicken livers, and brown on all sides. Reduce heat; cover and simmer 10 minutes, stirring occasionally.
3. Remove from heat. Add sour cream, paprika, s&p; stir well.
4. Cover and simmer 5 additional minutes; stirring occasionally.
5. Serve over hot, cooked noodles.

(Serves 2.)

We became friends with a couple who were also traveling on a boat in France. We spent some time in the same boatyard for weeks and occasionally shared meals together. Ursula who was born in Switzerland, and Mike, who was born in Bangladesh, have lived most of their married life in England. Mike, also, worked for a few years in Canada and the U.S. while Ursula stayed home there to raise their two daughters. Ursula is known along the waterways for her preparation of chicken curry. I have studied recipes for this dish from books and have gotten hints from Ursula and other friends. My version seems to satisfy our taste buds and includes an apple to make it more moist. This recipe does not include sophisticated, fresh spices that Ursula includes, but it remains simple and relies on the ingredients one commonly has in the cupboard. I was never very pleased with my attempts in preparing this curry until I observed Gwenda adding an apple to her curry. It works; the dish takes on a desirable moistness.

CHICKEN CURRY

1½ ounces butter
1 T. olive oil
4 medium-size servings of chicken
4 T. flour
2 medium-size onions. chopped
1 garlic clove
1 cooking apple, peeled and chopped
½ t. salt
½ t. cinnamon
1 T. curry powder
½ t. ginger
½ c. water
5 ounces yogurt
sliced tomatoes, salted peanuts, and chutney of your choice

1. Heat butter and oil; roll chicken in flour and fry until crisp on both sides. Remove.
2. Add onions and garlic to remaining butter and oil in skillet and fry until lightly golden.
3. Stir in apple, salt, and all other ingredients, except yogurt. Simmer 1 hour.
4. Stir in yogurt for further 5 minutes.
5. Serve over rice with sliced tomatoes, peanuts, and chutney—all in separate dishes.

(Serves 4.)

A couple of years ago when visiting Ursula and Mike in Carcassone in the south of France, we went to a restaurant which specialized in Kangaroo. I don't recall that they ordered this meal, but Hal and I had never had it so we went for it. It tasted similar to beef and was "OK," not something I'd probably order too often. But, it's fun to say that we have eaten kangaroo.

This recipe is probably one of my most recent favorites. When I have experienced a meal in a restaurant that really hits the spot, I decide to try to recreate it in my kitchen. Already, it has been requested by my English visitors and was well received by the Dutch and French guests, as well. This dish is meant to be savored so begin it with a nice white, dry wine.

CHICKEN SALTIMBOCCA WITH LEMON SAUCE

4 chicken breasts halves, skinless and boneless
8 large sage leaves or a sprinkle of ground sage
8 thin prosciutto slices (around 3 ounces)
½ cup + 2 t. flour
1 T. butter
1½ T. olive oil
2 T. white wine, dry
½ cup chicken broth
2 T. lemon juice

1. Place chicken between 2 sheets plastic wrap and pound to 1/3-inch thickness.
2. Sprinkle chicken with salt and pepper.
3. Add 2 sage leaves on each piece of chicken. Top with 2 prosciutto slices, pressing to adhere.
4. Spread ½ cup flour on a plate. Turn chicken in flour to lightly coat both sides.
5. Melt butter and oil in large skillet over medium-high heat.
6. Add chicken, prosciutto-side down. Cook 4 minutes. Turn over and cook about 3 minutes. Check for doneness.
7. Transfer to platter. Wrap chicken in tin foil and keep warm in the oven. Reserve drippings in skillet.
8. Whisk wine with remaining 2 t. flour in small bowl.
9. Add broth and lemon juice to skillet; bring to boil.
10. Add wine mixture and whisk until sauce thickens slightly, about 30 seconds.
11. Season with salt and pepper. Place chicken on individual serving dishes and spoon sauce on top.

(Serves 4.)

Prior to beginning this recipe, I suggest mixing the wine and flour together. And, I mix the broth and lemon juice, also Then, they are ready to be utilized immediately when you reach steps 8, 9, and 10.

Roger Apperley once served us Chicken Kiev, and it was as good as we remembered when dining in a nice London restaurant. However, I have to admit that I have been unsuccessful in a couple of attempts to prepare the basic Kiev dish. I have tied the chicken breasts with string, stuck them together with toothpicks, but I am disappointed that not enough of the butter/garlic stays within the serving. So, here is my simple solution, and I must say it has the flavor minus the difficult preparation.

CHICKEN KIEV, COUNTRY-STYLE

¼ cup breadcrumbs
2 T. Parmesan cheese
1 t. basil
1 t. oregano
½ t. garlic salt
¼ t. salt
2/3 cup butter, melted
4 chicken breasts halves, boned and skinned
¼ c. white wine, dry
¼ cup green onions
¼ cup fresh parsley

1. **Combine breadcrumbs, Parmesan cheese, basil, oregano, garlic salt, and salt.**
2. **Dip chicken pieces in butter, then, roll in crumb mixture. Set remaining butter aside. Place chicken in 2-quart shallow casserole.**
3. **Bake @ 375 degrees for 50 to 60 minutes.**
4. **To remaining butter, add wine, green onions, and parsley. Add to chicken and bake 3 additional minutes.**

(Serves 4.)

Vol-au-vent shells appear everywhere in Europe, often packaged in cellophane and available near the breads and other pastries. In the US I am familiar with the frozen product but probably availability differs with location. This recipe goes way back to our early 80's when we were first cruising the English countryside. Now, I probably serve this once or twice a year. It's another winner and as is true of most cooks, you ask yourself why you don't make this dish or that dish more often. When visiting in France, Karen, who used to be somewhat hard to please in the food line, really cleared the plate with this one. This is the same youngster who removed the cheese from a

Croque Monsieur (grilled ham and cheese sandwich) on the sidewalks of Paris's Champs Elysees. It's very true that French cheese is different from what we are used to in parts of the U.S. According to the authorities, there are some 300 varieties of cheese in France. I find that recipes do have different results, depending on where you obtain the ingredients. When Karen was served this meal back in Pennsylvania, she said it wasn't as she remembered. There you go.

CHICKEN IN PASTRY SHELLS
Poulet en Vol-au-Vent

2 whole chicken breasts
2 chicken bouillon cubes
4 T. butter
3 T. flour
1 cup chicken stock or canned chicken broth
¾ cup cream
salt and pepper, to taste
2 ounces Cheddar cheese, grated
1 (7-ounce) can mushroom pieces, drained
2 shallots or ¼ cup green onions
1 T. parsley
1 ½ t. prepared mustard
white wine, dry (enough to make mixture the right consistency)
4 patty-shell cases

1. Cook chicken breasts in simmering water with 2 chicken cubes for flavor until done, approximately 20 to 30 minutes. Set aside. Remove skin and cut into 2" pieces.
2. Melt butter in pan; remove from heat and stir in flour.
3. Add chicken stock and cream, stirring until combined.
4. Return to heat and allow sauce to thicken.
5. Season with salt and pepper; simmer for 2 minutes more.
6. Add grated cheese, mushrooms, shallots or green onions, parsley, mustard, and wine, stirring until cheese is melted.
7. Add chicken pieces, heating through over low heat.
8. Warm shell cases in oven until heated through.
9. Spoon mixture into shell cases.
10. Garnish with parsley.

(Serves 4.)

I know that Becky's favorite Chinese carry-out dish is Chicken In Garlic Sauce. I am looking forward to making this for her to see if it comes close to her liking. It's not Chinese in origin so may be altogether different.

CHICKEN IN GARLIC SAUCE

3 chicken breasts halves, boned and skinned
flour, for coating
4 T. olive oil
2 T. butter
5½ T. white wine
4 T. chicken stock
3 t. garlic
1 T. parsley
1 T. sherry
1 T. brandy
salt and pepper, to taste

1. Cut chicken into small chunks and coat with flour.
2. Add olive oil and butter and fry chicken in skillet on stove top.
3. Add white wine, chicken stock, crushed garlic, and chopped parsley; simmer to reduce the liquid by half.
4. Add sherry and brandy. Heat and serve.

(Serves 4 to 6.)

When I think about this recipe, I recall preparing many rounds when serving the wedding rehearsal dinner for Hal's son, Jim and his new bride. Jim's sister, Sarah, and I put many servings of this into the refrigerator the night before the dinner. While we were struggling in the kitchen, he was out enjoying his bachelor party. He returned around 2 a.m. after the food was prepared. That's OK as he has since that time often prepared food from his kitchen for us.

This is a great dish to take to someone's house. I place all the individual ingredients into plastic bags. Then, all that needs doing once you reach your destination is to put them together, place in a casserole and *voila*, dinner is in the oven. This way the chef can be a part of the conversation. After all, when you are away from family as much as we are, you want to make the most of the time you're together.

CHICKEN CASSEROLE

3 hard-boiled eggs
2 cups boned, cooked chicken
2 T. onion
1 cup celery
1 (10¾-ounce) can cream of chicken soup
1 cup slivered almonds
½ cup mayonnaise
½ t. salt, ½ t. pepper
1 t. lemon juice
½ cup butter cracker crumbs
Cheddar cheese, shredded

1. Cut eggs into pieces.
2. Cut chicken into pieces.
3. Chop onions and celery.

4. Combine all ingredients except crackers and cheese.
5. Place mixture in greased, 2-quart baking dish.
6. Top with mashed crackers and cheese.
7. Bake @ 350 degrees for 30 minutes.

(Serves 6 to 8.)

This recipe came as a part of a package—namely, my husband, Hal. For a time he and his son had been living alone. As a result, he had come up with several Daddy's Specials. Included was a quiche that he had obtained from a child's cookbook. Ever since, we have tried to locate a copy of this book but to no avail—not on any Internet source or any library search. It had something such as *1, 2, 3, Gourmet* in the title.

But, this is so jolly good and so easy that "even your little brother can do it," so said the book. You will always be proud to bring it to your table. You can choose your own variety of fillings. I especially like to prepare it using a can of good-quality crab as that is a food item I can keep with me at all times wherever I go. It's especially lovely as a vegetarian dish using spinach. (A quantity of chopped spinach from a can, drained, works sufficiently well. Sliced tomatoes on top are a nice addition.) For my vegetarian friends, I like to serve a first course of the Tomato Zuchini Grille. This combination, vegetarian or not, should please all cooks, regardless of their years in the kitchen.

QUICHE

Crust:
¼ pound butter, room temperature
1 cup flour
3 ounces cream cheese, room temperature
salt, a dash

Filling:
½ pound Swiss cheese, shredded
1½ cups whole milk
3 eggs, beaten
sprinkle of pepper
½ t. salt

Options to include:
¼ pound cooked, sliced ham in bite-size pieces, or 8 slices of crisply fried bacon, crumbled, or 1 7-ounce can of squeezed-dry crabmeat or 1 cup squeezed-dry chopped spinach with small slices of onion.

1. Mix by hand all crust ingredients: ¼ pound butter, flour, cream cheese, and salt. Press into a 9-inch pie plate or quiche dish.
2. Bake crust @ 375 degrees for approximately 8 minutes.
3. Add filling of your choice; bake 45 minutes.

(Serves 6 to 8.)

Just as in the curry version, I have taken examples from my mother and friends and how I want a good meatloaf to taste to make my rendition of meatloaf. In France, the stores often sell a mixture of veal, beef, and pork called *Tomate Farci*. This makes a nice dish but I tend to avoid veal for the same reason that I stay away from lamb.

I especially like the topping as it adds to the appearance, moistness, and taste. Here in the U.S., I rely mostly on ground beef and some ground pork, if I can find it.

MEATLOAF WITH TOMATO

3 pounds ground meat
2 medium onions
½ cup quick oats
1 egg
¼ cup ketchup
1 medium can tomatoes, not drained
bacon

Topping:
½ cup light brown sugar
¼ cup ketchup
½ t. Worcestershire sauce
¾ t. prepared mustard

1. **Combine meat, chopped onions, oats, beaten egg, ¼ c. ketchup, and tomatoes.**
2. **Form into a loaf shape on a baking pan and cover with bacon strips.**
3. **Mix topping ingredients (sugar, 1/4 cup ketchup, Worcestershire sauce, and mustard). Place over bacon.**
4. **Bake @ 350 degrees for 1 hour.**

(Serves 10 to 12.)

Who doesn't like to inhale the aromas from a slow cooker while you are busy with other tasks or as you are entering the house after a day at work?

BRAISED SWISS STEAK IN THE SLOW COOKER

2 pounds steak, cut 1" thick
2 T. dry bread crumbs
2 t. salt
¼ t. pepper
1 T. butter or margarine, melted
1 medium-size can stewed tomatoes
2 medium onions, thinly sliced
½ cup celery, chopped
1 garlic clove, crushed
1 T. Worcestershire sauce

1. Wipe steak with damp paper towels. Combine bread crumbs, salt, and pepper.
2. Place steak on board; sprinkle with half of crumb mixture; pound into steak with wooden mullet or the rim of a heavy saucer. Repeat other side. Cut steak into 6 portions.
3. Melt butter in large Dutch oven. Add steak; brown on both sides over medium heat.
4. Add tomatoes, onion, celery, garlic, and Worcestershire sauce; bring to boiling.
5. Reduce heat; simmer, covered 2 hours or until meat is tender.

This recipe works well in the slow cooker. I complete 4 steps of the recipe, then, place ingredients in the cooker for 6 to 8-hours on a LOW setting. The length of time will depend upon the tenderness of your steak.

(Serves 6.)

This, too, is a very recent addition to the Favorite File. Hal decided one Mother's Day to prepare all the day's meals. Using the crockpot, our small house had gorgeous aromas all day, peaking my interest in the final product. The cayenne pepper gave the dish a delightful kick and when served with dumplings (I admit to requesting the dumplings.), it was a big success. This meal is especially fitting for a cold winter's day.

Should you want to prepare this dish in a large pan or Dutch oven, brown the chicken, then, proceed with the other ingredients.

CLUCK–CLUCK STEW IN THE SLOW COOKER

1 T. vegetable oil
2 boneless chicken breasts, cut into bite-size pieces
4 cups water
4 chicken bouillon cubes
4 potatoes
2 carrots
2 medium onions
½ t. cayenne pepper
2 garlic cloves

½ t. pepper
1 large, fresh tomato
1 medium-size can corn, drained

1. Combine bouillon cubes and boiling water until mixed.
2. Place all ingredients except corn and tomatoes in the slow cooker; set cooker on high setting. After 1 hour, reduce setting to low. Allow 6 to 8 hours for chicken to become tender.
3. Add corn and tomato, diced; cook another 20 minutes.
4. Add more broth as needed; add flour or cornstarch for thickening as needed.

A recipe for dumplings is given as a part of the Pork and Sauerkraut recipe.

(Serves 8.)

In Arcachon, France, a leading producer of oysters, the only way they were prepared in restaurants was to be served raw. Now, I had the opportunity to get to like them raw as my father liked them that way, and I remember trying to get to appreciate them just to be in his favor. But, appreciation didn't occur. Not many years back, we attended an oyster festival with the Kraft family in St. Mary's County, Maryland. There, I found the oysters that had been steamed to be to my liking. The festival and seafood restaurants often have fried oysters on their menu and though I relish them, I prefer to avoid preparing fried foods at home. I save my craving for fried oysters for when I dine in a restaurant. But, of all the ways that oysters are cooked, the following is my very, very favorite. I followed my mother's recipe completely and can make it for a few or many by adapting the quantity. My good sister made this dish many times for an elderly woman friend of hers and, also, our father. And, my sister does not like scalloped or any other oyster dish.

While living in Paris one winter, we kept seeing oysters being sold in the shell at markets and at restaurant fronts. But, nowhere in the food stores did we see them shucked and packaged for sale in large quantities. Our curiosity finally caused us to stop and ask a question of a gentleman who was promoting the sale of oysters at a sidewalk café. We inquired if he sold oysters by the dozen and if so, how could we learn to shuck them ourselves. We had seen other people back in Maryland shucking oysters but not by the quart. He took an interest in this unskilled couple and showed us the fine points of shucking. He would have sold them to us shucked by him but we wanted to do it ourselves. He directed us to a store where we bought a proper tool. Before, Hal had tried shucking with a screw driver—not that effective. We returned with the right knife and bought enough oysters to make scalloped oysters for a Thanksgiving dinner. We invited our friends, John and Sheila, some 100+ miles away to come spend the holiday with us. Then, our refrigerator bit the dust; being able to entertain went down the drain. We searched for someone who could repair it and several business owners shook their head. No one at the marina could help us. We were told that when boat refrigerators stop functioning, people throw them away and buy new. Ugh! So, we had to cancel our invitation for Thanksgiving. We had a sad representation of your typical turkey-day dinner. The good news is we did have my favorite oysters.

My last supper! This is probably not going to happen as most likely I won't feel like eating. But, if I were asked to put together my most favorite meal, it would include the following. So, here is my number one, multi-star recipe which I gladly share with fellow oyster lovers.

SCALLOPED OYSTERS

6 cups butter crackers
¼ pound butter
42 ounces standard oysters
½ cup evaporated milk
1 t. Worcestershire sauce

1. Mix crushed crackers and melted butter. Place 1/3 of mixture in bottom of greased, 9x13 glass baking dish. A metal pan can cause scorching.
2. Top with half of the oysters.
3. Repeat with 1/3 of buttered crackers and remaining oysters.
4. Top with remaining buttered crackers.
5. Blend milk with Worcestershire sauce and pour along sides of dish.
6. Bake on top shelf of oven @ 325 degrees for 45 minutes.

(Serves 12.)

The quantity of ingredients can be reduced easily. If you like oysters, you may want the whole recipe as the oysters are good as leftovers the next day. Just warm the leftovers in the microwave and you end up a happy camper for two days' running. Yes, these days many of us call ourselves campers but in our RV's, we have ovens, large refrigerators, and most of the comforts of home.

Sometimes, you don't realize that guests enjoyed your offerings until later when they ask for the recipe. This is a simple one to prepare and gives you a touch of Chinese cuisine.

SWEET & SOUR CHICKEN

2 chicken breasts, split and skinned or 4 boned, skinless chicken breast pieces
1 (8½ ounce) can unsweetened pineapple chunks
1 cup cranberry sauce
2 T. vinegar
2½ T. brown sugar
½ cup chicken broth
2 T. cornstarch
2 T. water
1 green bell pepper

1. Place chicken in baking dish.
2. Drain pineapple reserving juice and set aside.
3. In a separate pan, combine cranberry sauce, vinegar, brown sugar, broth and reserved juice. Then, mix the cornstarch with 2 T. of water until smooth and add to the sauce mixture. Cook sauce until thickened.
4. Add pineapple chunks to sauce and pour over chicken.
5. Cover and bake @ 350 degrees for 35 minutes or until chicken is tender.
6. Uncover and add green pepper, cut into long, thin strips and baste with sauce.
7. Bake uncovered an additional 5 minutes.

(Serves 4.)

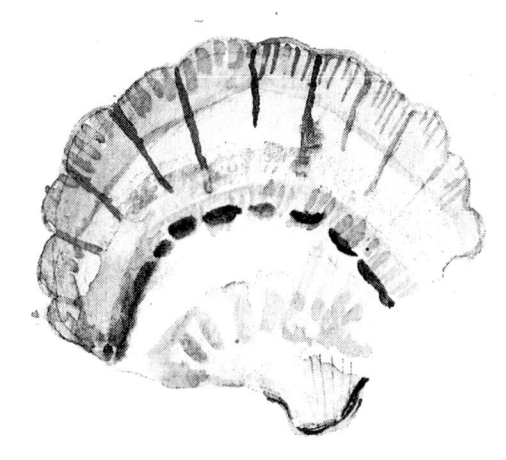

When we find that an electrical hook-up is available, it may mean that tonight's dinner will be prepared in the microwave. This is especially good when it is warm outside and one doesn't wish to add to the boat's indoor temperature. Plus, microwave cooking is an easy and quick way to put a meal on the table—leaving more time for the chef to relax, have a glass of wine, and reflect on the day's events.

This is quick and easy and what we would probably refer to as "comfort food." Little else is needed to accompany this main dish. I often serve an applesauce on the side which provides moistness to the meal. More than once I was told by Europeans that applesauce is not served with the main meal but is more of a dessert dish. They have many varieties of sauces on the store shelves that combine the apple with raspberries, or rhubarb, or other fruits.

CHICKEN NOODLE AU GRATIN IN MICROWAVE

1½ cups egg noodles
2 to 3 cups cooked chicken
½ cup milk
1 cup chicken stock (may need more liquid, either stock or milk, near the end of cooking for mixture to result in the right amount of moistness)
½ t. salt

1/8 t. pepper
1 cup Cheddar cheese, grated
¼ c. stuffed, green olives (If you like olives, increase to ½ cup.)

1. In a 2-quart casserole, place the noodles, chicken, milk, stock, salt, and pepper; mix well.
2. Cook in microwave at Power 70 for 8 to 10 minutes. Stir at least once during cooking. If noodles need more time, continue.
3. Add cheese and olives and cook on Power 20 for 5 minutes.

(Serves 4.)

A similar recipe to the following was given to me by Ruth. It never ceases to please us. We look forward to serving this once we are back in the U.S. Though cranberry juice is just now readily available in Europe, the sauce is not. For several years, the Nyes and Roberts would bring me cranberry juice from England and Spain, as it was not sold in France. It is a necessary drink for my health reasons. However, around the year 2000 we finally spotted the juice in a supermarket in the Burgundy region. From then on, it has become more and more popular. As for cranberry sauce, it had not been spotted though we have our search party out and about checking the shelves.

This is a recipe where ground turkey and turkey sausage can be substituted as the cranberry and chili sauces add adequate spice.

CRANBERRY MEATBALLS

1½ pounds ground beef
½ pound ground pork or mild sausage
2 eggs
½ t. garlic powder
1 medium onion
1/3 cup ketchup
2 slices of bread
¼ t. pepper

¼ cup dried parsley flakes

Sauce:
1 medium-size can jellied cranberry sauce, 16-ounce size
¾ cup chili sauce
3 T. light brown sugar
1 T. lemon juice

1. Mix all 9 ingredients for the meatballs, excluding the sauce. With your hands, make the mixture into balls, about 1½-inch in diameter.
2. Place in a 9 by 13 by 2-inch baking pan.
3. Mix all the sauce ingredients into a small bowl. Pour approximately 1/3 of the sauce over the meatballs, just enough to cover each meatball with some sauce.
4. Bake uncovered @ 350 degrees for 30 to 35 minutes. Remove from oven and pour off all the fat and discard as much as possible leaving the sauce more or less intact. Can use the item one uses to baste meat to remove the last bits of fat from the pan.
5. Add the remaining sauce and return to oven. Bake uncovered an additional 10 to 15 minutes.

(Serves 12.)

Here again one of the family, Sarah, remarked that she liked to make this for her gang. When I hear this, I think, "I should make that again." Sarah is one member of the family who is often asking for recipes, especially after she has just visited with us. Sometimes, if I cannot locate a particular recipe, I e-mail her and she sends me a copy. It's a really good feeling to know that someone has enjoyed a meal you served.

VEGETARIAN SPAGHETTI

1 to 2 t. olive oil
8 ounces fresh mushrooms
1 onion, sliced
1 zucchini, sliced
8 ounces broccoli, chopped
spaghetti for 2 people

Sauce:
4 to 5 T. white wine, dry
dash lemon juice

1. In oil, fry mushrooms, onion, and zucchini in a large pan, wok, or Dutch oven. Cook until it is *al dente*.
2. Steam broccoli 4 minutes in MW, drain well, and add to other vegetables.
3. Cook the pasta to desired tenderness and drain well.
4. Add the wine and lemon juice to the pasta pan along with broccoli, mushrooms, onion, and zucchini.
5. 5. Mix all ingredients well and cook just long enough to be well heated.

(Serves 2.)

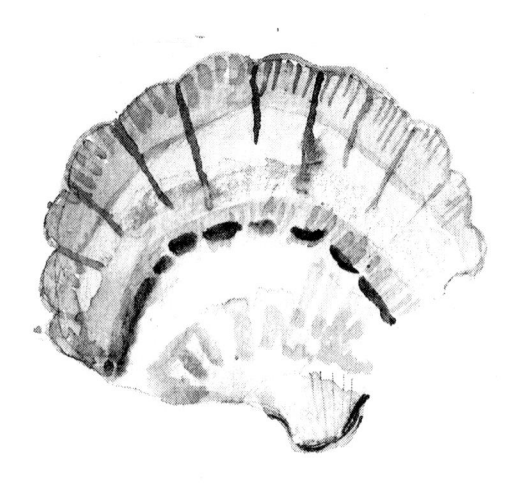

The following is so easy and yet so good! If you serve it in individual dishes, it's even more impressive. This is a super easy main course; your guests will think you spent more time in the preparation; let them think it.

PARTY SEAFOOD

4 cups shrimp, cooked, peeled, and deveined
2 (7-ounce) cans crabmeat
2½ cups celery, chopped
2/3 cup onion, finely chopped
2 t. Worcestershire sauce
1 t. salt
½ t. pepper
1 cup mayonnaise
1/3 cup butter
1½ cups fresh breadcrumbs

1. Lightly grease baking dish/pan/individual serving dishes. Drain shrimp, then, using your hands and paper towels, dry them as much as possible.
2. Squeeze crab by hand to get it as dry as possible.
3. Combine all ingredients except butter and crumbs and place in serving dishes or 8" square baking dish.
4. Combine crumbs and melted butter and sprinkle on top.
5. Bake @ 350 degrees for 35 minutes.

(Serves 6.)

This is a dish that I would most likely serve over the holidays or for a special occasion. Since turkey and ham are more traditional dishes for the holidays, I like to preface that special day with the pork roast.

FESTIVE PORK ROAST

1½ cups red wine, dry
2/3 cup firmly packed light brown sugar
½ cup ketchup
½ cup water
¼ cup vegetable oil
4 garlic cloves, minced
3 T. soy sauce
2 t. curry powder
1 t. ground ginger
½ t. pepper
1 (5-pound) boneless rolled pork roast
4 t. cornstarch

1. Combine first 10 ingredients in a large shallow dish or heavy-duty zip-top bag; add pork. Cover and seal and chill 8 hours, turning occasionally.
2. Remove pork from marinade, reserving 2½ cups marinade. Bring reserved marinade to a boil in a small saucepan.
3. Mix cornstarch with small amount of cold water. Add to marinade and cook stirring constantly, 2 or 3 minutes or until thickened. Cool.
4. Pat pork dry and place on a rack in a shallow roasting pan.
5. Bake pork @ 325 degrees for 2 ½ hours or until meat thermometer inserted into thickest portion registers 170 degrees, basting with ¼ cup reserved sauce during the last 15 minutes. Allow roast to stand 10 minutes before slicing.
6. Serve with warmed, reserved sauce.

(Serves 8 to 10.)

If substituting pork tenderloin, the baking time to reach tenderness will be lessened.

I have mixed results when frying pork chops. I usually stick with professional guidelines and fry on medium heat for 3 to 4 minutes on each side to get the best tenderness. However, that does not always produce those results. I have come to the conclusion that cooking tender pork has more to do with the pork itself. The pork will often melt in your mouth or become disgustingly tough. I recall that my mother would brown the chops on the stove, then, place them in the oven with some added water and bake until tender. I prefer to stick with just frying them on the stove top and adding this lovely cream sauce in the following recipe.

I was lucky one late afternoon while visiting one of our favorite towns in central France, *Moret-sur-Loing*. I purchased chops from the local butcher, took them back to the boat, and prepared dinner for the Tittensors who had just arrived from England. The chops melted in your mouth. I was lucky that day.

PORK CHOPS IN FRENCH MUSTARD CREAM SAUCE

4 (4-ounce) boneless, center-cut pork loin chops (approximately ½-inch thick)
½ t. salt, ½ t. pepper
butter/oil combination for frying
1/3 cup fat-free reduced-sodium chicken broth
1 T. French mustard (Vary amount according to your taste.)
1/3 cup fat-free half/half or fat-free evaporated milk

1. Sprinkle both sides of pork chops with salt and pepper. Coat skillet with oil/butter; place over medium-high heat until hot. Add chops and cook 3 to 4 minutes on each side or until nicely browned and middle of chop is sufficiently cooked. Depending on thickness of chops, cook time may need to be more. Remove chops from skillet and keep warm in the oven.
2. Add broth to skillet, stirring to loosen brown bits. Combine mustard and half/half; add to skillet.
3. Reduce heat and simmer 7 minutes or until sauce is thickened. To serve, spoon sauce over the chops.

(Serves 4.)

Don't serve the next macaroni dish too often as it's high in calories. However, once or twice or maybe three times a year is good. This French-take on macaroni and cheese gives a nice assertive flavor.

Nancy Makin, author of the book, *703, How I Lost a Quarter Ton and Gained a Life*, stated in a recent interview that given this great loss of pounds, she would still choose to have onion rings once a month. If I enjoy a rich dessert one day, I try to cut back the following day. Personally, if I am going to the trouble of preparing a recipe, I prefer to eat a smaller portion of the authentic rather than some substitute form that is tasteless.

MACARONI AND CHEESE WITH PROSCIUTTO

8 ounces small elbow macaroni (2 cups)
1½ cups (packed) grated Gruyere cheese (about 6 ounces), divided
1 cup whipping cream
1 cup whole milk
3 ounces thinly sliced prosciutto
3 T. Parmesan cheese, grated
1/8 t. ground nutmeg
salt and pepper, to taste

1. Butter a 9 by 13-inch glass baking dish.
2. Cook macaroni in large pot of boiling, salted water until tender but still firm to bite. Drain well.
3. Whisk ½ cup Gruyere, cream,

milk, prosciutto which has been coarsely cut, Parmesan and nutmeg in large bowl to blend.
4. Add macaroni and toss to coat. Season with salt and pepper.
5. Transfer to lightly-buttered baking dish. Sprinkle remaining 1 cup of Gruyere over.
6. Bake @ 350 degrees until cheese melts and the mixture sets and appears cooked, about 20 minutes. Serve warm.

(Serves 6.)

Well, I may say six but take that with a grain of salt. I've seen it consumed among three.

Simple and succulent and it meets the easy, simple preparation requirement. Often you can quickly tell if a recipe is going to be simple and easy to prepare by the number of ingredients and the few steps in preparation. It's a question of whether you have fifteen minutes or all morning.

CALIFORNIA GRILLED FISH

2 fish fillets
2 T. or more of tartar sauce
3 T. cheddar cheese, grated
2 T. dry breadcrumbs
1 t. coriander
black pepper and salt, to taste
paprika, to taste

1. Line grill pan with foil and spread the foil with butter.
2. Dry fish. Season with salt and pepper. Using "HIGH" setting of broiler, place grill pan as far away from heat as possible. Grill fish for approximately 10 minutes, 5 minutes on each side.
3. Remove fish from grill; spread fish with mixture of tartar sauce and cheddar cheese. Grill an additional 10 minutes or until middle of fish appears cooked.
4. Remove fish again, cover with mixture of breadcrumbs, coriander, a dash of black pepper, and paprika.
5. Grill until topping is nicely browned, just a few seconds

(Serves 2.)

This is not Dorothy Young.

Hal's sister, Anita, served this lovely dish and as a result of that, it became a huge favorite. It has been passed around by our English friends, as well. I often serve it to first-time guests on the boat because it's easy and oh, so delicious.

CHICKEN DIVAN

2 packages frozen broccoli florets or comparable amount of fresh broccoli
6 chicken breasts, halved, COOKED, and cut into bite-size pieces
2 cans (10¾-ounce each) cream of chicken soup
1 cup mayonnaise
2 T. lemon juice
1 cup cheddar cheese, grated
1 cup fresh breadcrumbs mixed with a tiny amount of melted butter
½ cup flake almonds, optional

1. If using frozen broccoli, cook long enough to separate spears.
2. If using fresh broccoli, remove long stems, cut into bite-size pieces; wash. then using paper towels or hand towel, drain very well.
3. Place broccoli in buttered 13x9x2-inch baking dish.
4. Place chicken on top.
5. Combine soup, mayonnaise, lemon juice, and cheese; pour over chicken.
6. Cover with buttered breadcrumbs; almonds are optional.
7. Bake @ 350 degrees for 30 minutes.

(Serves 10.)

I do not know if this is a popular main course which came from the Midwest but this was my mother's recipe. I like to purchase the thick chops already cut and ready for stuffing.

STUFFED PORK CHOPS

2 cups fresh breadcrumbs
¾ t. salt
¼ t. pepper
1½ T. parsley, minced
1 t. sage
1 T. onion, very finely chopped
margarine or oil or both for browning
6 thick pork chops ready for stuffing

1. Combine all stuffing ingredients.
2. Brown chops in margarine/oil combination, approximately 4 minutes on each side.
3. Stuff the chops. Add a little water and bake in oven.
4. Bake @ 350 degrees for 1 hour or until tender.

(Serves 6.)

It's New Years in Pennsylvania Dutch country and we're invited to join friends for a festive dinner to bring in the New Year. I was unaware of this traditional celebration dish until I found myself living in the area. When Hal's aunt was still able to prepare a dinner, this is the meal that she invited us to share with her. On an annual basis, she, her sisters or neighbors, would get together to can sauerkraut. She was preparing to preserve 20 jars of sauerkraut the day she died at age 97.

To make the meal complete, it is served with dumplings and mashed potatoes. To make it easy, I often use the simple dumpling recipe given on the box of commercial baking mix.

PORK AND SAURKRAUT

4 pounds of pork
1 ring of kielbasa, about 14 ounces
2 large cans of sauerkraut

Dumplings:
3 cups flour
½ cup sugar
3 t. baking powder
1 cup milk
½ t. salt
1 egg, beaten

1. Place roast in pan and cover with sauerkraut. Pour 1 quart water over it; sprinkle with pepper. Cover and roast @ 375 degrees for 2 hours or until pork is tender. It may take as long as 3 hours.
2. Add kielbasa slices and cover and bake 30 minutes longer. May need more water. Extend roasting time until pork is very tender.

Dumplings:
1. Mix dry ingredients; blend in milk and egg. Place by tablespoons across the top and cover. Steam (low heat) 20 minutes (until done in center.) Uncover and steam 10 more minutes OR follow the commercial baking mix directions on the box.
2. Serve with mashed potatoes.

(Serves 8 to 10.)

This is a lovely dish that can be prepared ahead of serving time, assuming that you have the time available. Just looking at it, you'll realize that you need a morning free.

CHICKEN CREPES

Crepe Batter:
2/3 cup flour
2 eggs
3 T. cooled, melted butter
1/8 t. salt
1 cup milk, divided

Chicken Filling:
¼ cup butter
¾ pound mushrooms, chopped
½ cup green onions, chopped
2½ cups cooked chicken, diced
½ cup sherry
½ t. salt
dash of pepper

Sauce:
¾ cup flour
2/3 cup sherry
1 can (10¾-ounces) condensed chicken broth, undiluted
2 cups light cream

½ t. salt
dash pepper

Final topping:
½ cup Swiss cheese, grated

Batter:
1. In medium bowl, combine flour, eggs, butter, salt, ½ cup milk. Beat until smooth. Beat in rest of milk. Cover and refrigerate for 3 hours or overnight.

Filling:
1. Heat butter in large skillet. Add mushrooms and onion; sauté 10 minutes. Add chicken, sherry, salt, and pepper. Cook over high heat, stirring until liquid is gone.

Sauce:
1. In a pan, blend flour with sherry. Stir in broth, cream, salt, and pepper. Over medium heat, bring to boiling, stirring. Reduce heat, simmer, stirring 2 minutes. Stir until blended. Add half of sauce to filling. Set aside other half.

Crepes:
1. Slowly heat a flat-surface skillet or I use the pancake grill, large enough to cook 2 crepes at a time. Brush surface lightly with oil or butter, rotate the surface so you spread the batter.
2. Cook over medium heat until golden; turn, brown other side. Cool on rack. Repeat to make 15.
3. Place ¼ cup of filling on each crepe; roll up. Arrange, seam side down, in single layer in buttered, shallow, baking dish.
4. Pour other half of sauce over crepes; sprinkle with the ½ cup grated Swiss cheese.
5. Bake at 425 degrees for 15 minutes or until bubbly.

(Serves 6 to 8.)

Grandma's Tip: I prefer to prepare the previous recipe through Step 2 ahead of time, then freeze crepes and sauce separately. Place wax paper between the crepes for freezing so they separate easily. The day before serving I remove them from the freezer into the refrigerator section. It is easy, then, to continue with Steps 3 and 4 prior to serving. You may need to increase baking time to compensate for the coldness of the crepes. The sauce can be warmed on the stovetop prior to putting atop the crepes and into the oven. This appears to be a long, difficult recipe but once you have done it, it becomes easier and believe me, the results are well worth the effort especially when you are retired and/or have free time to work in the kitchen.

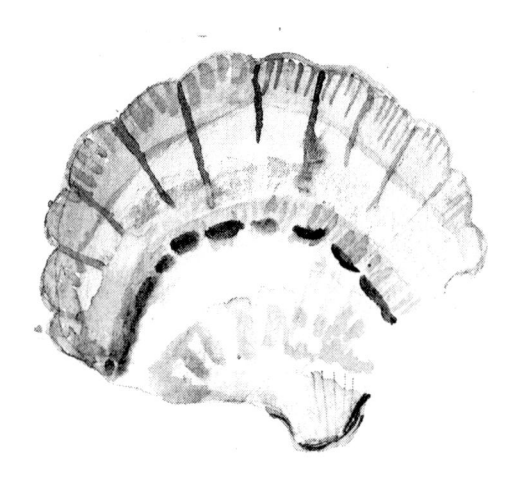

The next recipe was adapted from studying English cookbooks so have no knowledge of how it may differ from the original Spanish dish. The only time we visited in Spain, we dined in Continental restaurants with mostly English people in a very English-dominated part of the country. As a result, I left Spain without being immersed in Spanish cuisine. This dish represents a very savory offering and can serve a large group easily. The jury is out as to how it stands up to the original.

This dish is not restricted to Spain. Cuisines in Spain and France are intermingled somewhat because of their history and, also, because of a mobile society. We learn through TV and cookbooks about every imaginable ethnic region's cooking so it stands to reason that one can now accumulate a huge variety of recipes from books and the Internet.

PAELLA, PORTUGUESE-STYLE

4 chicken thighs, 4 chicken breast halves, boned, skinned and cut into 16 pieces
½ cup olive or salad oil
1 pound lean pork, cut into inch cubes
2 cups onion, chopped
2 garlic cloves, crushed
¼ t. pepper
1 t. dried oregano
2 t. salt
2 cups raw long-grain white rice or brown rice
1/8 t. saffron
1 pound Italian sausages, sliced
2 medium-size fresh tomatoes, peeled and chopped
1 bay leaf

3 cans (10¾-ounce each) condensed chicken broth
1½ pounds large shrimp, cooked, peeled, and deveined
10 ounces frozen peas, thawed
½ jar (4-ounce size) pimientos
2 lemons, each cut in 8 wedges

1. **Wash chicken and dry with towels. In hot oil in large skillet, brown chicken until golden, as many pieces at a time as possible. Remove as it browns.**
2. **Add pork cubes to skillet; brown well on all sides. Remove.**
3. **To drippings in skillet, add onion,**

garlic, pepper, and oregano; sauté stirring 5 minutes, until onion is golden. Add salt, rice, and saffron; cook, stirring—about 10 minutes.
4. Meanwhile, in another skillet brown sausages, turning on all sides—about 10 minutes. Drain and discard fat.
5. Place chicken, pork and sausage in roasting pan.
6. Add tomatoes, bay leaf and chicken broth to rice mixture and bring to boiling.
7. Add shrimp, then spoon evenly over chicken and sausage in pan.
8. Bake @ 375, tightly covered with foil, for 1 hour.
9. If mixture seems dry, add ½ cup or more of water.
10. Sprinkle peas over top, without stirring. Bake, covered, 20 minutes longer.
11. To serve turn Paella into heated-round serving platter or paella pan.
12. Garnish with pimiento and lemon.

(Serves 10.)

You will never catch me trying to make phyllo pastry. I know we are taught never to say "never," but I'm positive that there is no desire in me that would take me to that goal. The closest I have come is once I did attempt the French croissant, which turned out OK, but I was younger then. Still, I consider it too much work especially when you can buy croissants as good as or probably several degrees better than anything I might produce. However, I find the purchased pastry a wonderful product with many uses. It is important to follow the phyllo package directions carefully. The pastry is available almost everywhere so the following dish is doable. Again the sauce is outstanding.

All of the recipe can be prepared ahead of time.

CHICKEN IN PHYLLO
Kotopits

8 ounces frozen phyllo dough (10 to 12 sheets)
1 cup celery, chopped
¾ cup onion, chopped
1 T. butter or margarine
2 cups cooked chicken or turkey, chopped
2 T. chicken broth
2 t. dried parsley flakes
½ t. salt, 1/8 t. pepper
½ t. ground nutmeg
1 egg, beaten
6 T. butter or margarine, melted
hot cooked rice

Bechamel Sauce:
2 T. flour
2 T. butter or margarine
¼ t. salt
1¼ cups chicken broth
2 egg yolks, beaten
4 t. lemon juice

1. Thaw phyllo dough 2 hours at room temperature.
2. In a covered skillet, cook celery and onion in the 1 T. butter until vegetables are tender but not brown, stirring occasionally.
3. Add chicken or turkey and broth.
4. Cook and stir, uncovered, until all the broth is absorbed.
5. Stir in parsley, salt, pepper, and nutmeg. Remove from heat. Blend in beaten egg. Set aside.
6. For each roll, stack half the sheets of phyllo dough, brushing liberally with some of the butter or margarine between each layer.
7. Spoon 1¼ cups chicken mixture over phyllo layers to within 1-inch of edges.
8. Turn one short side over filling about 1-inch; fold in long sides.
9. Roll as for jelly roll starting with folded short side.
10. Place seam side down on a lightly-greased, shallow baking pan.
11. Repeat with remaining phyllo and filling.
12. Brush each roll with additional melted butter.
13. Score each roll into 3 or 4 portions.
14. Bake @ 350 degrees for 40 minutes or until rolls are brown and crisp.
15. During baking time, make the Bechamel sauce.
16. Cut rolls where scored.
17. Arrange on platter with hot cooked rice on bottom or side; rolls, on top. Spoon Bechamel Sauce over rolls. Pass remaining sauce.

Sauce:
1. In a saucepan, melt butter or margarine. Stir in flour and salt.
2. Add chicken broth all at once, cook and stir until mixture is bubbly.
3. Combine egg yolks and lemon juice. Stir about half of hot mixture into egg yolk mixture. Return to remaining hot mixture in pan.
4. Cook and stir 2 minutes more. (Makes 1½ cups sauce.)

(Serves 6 to 8.)

Sarah gathered ideas from several sources and served this special meal to us on one of our visits to Connecticut. She knew how much her father appreciated this particular dish. Here again, it looks longer and more complicated than it is as I have included the layering of ingredients to make the dish easier to put together. It is a bit long in preparation so save it for a special occasion. And, believe me, it will be worth your time and effort.

EGGPLANT MOUSSAKA

olive oil, enough to keep eggplant from sticking
2 eggplants (1½ pounds each)
1½ pounds of ground beef or lamb
1 medium onion, chopped
¼ t. nutmeg
½ t. garlic powder
1 (8-ounce) can tomato sauce
½ cup water
¼ c. fresh parsley or 1 T. dry parsley
salt and pepper to taste
Italian bread crumbs

Sauce:
1 quart milk (4 cups)
4 ounces butter
6 T. flour
1 cup grated Parmesan and Romano cheese, divided
1 t. salt
6 eggs, beaten

Filling:
1. **Peel and slice eggplants into ½-inch-thick rounds. Sprinkle with salt and leave to sweat for 30 minutes. Blot eggplants on paper towels.**
2. **In a skillet, brown eggplants in oil. Remove eggplants from**

skillet. Set aside.
3. Brown meat and drain. Return to a large pot or Dutch oven.
4. Add onions, nutmeg, and garlic powder. Cook 5 minutes.
5. Add tomato sauce, ½ cup water, parsley, salt and pepper to taste. Cook uncovered on low heat, stirring occasionally, until dry and no water remains. This takes about 2 hours
6. Lightly oil a 9 x 13-inch baking dish. Cover bottom with Italian bread crumbs.
7. After layering, pour cream sauce over all.
8. Bake @ 350 degrees in middle oven rack for 1 to 1½ hours. Allow to rest 20 minutes before serving.

Sauce:
1. Heat milk in saucepan until warm or in a microwave bowl. In another medium saucepan, melt butter and add flour. Stir in warm milk and whisk. Add ¼ cup of the cheese and salt, continuing to cook and stir until thickened.
2. In a small bowl, beat eggs until frothy. Stir in a few tablespoons of the warm milk mixture to the eggs, then, slowly add the eggs to the sauce mixture.

<u>Grandma's Tip:</u> I find it helpful in this recipe as well as the beef lasagna to have a <u>layering list</u> in front of me as I put these dishes together.

Layer as follows with sides of eggplant rounds touching :

1/3 of eggplant,
¼ cup of cheese
½ of meat mixture
1/3 of eggplant
¼ cup of cheese
½ of meat mixture
1/3 of eggplant
¼ cup of cheese

(Serves 10 to 12.)

Sometimes when I think that I may have served a particular dish to the same guests before and perhaps I should give them something new and different, I am reminded of how many occasions we sat at my mother's table and enjoyed the same dish, especially in her later years. Never did I tire or even give it a thought; if anything, it was great to be with my parents enjoying the togetherness and good food. Along with the ham loaf, she served potato salad (See Index.) and baby lima beans in a white sauce. I have not come across ground ham in any supermarkets. However, country stores often make up their own ham loaf mixture.

HAM LOAF

1½ pound ground ham
½ pound ground pork
¾ cup butter crackers, mashed
1 cup milk
1 t. prepared mustard
1 T. butter
¼ cup light brown sugar
¼ cup + 1 T. pineapple juice
3 to 4 pineapple slices from the can, enough to cover the bottom of a loaf pan

1. In a medium bowl, mix the ham, pork, crackers, milk, and mustard with your hands.
2. Melt butter and brown sugar in a small pan until butter is melted. Add the pineapple juice and bring to a boil. Continue to boil on medium heat for approximately 5 minutes or until mixture becomes somewhat thick.
3. Place butter, sugar, and juice mixture in bottom of a loaf pan.
4. Place sliced pineapples atop the mixture.
5. Place the meat mixture on top of pineapple.
6. Bake @ 350 degrees for 1½ hours.
7. Remove from oven, turn pan upside down onto a serving platter.

(Serves 8 to 10.)

The following recipe is a compilation from many versions. I have often enjoyed this dish at Anita's and at Ruth's, and it was from them that I got the inspiration to try it for us. Each time, I like it more and am always happy to have it again. Over the years I have adapted what I gleaned from them plus party cookbooks that proclaim it to be worthy of serving on a special occasion. You will probably adapt it to your tastes. It's very different and promises to leave a mark with your family and friends.

CHICKEN WITH DRIED BEEF

4-ounce package dried beef
6 chicken breasts, serving size, boned and skinned
6 strips of lean bacon
1 (10¾-ounce) can cream of mushroom soup
8 ounces plain yogurt
8 ounces sour cream

1. Arrange beef on baking dish.
2. Wrap bacon around each chicken breast; arrange over beef.
3. Combine soup, yogurt, and sour cream and arrange over beef.
4. Cover with foil.
5. Bake @ 300 degrees for 2 hours.
6. Uncover; bake @ 350 degrees for 25-30 minutes, basting several times.

(Serves 6.)

No salt is needed because of the salty dried beef.

Often I have tasted something in a restaurant that gave me motivation to try to duplicate it at home. In this example, it was quite easy to make a similar dish. I had eaten this omelet in a French restaurant in Washington, D.C. and now it's an adopted favorite. The potatoes can be cooked ahead of time.

OMELET FOR LUNCH OR EVENING

5 eggs, beaten
2 medium-size, cooked potatoes
1 small onion, chopped
2/3 cup plain yogurt
salt and pepper, to taste
butter for frying omlette

1. Fry cooked, sliced potatoes and onion until browned and tender. Add yogurt.
2. In a separate skillet or omelet pan, melt butter and prepare omelet.
3. When almost done, add the potatoes and onion mixture on top of one side of omelet. Add salt and pepper.
4. Fold omelet over and serve.

(Makes 2 large or 3 normal-size portions.)

Ask me to reflect upon past birthdays and number seventy comes to mind. We were spending an evening at Diana's place in Maryland on our way to our home in Georgia. And, she had assembled in one meal so many of my favorites. For appetizers, we had chicken livers wrapped in bacon. Then, as a main course we enjoyed a traditional dish of that region, stuffed ham. Though she has given me a recipe for the ham, I have to admit that I have not tried making it. It's one of those dishes that I enjoy but it's just easier to purchase it in their part of southern Maryland. She is able to get it from several sources in her area and it's fantastic.

This is the appetizer she served.

CHICKEN LIVERS WRAPPED IN BACON
Rumakis

¾ cup soy sauce, low sodium
¼ c. dry, white wine
½ clove garlic, peeled and crushed
1 t. ground ginger
6 chicken livers, quartered
¾ cup light brown sugar
12 oz. lean bacon, each strip halved crosswise

1. Mix soy, wine, garlic, and ginger.
2. Marinate chicken livers in the sauce at least 2 hours.
3. Retain the sauce; remove the livers.
4. Roll chicken livers in brown sugar, wrap with bacon, and secure with a toothpick.
5. Place in a glass baking dish, add sauce and marinate 30 minutes to 2 to 3 hours.
6. Bake @ 400 degrees for 30 minutes.
7. Serve with some of the sauce.

After we left Maryland in March, 2007 and settled into our winter home in Georgia, whom did I see walking down the street one Saturday morning? Diana, TJ, Christina and Sonny, a yellow Labrador had traveled all night to surprise me for my birthday. They walked past the house. To me, they looked similar to all other walkers who pass by in jogging clothes and hoods. My first comment was that I thought our neighbor was receiving weekend guests. However, these folks turned around and entered on our property. I couldn't believe my eyes.

It was Hal who had convinced me to have breakfast sitting at the dining table where I would have a bird's eye view of the front of the house. And, what had the Krafts brought with them on their all-night drive--a lunch, a dinner, and Sunday morning breakfast before they made their return road trip to Maryland. I remember lunch was Pork Barbecue sandwiches and breakfast was Breakfast Casserole, both appearing in this book. It turned out to be one glorious weekend that I shall never forget.

SANDWICHES

PORK BARBECUE

½ cup ketchup
½ c, water
¼ garlic clove, crushed
1 t. chili powder
½ t. Worcestershire sauce
¼ cup sugar
1 t. prepared mustard
slices of cooked roast pork (or beef or chicken)
6 sandwich buns

1. Add first 7 ingredients to a medium-size pan except meat.
2. Cook mixture 10 minutes.
3. Add meat and heat thoroughly.
4. Warm buns and serve.

It's quite easy to make the sauce part four times larger and a roast of medium size will require it. Plus, this dish can be stored in the refrigerator for a couple of days and/or frozen so nothing will go to waste. The amount of the pork is not given as you will need to adjust the sauce to the quantity of meat when you put the two together. This is a family favorite, not just mine.

On one occasion we were camping near New Orleans with John and Muriel. We left our campsite and went into the city to tour. I was not feeling well and was unable to partake in the Slave Market restaurant lunch the other three devoured. At least one of them, as I recall, ordered the Muffaletta sandwich. It looked so good so I was determined to try to duplicate it at some point in the future.

I have pulled recipes for the Muffaletta sauce from numerous magazines, and this is my estimation of what I missed on that day in New Orleans. The sauce can be prepared 2 or 3 days ahead; the flavor just gets better.

MUFFALETTAS

13 ounces green olives, drained and diced
1 carrot, diced
1 celery stalk, diced
1 large onion, diced
1 t. oregano
½ t. dried basil
1 t. garlic powder
2 T. dried parsley
¾ cup olive oil
4 hard sandwich buns
slices of salami
slices of roast beef
slices of Provolone cheese

1. Mix the first 9 ingredients in a jar, cover, and allow to stand at least 2 hours.
2. Remove part of the upper bread of the bun making a hole large enough to hold 2 T. sauce. Be careful not to put a hole in the top of the bun.
3. Add the sauce to the opened space in the top of the bun, then, add the meat layers to the bottom half of bun and close.
4. Heat buns in microwave for 1 minute, 30 seconds.

This is a very juicy sandwich. When eating this, a large table napkin is needed.

SHRIMP SALAD ON CROISSANTS

Use the large, sandwich-size croissants from the deli or a hard roll and cooked shrimp from the seafood department to save time. This is simply delicious. Should you have any leftover mixture, it's also an excellent appetizer served on crackers.

3 cups large shrimp, cooked, peeled, and deveined
1 cup celery, finely chopped
½ cup green olives, finely chopped
3 large, hard-boiled eggs, finely chopped

Dressing:
¾ cup mayonnaise
2 t. chili sauce
2 t. prepared horseradish, drained
¼ t. salt

1. **Combine first 3 ingredients; stir in eggs.**
2. **In a separate small bowl, combine the dressing ingredients, mixing well. The dressing will make approximately 1 cup.**
3. **Add sufficient dressing to moisten the shrimp mixture.**
4. **Chill before putting sandwiches together.**

(Makes 4 cups.)

I prefer the large-size shrimp because of texture, but I do cut them into small bite-size pieces for sandwiches and appetizers. If serving the mixture as a salad, I suggest leaving the shrimp whole.

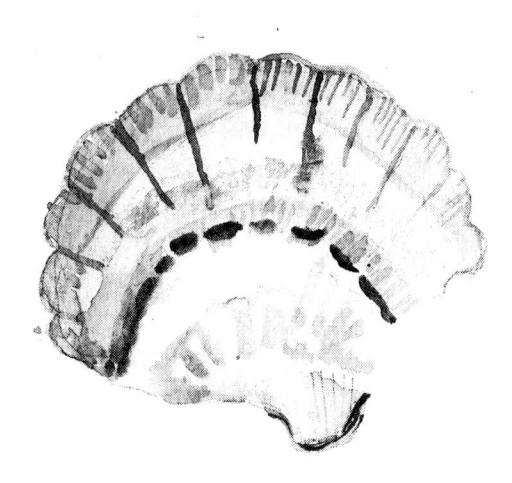

Rave reviews come your way and all it takes is canned tuna and a few common ingredients—unbelievable. Make the following filling ahead of time and enjoy more time with your guests.

TUNA FRANKS

12-ounce can tuna, drained
3 hard-boiled eggs, chopped
1 cup Cheddar cheese, shredded
½ cup mayonnaise
2 t. pickle relish, drained or 2 t. chopped pickle
2 T. onion, minced
15 stuffed, green olives, chopped
¾ t. salt
½ t. pepper

10 frankfurter rolls, whole wheat preferably

1. Combine all ingredients except rolls. Mix well.
2. Fill frankfurter rolls with tuna mixture.
3. Wrap each roll in foil.
4. Bake @ 375 degrees for 20 minutes.

(Makes 10 sandwiches.)

EGG SALAD PITAS

2/3 cup mayonnaise
2 T. pickle relish, drained
1 t. prepared mustard
¼ t. pepper
¼ t. celery salt
¼ t. paprika
¼ t. dried basil
¼ t. salt
6 hard-boiled eggs, coarsely chopped
½ cup Cheddar cheese, shredded
1 small onion, chopped
1 large carrot, shredded
2 bacon strips, fried crisply and crumbled (turkey bacon preferably)
3 (6") pita breads, halved (whole wheat preferably)
torn lettuce
2 medium tomatoes, chopped

1. Combine the first 8 ingredients.
2. Stir in eggs, cheese, onion, carrot, and bacon.
3. Spoon mixture, approximately ½ cup, into each pita half.
4. Add torn lettuce and chopped tomatoes.

(Serves 6.)

SEASONED TURKEY PATTIES

1¼ pounds ground turkey
½ cup fresh bread crumbs
½ cup onion, chopped
1 egg

1½ t. Worcestershire sauce
½ t. poultry seasoning
½ t. garlic salt
½ t. seasoned salt

4 sandwich buns

1. Mix all ingredients except buns and form into 4 to 5 patties, each ½ thick.
2. Fry over medium heat 4 to 5 minutes on each side until no longer pink inside.
3. Lightly butter the inside of the bun and warm in microwave.
4. I prefer adding ketchup to my turkey sandwich but the choice of topping is yours.

Grandma's Tip If you wish to grill or broil, brush the patties with barbecue sauce or butter while cooking. I usually make up the patties shortly after purchasing the ground turkey. I place them in the freezer, remove them the morning I am going to serve them, and have them readily available for an easy supper. It's easy to separate the patties after they have been in the refrigerator all day. If frozen, zap them in the microwave a few seconds until they part easily, and they are ready for the frying pan.

The following was my mother's recipe and has become a favorite for the extended family. Friends served these sandwiches for lunch on the boat in England requested the recipe as did our visiting friends from the Netherlands who liked the taste when the sandwiches were served to them during a Super Bowl gathering.

SLOPPY JOE'S, SOMETIMES CALLED SPANISH HAMBURGERS

1 pound ground beef
1 medium-size onion, chopped
2/3 cup ketchup
1 package butter crackers, approximately 30 to 35, crushed
½ cup milk or more
sandwich buns

1. Fry ground beef and onion until cooked; drain well.
2. Return to frying pan and add ketchup, then, crackers.
3. Cook an additional 2 to 3 minutes.
4. Add sufficient quantity of milk to give the mixture the right consistency.
5. Serve on warmed, sandwich buns.

(Serves 4 to 6.)

We prefer to serve this mixture on one side of a sandwich bun and eat the sandwich with a fork. Substituting ground chicken or turkey for the beef works well. When warming this recipe a second time, you will probably want to add more milk.

SALADS

Whenever we feel that we have overdone the rich foods and are at the top of our weight limit, we turn to our list of salads. One special salad is a plate of salad greens with some chopped celery or green pepper and carrots topped with cooked chicken, blue cheese dressing, and garlic croutons. This works as a speedy, easy plate if you have leftover, cooked chicken. One trick I use when I have not thought ahead on this meal is to remove frozen, cooked chicken, put it in a small saucepan with some chicken broth to heat until it is ready to serve. This works and keeps the chicken moist. My blue-cheese dressing recipe appears under Hamburger Sandwiches with Blue Cheese Dressing. See Index.

The following yogurt salad probably doesn't require a written recipe. Just add lots of fruit including some banana, chopped dates, raisins, dried cranberries, part of an apple, and any other favorite fruits. Vanilla yogurt is sweet so you do not need to add any sugar. When using plain yogurt, I add a bit of honey. For one person, half of a banana and half of an apple are sufficient.

YOGURT SALAD

½ apple, unless very small
4 to 8-ounces low-or-nonfat vanilla yogurt or flavored yogurt of your choice
1 rounded T. of raisins
1 rounded T. of dried cranberries
1 rounded t. chopped dates or prunes
½ banana, sliced
½ cup granola cereal

1. **Cut unpeeled apple into slices and place in bottom of serving bowl.**
2. **Add yogurt, raisins, cranberries, dates, and banana.**
3. **Top with cereal.**

Your quantities can be altered to suit. This is a favorite-favorite that is on our lunch table at least once a week.

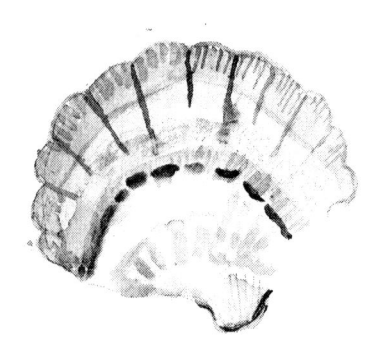

Even those folks who don't particularly like cauliflower will probably clear their plate of this one.

CAULIFLOWER SALAD

1 head lettuce
1 head cauliflower
1 large sweet onion
1 pound bacon, preferably turkey bacon
2 cups mayonnaise (1 cup can be light mayonnaise.)
½ cup Parmesan cheese
¼ cup sugar (A sugar substitute will work.)

1. In a large bowl, cut up and layer in order the following: lettuce, in pieces; cauliflower, cut fine; onion, chopped; bacon, fried crisply and crumbled.
2. Mix together mayonnaise, cheese, and sugar.
3. Pour mayonnaise mixture over the above ingredients. **DO NOT MIX.**
4. Let stand overnight.
5. Mix before serving.

(Serves 12.)

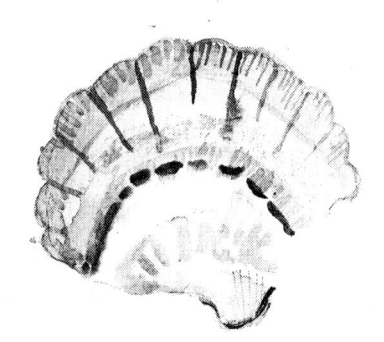

This next salad is one of those that I first experienced in a restaurant and is the one I so often serve prior to a seafood main course. For each serving, Thousand Island dressing mixed with a bit of mayo is spread over half of an avocado. I place salad greens and maybe some celery or green pepper on the plate with shrimp and the covered avocado on the side. I top the greens with a bit of the homemade French dressing, recipe in the Index, or any commercial vinaigrette dressing you prefer.

So often, the purchased avocados are not sufficiently ripe. I find that I often need to think ahead and buy them six or more days before serving.

Some markets provide varying stages of ripeness.

AVOCADO-SHRIMP SALAD

2 avocados, ripe
half mayonnaise-half Thousand Island dressing, approximately ¼ cup each
salad greens for 4
1 large stalk celery, chopped or ½ green pepper, chopped
small onion, chopped (optional)
2 cups large shrimp, cooked, peeled, and deveined
French dressing for lettuce greens only

1. Prepare mixture of mayonnaise/1000 island dressing to cover 4 avocado halves.
2. Cut up lettuce, celery or green pepper, and onion.
3. Prepare shrimp for serving.
4. Pare avocados and sprinkle with a bit of lemon juice to avoid discoloring.
5. Place one-half avocado on serving plate, top with the mixture of mayonnaise/1000 island dressing.
6. Place salad greens on plate and sprinkle French dressing over greens only.
7. Place shrimp atop the salad and serve.

(Serves 4.)

There is something about serving smoked salmon that communicates a lavish, sophisticated dish. Though it's expensive, it requires a small amount to make a salad tasty. It's a cut above. *(Serves 6.)*

SIDE SALAD WITH SMOKED SALMON

15 cherry tomatoes
1½ ounces smoked salmon
¼ cup green onions, chopped
salt and pepper, to taste (not much, needed, if any, because of salty salmon)
1½ ounces cream cheese, softened
½ t. milk
fresh dill sprigs

1. Combine halved tomatoes, salmon in pieces, chopped green onions, and s&p.
2. Mix cream cheese and milk and combine with the above.
3. Add dill and refrigerate until time to serve.
4. Place on lettuce leaves.

This French salad can be served as a main meal or it might be served along with a soup for lunch. I have tried various examples of this salad from restaurants and from friends' kitchens, and the salad varies considerably. But, this version keeps it easy and simple to prepare. I have read where no cooked vegetables are included, then, others will add them. Here again, it's a matter of pleasing your palate and, also, keeping it simple.

GREEN SALAD WITH TUNA
Salade Nicoise

½ cup salad oil
¼ c. red wine vinegar
½ t. salt
1 garlic clove, minced
4 eggs, hard-boiled (divided)
4 large potatoes, cooked
1 pound green beans, cooked
1 red onion
1 tomato
1 (4½-ounce) can pitted, black olives, drained
1 (2-ounce) can anchovy fillets, drained (If you don't like anchovies, omit them and salad will still be tasty.)
1 (7-ounce) can tuna, drained

1. Cook eggs to hard-boil stage. Leave 2 as a garnish.
2. In a jar, combine oil, vinegar, salt, and garlic; blend well.
3. In a large bowl, combine 2 eggs, sliced; potatoes, pared and cut into ½" slices; green beans, onion, tomato cut into wedges; olives, anchovy fillets, drained, and tuna, drained and cut into chunks.
4. Pour dressing over; toss thoroughly. Cover and refrigerate 1 hour.
5. Place pieces of lettuce into a salad serving bowl and add the refrigerated salad. Mix well.
6. Serve in the large bowl or on individual dishes.

(Serves 6.)

I was once served the above salad and the chef prepared it with fresh tuna. That was lovely, but remember, I'm mostly living on a boat or a camper and canned tuna makes it easy.

Friend Mary Cox prepared this layered salad for us during one of our visits with her and Tom in Florida. I have since served it frequently, as it makes a large amount and can be prepared ahead, very important in my book.

LAYERED SALAD

1 head lettuce
1 cup celery, diced
4 large hard-boiled eggs, sliced
10-ounce package frozen peas, cooked according to package directions
½ cup green pepper, diced
2 cups mayonnaise
2 T. sugar
8 slices of bacon, fried crisply and crumbled
4 ounces Cheddar cheese, grated

1. Break lettuce into bite-size pieces and place in large bowl.

2. Layer the remaining ingredients as follows: celery, eggs, peas, and green pepper.
3. Mix sugar and mayonnaise; spread, as if icing a cake, over the layered ingredients.
4. Sprinkle with bacon and cheese and chill. Will keep for a couple of days.
5. When ready to serve, mix salad and place in a clean salad, serving bowl.

(Serves 8 to 10.)

Here again, you can substitute turkey bacon and utilize half-real, half-light mayonnaise.

The following salad is often served in the summer months. It's not heavy and is refreshing. Similar contents are often referred to as "Waldorf Salad." If I have gorgeous grapes and crunchy apples available, I will often serve this, separately, of course. It goes well with anything that follows and is not so sweet that it turns some folks off.

FRESH FRUIT SALAD

1½ cups eating apples
1 cup celery, coarsely chopped
½ cup golden raisins
1½ cups red, seedless grapes
1/3 cup walnuts, chopped
2 T. mayonnaise
1 T. sugar
1/8 t. salt, dash of pepper

1. Combine apples, celery, raisins, grapes, and nuts.
2. Combine mayonnaise, sugar, s&p; stir well.
3. Gently blend the mixtures; serve on a lettuce leaf.
4. Serve immediately.

(Serves 8.)

This salad was served to us by Mary Jane, and I really liked it because it was different from anything I had eaten before. You will want to try this on yourself or include it with other salad choices as not everyone will relish it. So, try it; you might like it.

PASTA SALAD

3 cups bow-tie pasta, uncooked
4 ounces smoked turkey
4 ounces blue cheese
1 cup pecans, chopped
1/3 cup parsley, fresh
1 garlic clove, crushed
½ t. pepper
¼ cup olive oil
1/3 cup Parmesan cheese, grated

1. Cook pasta for 10 to 11 minutes or to your satisfaction; drain.
2. Chop the turkey and blue cheese into small pieces.
3. Add remaining ingredients and chill.
4. Serve on leaf of lettuce.

(Serves 6.)

Don't know why I serve this so infrequently. Every time I have it, I ask myself that question.

GREEK SALAD

2 large tomatoes, chopped
1/4th cucumber, sliced
1 small onion, chopped
¼ cup ripe olives
¼ pound feta cheese
lettuce greens

Dressing:
3 T. olive oil
1 T. lemon juice

salt and pepper, to taste
pinch of marjoram, dried

1. Mix ingredients except lettuce and separately mix dressing.
2. Chill separated mixtures 30 minutes.
3. Combine and serve on lettuce greens.

(Makes 2 large or 4 small servings.)

The French dressing recipe (See Tomato Salad with Homemade French dressing.) in the Index works well with this salad in place of the one above.

This salad is probably limited to those living in the U.S. as it calls for cranberries or I often substitute cranberry sauce. I have to admit to finding the sauce in Paris at the Thanksgiving store near the Bastille monument. (Yes, that's its name.) This Jello salad was a part of Hal's mother's Thanksgiving dinner. It never disappoints and is enjoyed by us all year long but especially over the holidays. Lenore's instructions were to make this two days ahead. Mother-in-law is always right, but I usually prepare this salad the night before or the morning of serving day.

CRANBERRY JELLO SALAD

2 c. ground cranberries (or whole cranberry sauce and no sugar)
2 c. sugar
2 regular-size or 1 large box of gelatin (cherry, strawberry, or other variety)
3 c. boiling water
½ c. nut meats (I use walnuts.)
1 c. celery, chopped
1 orange (ground or in segments)

1. Chop cranberries in food processor or a junior mouli.
2. Add sugar and let stand.
3. Combine Jello and boiling water and let cool in refrigerator for 30 minutes.
4. Combine walnuts, celery, and orange and add to cooled Jello.
5. Add sweetened cranberries and pour into a large mold that has been sprayed with a no-stick spray.

(Serves approximately 12 to 14.)

I like to add one can of black cherries, drained, to the above. If I do not have access to fresh cranberries, I exclude the sugar and substitute a medium-size can of whole cranberry sauce. A small can of drained, crushed pineapple is a nice addition.

My mother would fry the chicken gizzard along with her memorable fried chicken and I don't recall who chose to put it on their plate but the gizzard was always a bit chewy. Mother always fried her chicken with the skin on and in all butter. This is something the recent generation does not do; however, my mother and father who dined on this many Sundays in their lifetimes lived to be 91 and 95. So, it's not all what we eat obviously. But, let's get back to the following recipe.

The gizzards cooked in Ohio were not a tender piece of meat. The first time I tasted a gizzard in France, I could not believe it. It melted in the mouth. It's a mystery how a chicken gizzard can be so different. In France, gizzards are available in the refrigerator section of the supermarket or from a can. I have no information regarding the canned product being available in the U.S. I have not been able to locate it. However, it's one dish I look forward to enjoying when I'm in France.

It was actually a mistake that I was served the gizzards in the first place. I had seen the restaurant's menu offering chicken livers (They had the English words listed under the French.) and made them my selection. However, when the main course was delivered to the table, gizzards were served, not livers.

GIZZARD SALAD
Salade Gessier

1 can cooked gizzards, drained or fresh gizzards from deli or store, fried crisply
lettuce greens
stalks of celery, chopped
1 large carrot, chopped
1 small onion, chopped, (optional)

French dressing (See index.)

1. **Prepare gizzards and set aside.**
2. **Combine lettuce greens, celery, carrot, and onion; add to gizzards.**
3. **Top with French dressing**

(Servings depend on quantity of gizzards.)

The following salad is a simple combination of flavors that makes a good introduction to a main course. Any spicy French dressing with a tomato base will be acceptable. It is similar to a house salad served at our favorite, local restaurant. One of the benefits of dining out is that you may be introduced to something entirely different from the dishes you prepare at home. It can often open your eyes to new combinations of foods and give a lift to your home cooking.

EGG AND BEET SALAD

homemade croutons for 4
olive oil
garlic salt, to taste
1 cup beets, chopped
4 hard-boiled eggs, sliced in half
lettuce greens
tomato-based commercial salad dressing

1. Cut stale bread into croutons; fry in sufficient amount of olive oil to slightly dampen the croutons. Add garlic salt while frying. Fry until croutons are crisp.
2. Rinse and drain beets and chop.
3. Hard boil the eggs; slice in half.
4. Prepare salad greens for 4.
5. Place lettuce greens on individual salad plates; add 1 sliced egg to each;
6. Place beets atop salad; add croutons, and pass the dressing.

(Serves 4.)

SOUPS

High on my list of favorite soups is the next one. Sarah has made it probably as many times as I have and she has shared it at group gatherings. I especially like putting it together when I am clearing the food products from the refrigerator prior to leaving the house or boat. It's great for using up the last of the potatoes, celery, and carrots.

When I need to serve a very simple supper, I offer this soup along with ham on warm, buttered rolls. For some reason, I have gotten into the habit of serving this combination to family and friends the first day they arrive on the boat. I figure they have eaten various meals at various times while traveling, and the best solution is a quick meal and the opportunity to crash, if necessary. Plus, the soup is extremely tasty.

POTATO SOUP

2 stalks celery, sliced
1 medium onion, chopped
2 T. butter or margarine, melted
6 medium potatoes, sliced
2 carrots, sliced

3 cups water
5 chicken bouillon cubes
¾ t. seasoned salt
½ t. dried thyme
dash of garlic powder

dash of pepper
2 cups whole milk
1 cup Cheddar cheese, shredded

1. Saute celery and onion in butter in a large Dutch oven until tender.
2. Add remaining ingredients (except milk and cheese); cover and simmer about 20 minutes or until vegetables are tender.
3. Remove from heat. Mash vegetables with a potato masher.
4. Add milk and cheese; cook, stirring constantly, until cheese is melted.

(Makes 10 cups.)

There is a café that we frequent during our winter stay in Georgia. They serve the most delicious crab chowder and people rave about it from afar. The owners of the café are our realtors and even then wouldn't give us the recipe so Hal and I worked on a duplication of this and have come up with a close match-up but not quite as good as theirs. However, it's a lot cheaper and more personal when you have made it yourself.

CRAB CHOWDER

1 T. olive oil
1 carrot, chopped very finely
½ cup onion, chopped
1 stalk of celery, chopped very finely
2 potatoes, diced and 2 cooked potatoes, mashed
¼ cup butter (2 ounces)
¼ cup flour
1 chicken bouillon cube dissolved in 2 ounces boiling water
1 quart + 1 cup half&half
4 ounces white wine, dry
1 t. salt and pepper
pinch of white pepper
1 pound fresh crab
¼ t. paprika
pinch of Old Bay Seasoning

1. Fry carrot, onion, celery, and diced potatoes lightly in oil.
2. Melt butter, then, add flour off heat. Return to mixture. Add mashed potatoes, chicken broth, half and half, white wine, salt, and seasonings, stirring until well blended.
3. Add crab. Place in a crock pot on low heat or in a Dutch oven. If using a crock pot, you can begin on High Heat for the first 45 minutes, then, turn to Low Heat for a further 5 hours or until chowder vegetables are tender.
4. Taste for seasonings, adding more paprika and salt and pepper.
5. Before serving, check the seasonings and add as needed.
6. For presentation, sprinkle individual servings with paprika.

(Serves 12.)

If you are like me and hate paying the high price for one can of commercial soup, then, you will feel good about preparing the following soup. It goes a long way and costs much less, and you are in charge of the quantities of the seasonings.

CHICKEN AND RICE SOUP

1½ cups rice, cooked
1 t. olive oil
2 garlic cloves, minced
3 (10¾-ounce each) cans chicken broth or 3 chicken bouillon cubes in
3 cups boiling water
1 cup cooked, diced chicken (I like a mixture of thigh meat and breast meat.)
2 cups frozen peas-and-carrots, thawed
salt and white pepper, to taste

1. Prepare rice.
2. Heat oil in medium pan over medium heat; add garlic and sauté 30 seconds.
3. Add broth, chicken and peas and carrots and bring to a boil.
4. Reduce heat to low and simmer 10 to 15 minutes.
5. Stir in cooked rice
6. Season to taste.

(Serves 6.)

The French have a favorite soup that is referred to as "country fare." A French family including three children came to spend the weekend with us on the boat and the plan was the children would sleep in their tent. Only problem with the plan was that the guests forgot to bring stakes for the tent so the children ended up sleeping on the floor of our boat, not a problem for the adults but maybe for the kids. They brought this soup with them and what follows is my attempt to duplicate their Pistou.

VEGETABLE AND PASTA SOUP
Soupe au Pistou

2 large carrots
2 medium-size zucchini
1 garlic clove, crushed
3 handfuls of fresh green beans
2 large cans of white beans
3 medium-size cans tomatoes
3/4 cup pasta shells
1/3 cup fresh basil, chopped
¼ cup olive oil
1 cup Gruyere cheese (3 ounces), grated

1. Cook chopped carrots; chopped zucchini; garlic clove; trimmed green beans; white beans; tomatoes, chopped; pasta; and the basil in boiling water, enough to cover.
2. Add 2 cups of chicken broth and cook until vegetables are tender.
3. Before serving, add olive oil, and cheese.
4. Cook 5 minutes.

Most French folks separate the body of the soup from the *pistou*. However, I have simplified it by placing all ingredients into one pot. It may not be quite as authentic my way but in this case, simplicity prevails. The quantity of ingredients can be halved easily.

Picture this: In the 1950's and 1960's their family restaurant was situated close to the Pennsylvania Turnpike Exit in Bedford and very near the Blue Knob Ski Resort. Skiers and other travelers came in from the cold and ended up sitting down to this mouth-watering bowl of chili. On a cold day, it makes you want to go to the kitchen immediately to make a pot for your own crowd.

Reube and Doc had so many good recipes from their 25 years of operating the restaurant. Once they retired, we often got together to enjoy good food and each other's company.

The tomatoes and kidney bean cans vary from 14.5 ounces to 15.5 ounces. I call them all medium size, and any slight variance is not important.

CHILI SOUP

1 pound ground beef
2 green peppers, chopped
1 large onion
4 celery stalks, chopped
salt and pepper, to taste
3 t. chili powder (good, rounded teaspoons)
1/8 to ¼ t. red pepper
1 t. cumin
4 ounces tomato paste and 4ounces water
3 medium-size cans of Italian-style, diced tomatoes
3 medium-size cans of kidney beans

This is a basic soup mix and you can add various ingredients according to your own tastes. I think it doesn't need much in addition.

1. Fry beef and drain. Fry peppers, onion, celery, s.&p., chili powder, red pepper, and cumin with the beef until celery is cooked.
2. Add tomato paste, 1 or 2 cans of water the size of the paste cans, the tomatoes and kidney beans.
3. Cook until heated through.

(Makes 12 cups.)

DESSERTS

Ruth came up with this delightful dessert, and it certainly gives the traditional pumpkin pie a run for its money. Be careful that you use the pumpkin pie filling, not the puree pumpkin, when making it. My first attempt was a disaster because I had failed to note the difference; when I took that first bite, it was a shock to my tastebuds.

When in Europe, we have to buy the fresh pumpkin and cook it down before we can start the recipe. We did it once or twice, just to impress our foreign guests and introduce them to this American dish but I don't plan getting that *"cordon bleu"* as long as canned pumpkin is on the shelf. Hal prefers this cobbler over the pumpkin pie he makes.

PUMPKIN COBBLER

4 ounces butter
1 cup self-rising flour
1 cup sugar
1 cup milk
1 t. vanilla extract
2 eggs
5-ounce can evaporated milk
1 large-size (30 ounces) can pumpkin pie filling (not plain pumpkin) MAKE CERTAIN OF THIS.

1. Cut butter into 4 pieces. Place in a 9 by 13-inch baking dish. Place dish in oven to melt butter.
2. Meanwhile in medium bowl, mix together flour, sugar, milk, and vanilla.
3. Remove melted butter from oven, pour flour mixture into dish. **DO NOT STIR**; set aside.
4. Break eggs into a mixing bowl. Whisk them; add evaporated milk and pumpkin pie filling. Stir to mix well.
5. Slowing pour or spoon filling mixture on top of crust batter in pan. **DO NOT STIR**. Crust batter will rise to cover pumpkin as it bakes.
6. Bake @ 350 degrees 50 minutes to 1 hour; bake until crust is dark golden brown on top. Let rest 20 minutes to 1 hour before serving. (You can keep this cobbler in refrigerator and warm individual servings in microwave for 10 to 15 seconds just before serving.
(I like a small dab of vanilla ice cream on the side.)

(Serves 12 to 16.)

Back in the days when Hal and I were both working in our careers, we had the opportunity to taste this dessert for the first time. One of the teachers at his school used to make this for the staff. And, it was often on the dessert menu of a restaurant we visited. So, again, I was motivated to try my turn at making it. Though it looks complicated, it turned out to be fairly easy and as good as any we had eaten previously.

BAKLAVA

Syrup:
- ¾ c. sugar
- 1/4 c. water
- 1½ cups honey
- 2-inch cinnamon stick
- 4 lemon slices
- 4 orange slices

Pastry & nut mixture:
- 1 package (1 pound) prepared phyllo pastry (15x12-inch)
- 1½ cups butter, melted
- 2 cups finely chopped or ground walnuts
- 1 cup finely chopped or ground blanched almonds
- ¾ cup sugar
- ½ t. ground cinnamon
- ¼ t. ground nutmeg
- 1½ cups butter, melted

Syrup:
1. In medium pan, combine sugar and ¼ cup water. Bring to boiling, stirring to dissolve sugar. Add honey, cinnamon stick and lemon and orange slices. Reduce heat; simmer, uncovered 10 minutes. Strain; cool. Should measure 2½ cups.

Pastry:
1. Remove pastry leaves from package. In small bowl, mix walnuts, almonds, ¾ cup sugar, the cinnamon and nutmeg. Place 2 pastry leaves in a 9 by 13-inch baking pan. Brush top leaf with some of the melted butter.
2. Sprinkle pastry with 1/3 of nut mixture.
3. Keep unused pastry leaves covered with damp towel to prevent drying when not in use.
4. Add 6 more leaves, brushing every other one with butter. Sprinkle pastry with 1/3 of nut mixture.
5. Continue stacking leaves, 14 in all, and buttering every other leaf. After 6 leaves, sprinkle with 1/3 of nut mixture. Trim edges, if necessary. Stack any remaining pastry leaves on top, brushing every other one with remaining, melted butter. Butter top pastry leaf. Trim edges, if necessary.
6. With a sharp knife, cut through top layer on long side, making 8 diagonal cuts at 1½-inch intervals. Then, starting at one corner make 9 cuts, on diagonal at 1½" intervals, to form diamonds. Cut through the top layer only; do not cut through the layers.
7. Bake @ 325 degrees for 1 hour or until golden and puffy. Turn off the heat. Leave in oven 1 more hour, then, remove.
8. Pour cooled syrup over hot baklava. Following the diamond pattern, cut all the way through the baklava. Cool in pan—to absorb syrup—on a wire rack.

(Makes about 35 pieces.)

BLONDE BROWNIES

2 cups sugar
1½ cups flour
2 t. baking powder
1 t. salt
2 cups dates, pitted and chopped
2 cups pecans, chopped
4 eggs, well beaten
powdered sugar for topping

1. Mix sugar, flour, baking powder, and salt in medium-size bowl.
2. Add dates and pecans.
3. Fold in eggs.
4. Pour into two (8-inch square) greased pans.
5. Bake @ 350 degrees for 15 minutes.
6. While still warm, cut into small squares and sprinkle with powdered sugar.

(Makes 18-20.)

The following didn't used to be one of my favorite desserts but it has always been high on Hal's list. He will order it in restaurants if he has not had too much to eat prior to the dessert course. And, Barbara once put it on the table saying that it was made with all commercial products. We have always appreciated the wonderful meals that Barbara has prepared for us and this dessert gave her more high marks. In my local stores, I was unable to locate the mascarpone cheese and the prepared custard. So, I have put together my best effort trying to substitute ingredients easily obtained in the States. The family gave it high marks.

TIRAMISU

6 egg yolks
1¼ cups sugar
1¼ cups cream cheese
1¾ cups whipping cream
2 packages (3-ounces each) ladyfingers
5 T. coffee liqueur
1/3 cup strong, black coffee
sweetened whipped cream
unsweetened cocoa powder for garnish
flake almonds for sprinkling on top

1. Combine egg yolks and sugar and whip until thick and lemon colored, about 1 minute. Place in top of double boiler over boiling water. Once the water has returned to boiling, reduce heat to low and cook 8 to 10 minutes, stirring constantly.
2. Remove from heat and cool to room temperature.
3. Add cream cheese, beating well.
4. Whip the cream until stiff peaks form.
5. Fold into egg yolk/cream cheese mixture; set aside.
6. Lay half of the halved fingers on a baking sheet. Mix the liqueur and coffee together and brush with half of coffee and liqueur mixture.
7. Spoon half of the egg yolk-cream mixture onto ladyfingers. Allow fingers to chill for 10 minutes.
8. Repeat the same process of ladyfingers, the coffee liqueur and coffee mixture, cream layer, and 10 minute chilling time.
9. Garnish with sweetened whipped cream, cocoa, and almonds.
10. Cover and refrigerate several hours or overnight.

(Serves 10 to 12.)

<u>Grandma's Tip:</u> The above ingredients do not run so they can be placed on any-size baking sheet. Since I have no double boiler in any of my galleys/kitchens, I utilize a 1-quart glass measurer and place it into a pan of water; works well. And, the tiramisu stays nicely a second or third day, should there be leftovers.

The following dish is definitely an English dessert. To vary, you may use other fruit and jam; strawberries, cherries, or peaches. Replace half the juice with medium sweet sherry for an even more English touch. Can be prepared a day ahead.

ENGLISH TRIFLE

Cake:
4 ounces butter, softened
4 ounces sugar
2 eggs
6 ounces flour
1½ t. baking powder
Small amount of milk

Part of Filling:
Raspberry jam
1 medium-size can apricots
1 medium-size can raspberries (or blackberries)

Custard:
4 ounces sugar
2 ounces flour
1 ounce cornstarch
2 eggs
20 ounces whole milk
½ t. mace
2 ounces butter
½ pint whipping cream

Cake:
1. Cream the butter and sugar. Add eggs and fold in the flour and baking powder.
2. Mix to soft, dropping consistency, adding a small amount of milk.
3. Spoon onto greased baking pan.
4. Bake at 350 degrees for 30 minutes.

Part of Filling:
1. Cut cake in half. Spread with jam and sandwich together.
2. Cut into 1" cubes and place in bottom of trifle dish.
3. Drain apricots and raspberries, reserving juice. Arrange fruit on top of cake.
4. Pour juice over fruit.

Custard:
1. Make a custard by blending sugar, flour, corn starch, and eggs in a bowl until mixture is smooth.
2. Heat milk gently. Stir milk gradually into the custard mixture. Add the mace.
3. Place custard in pan and cook over low heat, stirring constantly until it thickens and just begins to boil.
4. Remove pan from heat and beat custard until smooth.
5. Cut the butter into pieces and add to custard.
6. Stir until completely melted and blended; add to trifle dish.
7. Top with whipped cream and chill.

(Serves 8 to 10.)

One of my mother's desserts and one that the family really enjoyed is the following date pudding. We did not have it often, maybe once or twice a year usually during the holidays, but I still think about it, remembering all the good times we shared. And, I do not save it for the holidays. It's unique and is something that generally people find unfamiliar but truly enjoyable.

DATE PUDDING

1 cup dates, chopped
1 cup nuts, chopped
1½ T. flour
¼ c. sugar
3 t. baking powder
2 eggs, separate yolks from whites.
vanilla ice cream or whipped cream

1. Mix dates, nuts, flour, sugar, baking powder, and 2 egg yolks.
2. Beat egg whites and fold into other mixture.
3. Bake in greased pan @ 350 degrees, about 20 minutes.
4. Serve warm with vanilla ice cream or sweetened whipped cream.

Serves 8 to 10.)

One day I got brave and started this recipe by putting sugar alone in a pan and turning on the heat, worrying that this was going to be a disaster. I imagined another pan going into the bin. To my surprise, it melted without sticking into a lovely, golden syrup. And, that was the beginning of a successful attempt at a delightful dessert. This dessert should be prepared 2½ hours before serving.

CREME CARAMEL

½ cup sugar, divided
4 eggs
2 cups whole milk
1 t. vanilla extract
¼ t. salt
6 lemon-peel twists, optional garnish
6 small nontoxic leaves, optional garnish

1. Preheat oven to 325 degrees.
2. Heat ¼ cup sugar over medium heat until melted and light caramel color, stirring constantly.
3. Immediately pour into prepared custard cups.
4. In a large bowl with wire whisk or fork, beat eggs and ¼ cup sugar until well blended.
5. Beat in milk, vanilla, and salt until well mixed; pour mixture into custard cups.
6. Place custard cups in 13x9" baking pan; fill pan with hot water to come halfway up sides of custard cups.
7. Bake 50 to 55 minutes until knife inserted in center of custard comes out clean.
8. Remove cups from water in baking pan; cover and refrigerate until chilled, about 1½ hours.
9. To serve, unmold each custard onto a chilled dessert plate, allowing caramel topping to drip from cup onto custard. Garnish.

(Serves 6.)

Often when Hal and I are dining in a French restaurant, he will select the following dessert as it is another one of his favorites. In the past, I made it so seldom as it did take considerable time. However, just recently I discovered a way to make it in the microwave. I was "chuffed" as the English say, with the results. I like it when the job can be made more simply and in less time. And, you can make the custard ahead of time.

FLOATING ISLAND IN THE MICROWAVE
Ile Flottante

2 egg yolks, room temperature
¼ cup sugar
1½ t. cornstarch
1½ cups whole milk
½ t. vanilla extract
2 egg whites, room temperature
4 T. sugar
½ t. vanilla extract

1. Place egg yolks, ¼ cup sugar, and cornstarch in medium-sized pan. Mix well.
2. Gradually stir in milk, heat uncovered 4 to 5 minutes or until just about boiling. Do not boil.
3. Stir mixture occasionally during last half of cooking, add the ½ t. vanilla, and chill until ready to serve.
4. Just before serving time, beat egg whites until stiff but not dry, beating in 4 T. sugar, 1 T. at a time, until soft peaks can be formed.
5. Beat in ½ t. vanilla.
6. 6. Divide custard into 4 dessert dishes. Place in microwave and heat uncovered 45 seconds to 1 minute.
7. Add spoonfuls of beaten egg whites atop custard.
8. Brown under grill for a few seconds, just to make it look more appetizing.

(Serves 4 to 6.)

<u>Grandma's Tip:</u> A helpful hint and one that I am using myself when following an old recipe is to question whether or not a step in the preparation process can be shortened by utilizing the microwave.

PIES

From early childhood in the U.S., peanut butter becomes the youngster's staple food. Add chocolate to it, and you are over the moon. As they say in the television ads, chocolate and peanut butter are a great combination. It's hard to imagine that people who grew up in other countries don't share that same love for it. But, then, we don't appreciate the English folks' fondness for marmite. It's a fact that I could add pounds in no time, just trying to satisfy my desire to consume chocolate and peanut butter in cookies, pies, and ice cream. That stems from childhood and will stick with me until food is no longer appreciated. I recall my mother had Reese's peanut butter cup candies that she kept in a cupboard; no one ever bothered her special stash. I try to avoid purchasing peanut butter in France as a medium-size jar can cost $6.

Back in the 80's I had found a pie in a Florida restaurant that bragged that their pies were homemade. They had a display of them and naturally, I chose to try the peanut butter one. When it was served and I inquired of it, they said that it was the only one not made by them. It actually came from Hershey, Pennsylvania. I suppose more than one restaurant relies on that source. More recently when dining in a restaurant near our Pennsylvania home, the Jean Bonnet Tavern in Bedford, I came across the best peanut butter pie that I had ever consumed. Over the years I have tried many varieties and the following is tops in my book. Get it? My book?

Being a subscriber to <u>Bon Appetit</u>, I wrote to them to see if they would write the restaurant to obtain the recipe. The magazine features several restaurant recipes each month. This, they did, though I don't think the recipe was ever published. The magazine editor did write a letter to me and included a copy of this pie. We have dined at this restaurant near to us many times, and I told the pastry chef that I was the one who had inquired through the magazine.

It's easy, it's delicious, and it's a keeper. It's worth several gold stars. Thanks, <u>Bon Appetit</u> and Jean Bonnet Tavern. We continue to go there often and sometimes, we even order the pie.

CHOCOLATE & PEANUT BUTTER PIE

Crust:
1 1/3 cups graham crumbs
1/3 cup sugar
8 T. butter, melted

Filling:
12 ounces cream cheese, softened
1½ cups peanut butter, smooth
1½ cups sugar
1 cup whipping cream (whipped)

Topping:
2/3 cup whipping cream
2 T. butter
1/3 cup light brown sugar
2 ounces semi-sweet chocolate, finely chopped or chocolate bits
1/8 t. salt

Crust:
1. Mix pie crust ingredients and place in 9-inch shell.
2. Bake @ 350 degrees for 8 minutes.

Filling:
1. Beat whipping cream.
2. **Using same beaters, mix cream cheese, peanut butter, and sugar. Fold in whipped cream.**
3. **Spoon onto crust and refrigerate at least 4 hours.**

Topping:
1. **Bring whipping cream to boil with butter.**
2. **Add brown sugar and simmer, stirring frequently for about 2½ minutes or more to reach some thickness.**
3. **Add chocolate and salt and over low heat, whisk until smooth.**
4. **Allow topping to cool to room temperature.**
5. **Drizzle sauce over top.**

(The crust and filling make enough for a 10-inch pie.)

Grandma's Tip: When placing crust into pie plate, use the bottom of a measuring cup or a similar item and press the crust down. The top rim may appear uneven but just a light touch will improve the looks. A bit of unevenness just makes it look more homemade, right? It is your choice as to whether or not you wish to warm the topping before putting onto the individual servings. You can add the topping over the entire pie at the time of making. You can add it to an individual serving without warming it or you can warm it slightly.

PIE CRUST

I have used the following crust recipe for years; however, living on a boat or a camper limits my desire to start from scratch. I find it too easy to procure the prepared crusts, both for pies and tarts and for pizzas. Recently when listening to the justly famous chef Paula Dean of Savannah, Georgia, she was using prepared pie crust. If she does it, I don't feel so guilty.

8-inch pie:
1½ cups flour
½ t. salt
½ c. shortening
5 T. cold water

9-inch pie:
2 cups flour
1 t. salt
2/3 cup shortening

7 T. cold water

1. **Cut flour, salt, and shortening with a pastry cutter or 2 knives close together until it is well mixed.**
2. **Blend the mixture thoroughly.**
3. **Add icy, cold water. Shape into a ball and refrigerate for 30 minutes or longer.**

The dough will roll out easier if left 10 minutes or so at room temperature.

Back in Ohio, it is common for communities and churches and schools to organize a cookbook to make money for different charities and causes. My sister, Kate, submitted a pie very similar to this one. Strawberries really become a favorite item in Ohio as the month of July arrives. As a youngster I picked strawberries at a nearby fruit farm. I and my friends had a good time while earning a bit of change.

STRAWBERRY PIE

1 9-inch baked pie shell
4 cups fresh strawberries, divided
2/3 cup water
4 T. cornstarch
2 T. cold water
¼ cup of hot liquid from pan of strawberries
1 c. sugar
1 T. butter or margarine
½ pint whipping cream (optional)
sugar to sweeten cream

1. Wash, hull, and slice strawberries into large, bite-size pieces
2. Combine 1 cup strawberries with 2/3 cup water minus 2 T. in a pan; bring to boil, then, simmer 4 to 5 minutes.
3. Mix thoroughly the cornstarch with 2 T. cold water. Remove ¼ cup of the hot liquid from the pan of strawberry/water mixture and add to cornstarch/water mixture. You can accomplish this task while the strawberries are simmering.
4. Add the sugar to the cornstarch/water mixture, then, after the 5-minute simmering time, put this mixture in the pan with the strawberries and remaining liquid.
5. Continue cooking and stirring until the syrup thickens, approximately 1 minute to 2 minutes.
6. Remove from heat; add butter or margarine. Mix well.
7. Place the remaining fresh berries into the baked pie shell and top with the syrup.
8. Chill in refrigerator at least 4 hours.
9. Top with sweetened, whipped cream when serving (optional).

To avoid lumps, it is necessary to add the cold water to the cornstarch before mixing it with the hot mixture.

As early as in the 1970's, I was served a pecan pie at my sister Kate's house. Back then, I wasn't as concerned about calories. Still I will enjoy a good dessert, then try to watch the calorie count the following day. Well, pecan pie is one of those special treats that appears on many restaurant menus all over the U.S. and especially in Georgia, and its calorie count is at the top of the pie chart. I have adapted the following to include chocolate.

CHOCOLATE & PECAN PIE

1 10-inch unbaked pie shell
3 T. butter
3 squares (3 ounces total) unsweetened chocolate
2 cups sugar
1 T. flour
1/8 t. salt
4 eggs
½ t. vanilla extract
1 cup pecan halves

1. Place butter and chocolate in microwave on 50% power until both are melted.
2. Mix sugar, flour, and salt thoroughly.
3. In a mixing bowl, beat eggs slightly. Stir in both butter and sugar mixtures until well blended.
4. Mix in vanilla extract and pecans.
5. Pour into pie shell.
6. Bake @ 375 degrees for 30 to 35 minutes or until set but center ripples when being gently shaken.
7. Cool completely on wire rack. Do not refrigerate; serve at room temperature.

The following recipe is for the more traditional pecan pie. Lenore gave me her recipe and from it and some practice, I have come up with a more simplified recipe. It requires no prior cooking, just place all well-mixed ingredients into a pie shell and stand back.

PECAN PIE

1 cup brown sugar
1 cup light corn syrup
4 eggs, beaten
1 cup pecans, chopped
1 8-inch or 9-inch pie shell
2 t. light rum, optional

1. Mix the sugar, corn syrup, eggs, and pecans plus the optional rum until very well blended. Place in pie shell.
2. Bake @ 425 degrees for 5 minutes; lower heat to 300 degrees and bake for about 1 hour. Be sure your oven is preheated before beginning the baking process.

I place individual servings in the microwave for a few seconds, then, top with vanilla ice cream.

This is a pie that I serve most often because it is so easy and oh, so good.

DUTCH APPLE PIE

1 prepared 9-inch pie crust, unbaked
5 ½ cups cooking apples; it requires 5 or 6 apples. (Granny Smith is my choice.)
1 T. lemon juice
½ c. sugar
¼ cup light brown sugar

3 T. flour
¼ t. salt
½ t. cinnamon
¼ t. nutmeg
Topping:
¾ c. flour
¼ c. sugar
¼ c. light brown sugar
1/3 cup butter, room temperature

1. Peel and slice apples; add lemon juice, ½ cup sugar, ¼ cup light brown sugar, 3 T. flour, ¼ t. salt, ½ t. cinnamon, and ¼ t. nutmeg. Set aside.
2. Prepare topping. Mix ¾ cup flour, ¼ c. sugar, ¼ cup light brown sugar; cut in butter until mixture resembles coarse breadcrumbs.
3. Place apple mixture in pie crust; add topping.
4. Bake @ 375 degrees for 50 to 60 minutes.

Check after 50 minutes. You may need to turn pie in oven and/or cover. I usually bake for 10 additional minutes to be certain that the apples are suitably tender.

You may choose to decrease the amount of sugar and butter in this recipe. As with most recipes, you will want to add and/or subtract quantities to your liking. Over the years, I have added less sugar and butter and the pie remains tasty.

Move on down one more state from Georgia y'all and you're in Florida and that calls for another kind of pie. Georgia promotes their pecans and Florida, their key limes. We had never experienced this kind of pie up north and found it to be a refreshing and cooling dessert. My aunt was the one who introduced me to this particular pie. As long as you can buy lime juice, you should be in business. A friend recently brought us a bottle of lime juice in a fancy bottle as a present. Now we "have to" make the pie and endure the results.

KEY LIME PIE

1 prepared 9-inch graham-cracker pie crust
4 egg yolks
2 cans condensed milk, 14-ounces each
1 cup lime juice
whipped cream, sweetened

1. Beat egg yolks until frothy; add milk and then, the lime juice. Beat well.
2. Bake @ 350 degrees for 15 minutes.
3. Add sweetened, whipped cream. (optional)

CAKES

If you ask my siblings, they will probably tell you that our mother's best cake was chocolate angel food with brown sugar icing; I agree. I once tried to ice the cake with her icing mixture but it was a total disaster. How she ever got it to a spreading consistency, then managed to cover the cake is beyond any of us. The cake is simple enough, but she was able to beat by hand the icing until a certain point before it turned to fudge. And, it was next to impossible to layer it onto the cake. So, I attempted to make a nice chocolate cake and cover it with the following icing to reach some similarity to our mother's masterpiece. Her chocolate angel food is, also, presented below.

DEVILS FOOD CHOCOLATE CAKE WITH PENUCHE ICING

3 ounces of unsweetened chocolate
6 ounces butter, room temperature
1½ cups sugar
1½ t. vanilla extract
3 eggs
2½ cups cake flour
1½ t. salt
1 1/8 t. baking soda
1 cup + 2 T. ice water

Icing: Makes 3 cups.
6 ounces butter
1½ cups firmly-packed light brown sugar
1/3 cup whole milk
3 cups powdered sugar

1. Butter 3 (8-inch round) pans. Line with wax paper and butter.
2. Melt chocolate in microwave (approximately 20 seconds).
3. In bowl, cream with electric mixer the butter, sugar and vanilla.
4. Beat in 3 eggs, 1 at a time and add chocolate mixture and beat more.
5. In a large bowl, mix cake flour, salt and baking soda.
6. Beat into the chocolate mixture with the ice water, alternating until both flour mixture and water are incorporated.
7. Bake @ 350 degrees for 25 minutes.

Icing:
1. Melt 6 ounces butter; stir in brown sugar and bring to a boil. Cook over low heat, stirring 2 minutes.
2. Add milk and cook over medium-heat until it comes to a boil.
3. Transfer to mixer bowl and let it cool.
4. Beat in 3 cups powdered sugar, a little at a time. Beat until smooth. Add more milk, if necessary.

My mother was known in the village for her angel food cake. At carnivals and school events organized to make money for charities, her cake would often reach the highest bid. Interestingly enough, the grandchildren should know that the other cake at the carnival as appreciated as my mother's was that of my future mother-in-law's. She made a hickory-nut cake that won a blue ribbon at the county fair.

ANGEL FOOD CAKE, PLAIN OR CHOCOLATE

1 1/3 cups of whites of eggs
1 1/3 t. cream of tartar
1 t. salt
1 cup cake flour
1½ cups sugar
1 t. vanilla extract
2 T. cocoa powder
To make the plain angel food a chocolate one, remove 2 T. flour and add 2 T. cocoa powder.

1. Beat the egg whites until stiff, but not dry.
2. About half way through the beating, add cream of tartar and salt, then finish beating.
3. Fold the cake flour and sugar slowly, a bit at a time, using a strainer to make it nicely sifted.
4. Add the vanilla extract at the end. Place the mixture in an angel food cake pan.
5. Bake @ 325 degrees for 1 hour.

STRAWBERRY SHORTCAKE

2 cups flour
2 T. sugar
3 t. baking powder
1 t. salt
½ cup shortening
1 egg
1/3 cup whole milk
1 quart fresh strawberries
¾ cup sugar
vanilla ice cream or sweetened whipped cream, optional

1. Mix flour, sugar, baking powder, and salt.
2. With pastry blender or 2 knives, cut shortening into dry ingredients until mixture resembles coarse crumbs.
3. Beat egg with milk. Add to flour mixture, stirring only until all ingredients are moist.
4. On lightly-floured board, divide mixture in half and pat the mixture to fit onto 2 (8-inch) greased and floured cake pans.
5. Bake @ 450 degrees for approximately 15 minutes. Watch near the end of baking time and remove before it becomes brown and crisp along the edges.
6. Cool. Prepare strawberries and mix with sugar.
7. Once cool, put layers together with strawberries between layers.

(Serves 12.)

Can easily be halved.

It is often my goal to have as many foods prepared ahead of time when getting ready for family or friends arriving for a weekend. This cake is not only pretty to place on your breakfast table but delicious. It can be baked ahead of serving day, then glazed once defrosted.

SOUR CREAM & WALNUT COFFEE CAKE

Cake:
¾ cup butter, softened
1½ cups sugar
3 eggs
2 t. vanilla extract
3 cups flour
1½ t. baking powder
1½ t. baking soda
½ t. salt
2 cups sour cream
¾ cup light brown sugar
2 t. ground cinnamon
1 cup walnuts, coarsely chopped

Glaze:
1½ cups powdered sugar
2 T. whole milk
½ t. vanilla extract

Cake:
1. Cream butter and sugar until fluffy; add eggs, 1 at a time, beating well after each addition.
2. Stir in vanilla.
3. Combine flour, baking powder, baking soda, and salt.
4. Add to creamed mixture, alternately with sour cream. Mix well.
5. Combine brown sugar, cinnamon, and walnuts, mixing well.
6. Spoon 1/3 of batter into greased and floured 10-inch tube pan.
7. Sprinkle with 1/3 of nut mixture.
8. Repeat layering.
9. Bake @ 350 degrees for 1 hour or until done.
10. Let stand 5 minutes before removing from pan.
11. Place on serving dish and drizzle with glaze.

Glaze:
1. Mix all ingredients well, adding more milk if needed.

(Serves approximately 12.)

I think most cooks would agree that it is from friends and family gatherings that we get some of our best recipes. Our neighbors used to give us an apple cake at holiday time. The following cake, though extremely high in calories, is a delicious cake that is so delectable, especially when served warm with vanilla ice cream. If you are concerned that it is so rich and full of calories, then take a smaller portion, but you must try it.

APPLE CAKE

Cake:
- 3 cups cake flour
- ½ t. salt
- 1 t. baking soda
- 1½ cups corn oil
- 2 cups sugar
- 3 eggs
- 1 t. vanilla extract
- 3 cups apples, peeled and sliced
- 1½ cups pecans, chopped

Topping:
- 1 cup light brown sugar, well packed
- 1 t. vanilla extract
- 4 ounces butter or margarine
- ¼ cup whole milk

Cake:
1. Mix flour, salt, and soda.
2. Beat oil, sugar, eggs, vanilla.
3. Blend the two mixtures.
4. Add the apples and pecans.
5. Bake 1 hour @ 325 degrees (300 degrees if using glass) in a greased, 9 by 13-inch baking dish.

Topping:
1. Cook the topping ingredients for 2½ minutes. Once it has reached boiling, reduce heat to medium heat.
2. Pour over warm cake.

(Serves 12 to 16.)

This is a quote from TJ who was 15 at the time: "Grandma, you could make these and sell them." We took three of these cheesecakes to his sister Christina's high school graduation. Up to now, I have been unable to avoid having cracks in the top. I have tried all the many hints given to avoid the cracking but have not cracked it yet. I solve my problem by covering it with a light topping of sweetened whipped cream and a few strawberries, but then it isn't plain, is it?

PLAIN CHEESECAKE

Crust:
- 1¼ cups graham cracker crumbs
- 1/3 c. butter, melted
- ¼ c. sugar, optional

Filling:
- 4 (8-ounce) packages cream cheese, room temperature
- 1¼ cups sugar
- 2 t. flour
- 4 eggs
- 2 t. whole milk
- 1 t. grated orange rind, optional
- 1 t. grated lemon rind, optional

- dash salt
- whipping cream, ½ pint
- chocolate shavings, optional
- OR fresh raspberries or strawberries, optional

Crust:
1. Combine crumbs and butter (& sugar, if using). Press into bottom and up the side (about an inch) of a buttered, 8-inch springform pan; set aside.

Filling:
1. Beat cream cheese at medium speed of electric mixer until light and fluffy. Gradually add 1¼ cups of sugar and flour. Mix well.
2. Add eggs one at a time, beating well after each one.
3. Add milk, rinds, and salt. Mix well.
4. Spoon into pan. Bake @ 375 degrees for 15 minutes. Reduce temperature to 300 degrees; bake 1 hour.
5. Turn off oven, allowing cake to cool in oven 30 minutes.
6. Cool to room temperature and refrigerate for 8 hours.
7. Remove cake from pan and serve or freeze it. Run a knife around the cake's side and carefully remove.
8. Top with sweetened, whipped cream and fresh fruit, if using.

(Serves 12 to 16.)

A new dessert has come into the family favorites because the oldest granddaughter, Christina, brought it to Grandpa's birthday celebration. It's really, really nice and we have to be careful to be fair when sharing what's left after the first round. We laughed when she said that her roommate who watched her preparing it had to watch her take it away. We saw to it that there was a serving remaining that could be taken back to the roommate. But, it's a fact, any leftovers are to be treasured and portioned out fairly.

Here again, Christina is into a promising career and young enough to be very much a part of the social scene, so for her to take an evening out and bake a special cake for her grandfather was indeed very sweet, sweet meaning both Christina and the cake. It was her first offering from her kitchen to our family gatherings. Good going, Christina. We won't go into how difficult it was for her to smash the ginger snaps without the aid of a food processor.

PUMPKIN CHEESECAKE

Crust:
8-ounces gingersnap cookies (about 32 cookies), made into crumbs.
½ cup finely chopped pecans, optional
4 T. unsalted butter, melted
2 T. sugar
1 t. ground cinnamon

Filling:
3 T. flour
1½ t. ground ginger
1 t. ground cinnamon
¼ t. freshly grated nutmeg
4 (8-ounce packages) cream cheese, room temperature
1½ cups sugar
1 (15-ounce) can unsweetened pumpkin puree
3 T. bourbon
2 t. vanilla extract
4 large eggs
whipped cream, for serving

Crust:
1. **Place gingersnaps in food**

processor and whirl until finely ground. Add pecans, melted butter, sugar, and cinnamon. Process just until combined and the mixture holds together. Transfer the cookie mixture to a 9-inch nonstick springform pan and pat out evenly to make the crust, lining the sides of the pan about 1½ inch high.
2. Bake @ 325 degrees for 10 minutes. Cool completely on a wire rack.

Filling:
1. In a small bowl, whisk together flour, ginger, cinnamon, and nutmeg; set aside. In a separate bowl, beat cream cheese and sugar on medium speed until light and fluffy, about 2 minutes. Add pumpkin, bourbon, vanilla, and flour mixture. Beat to combine. Add eggs, one at a time, beating to incorporate after each addition.
2. Pour batter into prepared crust. Wrap the outside of the springform pan with a double layer of aluminum foil. Place in a roasting pan. Add enough hot water to come halfway up the sides of the springform pan. Bake @ 325 degrees until cake is set in the center, about 1 hour and 45 minutes.
3. Remove from water and cool on a wire rack. Remove foil and refrigerate for at least 4 hours or overnight. To unmold, release the sides of the pan and slide onto a serving plate. Serve with sweetened, whipped cream.

(Serves 10 to 12.)

On the boat without a food processor, I used a hammer and a plastic bag.

BREADS

MOTHER LENORE'S TURKEY STUFFING

3 packages (1 pound each) stuffing
salt and pepper to taste
¼ cup fresh parsley, cut fine
1 egg, beaten
½ cup margarine or butter, melted
½ cup celery, chopped

I was given the ingredients only but suggest the following:
1. Saute the celery in margarine or butter.
2. Add stuffing, salt and pepper, parsley and egg.

Lenore used this as stuffing for the turkey and served any surplus in a separate dish. If using a baking dish, be sure to grease it well.

I prefer to serve a dressing as a side dish with the turkey rather than as stuffing. The following are three of my favorites.

YANKEE OYSTER DRESSING

12 slices Italian bread
olive oil or oil spray
1½ cups onions, chopped
1½ cups celery, chopped
3 T. fresh parsley, chopped
½ t. salt
½ t. sage
¼ t. thyme
¼ t. pepper
1/8 t. white pepper
1/8 t. ground bay leaves
12 ounces standard oysters
2 (10¾-ounce each) cans chicken broth (unsalted)

1. Cut bread into cubes and bake @ 350 degrees for 10 minutes, turning once.
2. Saute onions and celery in oil to tender stage.
3. Add next 7 ingredients and sauté 1 minute.
4. Combine bread cubes, the oysters, and the onion/celery/seasoning mixture.
5. Lastly add the broth but not all at once. Perhaps add 1½ cans and check to see if you are content with the amount of moistness.
6. Bake uncovered @ 400 degrees for 1 hour.

I have combined my mother's more crusty-type dressing with others that are more moist to get the consistency that I like best. You can vary the broth ingredient to suit yourself.

THANKSGIVING DRESSING

4 ounces butter
1 medium onion, chopped
1 cup celery, chopped
14-ounce package stuffing mix or toasted, white bread, broken into pieces, approximately 14 slices
1 egg
1 cup chicken broth
1 t. sage
1 t. poultry seasoning
salt and pepper, to taste
1/3 cup fresh parsley, tightly packed

1. Melt butter and fry onion and celery until tender but not browned.
2. Combine all other ingredients and place in a greased baking dish.
3. Bake @ 350 degrees for 45 minutes.

In place of the stuffing mix, I toast white bread, cut it into pieces larger than those found in stuffing mix packages.

This is a dressing that is very popular in the southern region of the U.S.

CORN BREAD DRESSING

4 cups corn bread, in pieces
2 cups toasted bread, in pieces
10 saltine crackers
3 stalks celery, chopped
1 small onion, chopped
2 cups chicken broth
2 ounces butter
salt and pepper, to taste
1 t. dried sage

1. Mix in a large bowl the corn bread and toasted bread.
2. Mix in crackers, mashed.
3. Add celery and onion to chicken broth and butter.
4. Boil for 15 minutes; cool.
5. Mix the liquid with the breads; add the salt, pepper, and sage.
6. Bake @ 350 degrees for 1½ hours.

The following is one of two breads that I make frequently when I am in my house and have the use of the Bread Machine. My Bread Machine is a small version that makes a cylindrical loaf, five-inches in diameter and six-inches high. The muffin bread can be sliced and toasted and is lovely with a butter and jam spread. The other, the Cuban bread, comes very close to French bread that we enjoy when we're not in France.

ENGLISH MUFFIN BREAD

1 package dry yeast
1½ cups white flour
1 cup whole wheat flour
¾ t. salt
1½ t. sugar
1 t. oil

1 cup warm water

1. Adapt the quantities to the size of your machine and follow the directions that your machine recommends.

CUBAN BREAD

1 cup + ½ of a 1/3 cup water
1¼ t. sugar
2 t. salt
2½ cups bread flour
2 t. dry yeast

1. Place yeast in bottom of bread machine and follow the directions that your machine recommends.

GARLIC BREAD

1 large garlic clove, peeled
1/8 t. salt
2 T. unsalted butter
1 heaping t. parsley, minced
4 thick slices of French or Italian bread

1. Mash garlic with salt to form a paste.
2. In small skillet, melt butter and add garlic paste. Saute until butter has a garlic aroma.
3. Toss in parsley.
4. Spread bread with mixture; wrap in heavy-duty foil.
5. Bake @ 350 degrees for 5 minutes.
6. Open foil and bake 5 minutes longer.

CINNAMON ROLLS

2½ cups lukewarm-to-hot water
2 packages quick-rise yeast
1 box yellow cake mix (18.25-ounces)
1 cup flour
2 eggs
½ cup oil
1 t. salt
5½ cups flour
soft margarine, sugar, and cinnamon
raisins, optional

Icing:
½ cup powdered sugar
½ t. vanilla extract
enough milk to make the right consistency

1. Dissolve yeast in water for 3 minutes.
2. Add cake mix, 1 cup flour, eggs, oil, and salt. Beat until bubbly.
3. Add balance of flour to make soft dough.
4. Knead lightly, cover, and let rise until double in a warm place.
5. Roll out about ¼-inch thick; it's easier if the dough is divided in half.
6. Spread with margarine and sprinkle with sugar and cinnamon. Raisins may be added, also.
7. Roll as for jelly roll and cut. Let rise until double.
8. Bake @ 350 degrees for 20 to 25 minutes.

Icing:
1. Mix approximately ½ cup of powdered sugar with vanilla extract and a small amount of milk to give it the right consistency for coating the rolls. Adapt the amount of icing to your liking. I like to warm the rolls in the microwave just a few seconds, then add the icing at serving time. The use of the cake mix in this recipe makes the rolls very light in texture. They are light and mouth-watering wonderful served warm.

(Makes about 24 nice-sized rolls.)

ECLECTIC CATEGORY

HAL'S HEALTHY HEART COOKIES

1½ cups flour
½ t. salt
½ t. baking powder
¾ t. baking soda
1 t. cinnamon
¼ c. sugar
¼ c. brown sugar
1/3 cup oil
½ cup molasses

2 eggs
1½ cup quick oats
1 cup pecans

1. Mix all ingredients well.
2. Bake on greased/floured cookie sheet @ 350 degrees for 12 to 15 minute.

Additional Favorite Recipes Main Courses and Casseroles

A sugar substitute can replace the two sugars. Using regular sugar, my rough estimate on calorie consumption came to 86 calories/cookie.

(Makes 18 to 20.)

This was a dish that my mother made frequently and it was always appreciated. She did not use raisins in her recipe and, therefore, I grew up not caring for them in my pudding. People often associate raisins with rice pudding, and you may wish to include them. Recipes often call for raw rice making the baking time over 2 hours. This is a shortcut but still very good.

RICE PUDDING

1½ cups cooked rice
2 eggs
1 cup sugar
¼ t. salt
1 t. vanilla
1 medium-size can evaporated milk
2 cups half and half
½ t. nutmeg

1. Mix beaten eggs with rice. Add remaining ingredients. Place in loaf pan.
2. Place mixture into another pan of lukewarm water.
3. Bake @ 375 degrees for 1 hour, stirring every 5 minutes for the first half hour, then, sprinkle with nutmeg and do not stir any more.

(Serves 4 to 6.)

This next one beats any other homemade caramel corn I have tasted and it's so very easy. You do need a large microwave. The ones on our boat and recreational vehicle are not large enough. You also need to have a paper grocery bag.

CARAMEL POPCORN IN THE MICROWAVE

3 quarts of popped corn, not microwave popcorn but plain popcorn
1½ cups peanuts
1 cup packed light brown sugar
½ cup margarine
¼ cup light corn syrup
½ t. salt
½ t, baking soda

1. In paper bag, place the popped corn and peanuts.
2. In a microwave bowl, place the brown sugar, the margarine, corn syrup, and salt. Microwave 3 to 4 minutes, stirring after each minute until the mixture boils.
3. Microwave 2 minutes longer.

4. Stir in baking soda
5. Pour into paper bag and shake.
6. Microwave for 1½ minutes, then shake.
7. Microwave for 1½ minutes, remove from bag, and cool.

I have researched shortbread using recipes from both the U.S. and the British Isles. Muriel gave me her recipe for Cherry Almond Shortbread, and my attempt did not measure up to hers. When she served the shortbread in her home, it was very, very nice. So, I figure that translating the metric weight measurements got me into trouble. By combining recipes from numerous sources, this is now my favorite shortbread. I like adding the cherries and almonds as it makes it different from the norm and is especially nice for the holidays, though good any time.

This shortbread and the almond cocoons placed in cookie tins were shipped to family for the holidays. They traveled well and seemed to be winners.

CHERRY ALMOND SHORTBREAD

2½ cups flour
1 cup butter, softened
1 cup sugar
1 generous ounce ground almonds
2 ounces glace cherries, cut into small pieces

1. Beat butter at high speed on electric mixer until it is light and fluffy.
2. **Mix with sugar, continuing to beat.**
3. **Remove 1 generous ounce of flour and replace with 1 generous ounce of ground almonds. If you have no ground almonds, you can

Additional Favorite Recipes Main Courses and Casseroles | 187

grind the slivered almonds in a food processor.
4. At medium speed, add flour/ground almond mixture, a bit at a time.
5. Add cherries, by hand.
6. Form into a large ball
7. Roll on a floured surface to ½-inch thickness, making it approximately 8-inches by 10-inches.
8. Lightly butter or use flour-butter spray on a baking pan.
9. Cut into vertical strips every 2 inches and, also, horizontally. Punch the top with a fork to make marks all over. Place shortbread on pan. (I place 2 pieces at a time on the pan, making sure they are separated before baking.)
10. Bake @ 325 degrees for approximately 20 minutes, checking before that time. The shortbread should be just starting to brown a bit on the edges. The most important part of this baking process is to remove the shortbread before it gets too done.

(Makes approximately 30 pieces.)

<u>*Grandma's Tip*</u>: The first time I made these I over-baked them. However, by zapping them a few seconds in the microwave just before serving made even the overdone ones acceptable. It's a pleasant thing to take a rest with a cup of tea or coffee and a warmed piece of shortbread. Before eating, zap the shortbread for 8 seconds in the microwave—enjoy.

When a little girl, I used to be given pieces of peanut butter fudge that tasted better than any candy I had ever eaten. Then, too, I was already hooked on peanut butter. A woman who lived next door to the food store where I spent time made this fudge and my mother would buy it from her. You're wondering why I spent idle time in the store. Well, in the 1950's the store was a gathering place of my school friends. I lived just outside the village but close enough to ride a bicycle there. The post office was a part of the store and opposite that was an area where the owners had a few chairs and a coal stove. My best girlfriend lived across the street, another reason for being at the store. The manager didn't seem to mind our congregating; it was the town's teenage hangout. Though I never obtained the woman's peanut butter fudge recipe, I developed the following recipe for two pounds and it brings back such good memories.

PEANUT BUTTER FUDGE

2 cups sugar
¼ cup light corn syrup
½ cup milk
¼ t. salt

2 T. butter or margarine
1 t. vanilla extract
1 cup crunchy or smooth peanut butter
½ cup finely chopped peanuts (optional)

1. Combine the sugar, corn syrup, milk, and salt in a medium-sized pan.
2. Cook over low-to-medium-heat, stirring constantly, until sugar dissolves.
3. Cover the pan for 1 minute to allow the steam to wash down the sugar crystals that cling to side of pan, or wipe down the crystals with a damp cloth.
4. Uncover the pan; insert candy thermometer. Cook at the low-medium setting without stirring until candy thermometer reaches 236 degrees (soft ball stage.)
5. Remove from the heat; add butter. Cool the syrup until lukewarm, 110 degrees
6. Add vanilla, peanut butter.
7. Beat until candy begins to thicken and loses its high gloss.
8. Turn immediately into a buttered, 8x8x2-inch pan. Score with a sharp knife into small squares; cool.
9. When completely cool, cut squares all the way through. Store 2 to 3 weeks in a tightly-covered container with foil or plastic wrap between layers.

This candy was prepared in friend Mary's kitchen in Florida while we sat at the kitchen bar and visited. We left the following morning and I did not give it another thought. On our return from visiting her and Tom, we stopped in Maryland to visit Diana and family. When we arrived and the already-mentioned birthday party occurred, one of my presents that day was a box of Tiger Butter.

TIGER BUTTER

1 pound chocolate bark
1 pound white chocolate
¾ cup peanut butter

1. Melt each chocolate separately. This can be accomplished easily in the microwave, approximately 90 seconds at a time until you reach the desired consistency. Be sure to mix with a spoon after the 90 seconds. Add peanut butter to melted white chocolate. Stir in well.
2. Spray a 9x13" dish with an oil or butter spray.
3. Add melted chocolate bark to pan.
4. Place white chocolate/peanut butter mixture on top.
5. Swirl it with a knife.
6. Cut into small rectangle pieces.
7. Cool in refrigerator, then store in covered container.

(Makes approximately 60 pieces.)

My mother would prepare these waffles, usually as an evening meal. I always felt a bit guilty eating them as she was still standing at the kitchen counter making them, trying to keep up with her family's appetite. This is one of the reasons that we now bring the electric waffle iron to the dining table. At least we can all visit and relax while the waffles are in the making.

WAFFLES

2 cups cake flour
3 t. baking powder
½ t. salt
2 T. sugar
2 egg yolks
1 2/3 cups milk or 1 1/3 cups or 2 cups (See below.)
½ cup salad oil
2 egg whites

1. Preheat waffle iron.
2. Mix four, baking powder, salt, and sugar into mixing bowl.
3. Beat egg yolks in another bowl; add milk and oil. Pour liquid into dry ingredients all at once and stir until smooth.
4. Beat egg whites until stiff peaks form; fold gently into batter.
5. Bake in waffle iron. If there is no automatic light in the iron, the waffles are done when steam no longer appears.

(Makes 7, 4-sectioned, 7-inch round waffles.)

If you want them fluffier, decrease milk to 1 1/3 cups. For crispier waffles, increase milk to 2 cups.

This custard can be served as a separate dessert or as a topping on a cake or fruit.

VANILLA CUSTARD SAUCE IN MICROWAVE

1 cup 2% milk
1 T. cornstarch
1 egg. beaten
¼ c. sugar
½ t. vanilla extract

1. Combine milk and cornstarch in 1-quart bowl. Stir well. Microwave uncovered 3 minutes, stirring after each minute.
2. Combine egg and sugar, stirring well. Gradually stir in 1/4th of the milk, then all of it.
3. Microwave on 50% Power. Cook 1½ to 2 minutes stirring every 45 seconds, then in 15-second intervals until it bubbles. This will vary somewhat due to the wattage of microwaves.
4. Stir in vanilla extract.
5. Cover and refrigerate until needed.

STIR FRY SAUCE

3 T. dark brown sugar
1/3 cup cornstarch
2 t. ground ginger
4 garlic cloves, crushed
½ cup soy sauce
½ cup dry sherry
¼ t. red pepper sauce
3 T. red wine vinegar

2½ cups beef or chicken broth

1. Mix first 8 ingredients well. Add broth.
2. Mix well. Refrigerate 10 days to 2 weeks OR freeze 3 months. If frozen, thaw for 2 hours.

(Makes 4 cups.)

I particularly like this when stir frying vegetables with beef or chicken.

Reube prepared the following recipe for their restaurant. It made 1 gallon or 50 servings. Fifty servings are a bit much so the following is adjusted for family consumption. The amount you plan to use for each meal can be frozen separately.

BARBECUE SAUCE

1¼ ounce butter
1¼ cup onion, chopped
¼ cup sugar
¾ t. black pepper
¾ t. dry mustard
¾ T. paprika
¼ cup Worcestershire sauce
¾ t. hot sauce

1½ cups ketchup
¾ cup vinegar
¾ cup water

1. **Simmer all ingredients until it is a bit thick, 1½ to 2 hours.**
2. **Keeps really well in the refrigerator for a week or more.**

(Makes 6 cups.)

The following cocktail is one that we serve when a large number is visiting, and we prefer to offer just one drink rather than prepare individualized requests. Only occasionally, then, do we open up the entire bar. If I have the Frosty Sours mixed, people will often want them anyway, except for those folks who prefer their scotch or vodka straight. We prepared these when at my parents' 65th wedding anniversary party.

FROSTY SOURS

1/3 cup bourbon
6 ounces frozen lemonade concentrate
1 T. frozen orange juice concentrate
cracked or cube ice
3 or 4 cups ginger ale

1. **Combine the bourbon, lemonade, and orange juice concentrates in a blender.**
2. **Add the ice, then the amount of ginger ale to your liking.**

This is another recipe from Doc and Reube. They are both good cooks. We have such fond memories of making mincemeat at their house. We would start in the morning and it would take most of the day. Their recipe was the American version using beef. Later, we learned the mince pies in England did not include beef, nor do the commercial jars of mince in the United States—Nonesuch brand. Their recipe included a good portion of rum and we would add some rum to glasses of fresh cider that spurred us on to continue peeling apples.

Doc would also spend a good part of a day monitoring his pot of ham, ham bone, and beans. It, too, was out of this world. Since Doc is no longer around and Reube no longer cooks, we rely on memories. The closest we get to mince pies is when Hal prepares them for the holidays using the commercial mince.

However, this is one of the recipes in my file from Reube. It wasn't until I moved to Pennsylvania that I was served this warm dressing over greens.

SWEET AND SOUR BACON SALAD DRESSING
Pennsylvania Dutch

6 bacon strips, fried crisply
2 T. flour
6 T. sugar
1 t. dry mustard
1 cup cider vinegar
1 cup water
2 eggs

1. **Fry bacon and crumble**
2. **Remove half of the drippings.**
3. **Add the flour, sugar, mustard, vinegar, and water. Add crumbled bacon.**
4. **Add beaten eggs; cook until thick, stirring constantly. If too thick, add a bit of water. Serve over lettuce.**

VIII

My Favorite Foods That I Order But Do Not Prepare

Though the following is a French thing, I feel sure that there are restaurants in the cities of the U.S. that serve **MUSSELS**. I don't get around much so do not have the answer. I am a faithful reader of <u>Bon Appetit</u> and <u>Gourmet</u> magazines. (Ruth, gives me her copies after she has read them.) I am no longer able to subscribe to any magazines. Because of the mobility, I cannot rely on the postal service to hold them for me. After so many months, they send them to some place on Mars. I do plead guilty to hoarding old issues, thinking that someday I might be bedridden but still able to read. There is a great deal of historical writing in them and when I pick up a back issue, I sometimes find an article which is now more meaningful since I have traveled there.

I have not lived in a large city ever, though one of my unfulfilled dreams is to live in selected cities for one year, rent an apartment and become familiar with the area before moving on to another. I doubt that I shall ever follow this dream though I did come close to it when we lived on Oasis one winter in Paris. We have talked about taking a boat to Montreal and living there for a time as it's a combination of English and French. We dropped in for a couple of days not long ago and were impressed with the people and the beauty of the city. We liked the result of the melding of the two languages. I particularly enjoyed browsing the supermarket and seeing food items that we had liked while living in England and France.

Most cities of size have restaurants specializing in serving mussels. One enjoys the experience but doesn't necessarily go away feeling full. It provides a nice, social setting for a group of people or at least another couple. The sauce served with the mussels comes in many varieties and crusty bread is a necessity for soaking up every last drop.

A more tasty treat, personally speaking, came about when we were taken to another specialty restaurant in Belgium. When it came time to order, the wife ordered the **EEL** and Hal followed her lead. The husband ordered pork chops. I was in a quandary but the "Don't knock it until you try it," plugged in and I went for the eel. By then, the husband was feeling guilty so he changed his order to eel. The eels were unbelievably tasty. Probably it was the sauce/gravy that made the eels so rich but I would go back there again. You will not find a recipe for eels in the Index. With a good taste in our memory, we once bought smoked eel in Copenhagen. We ended up throwing it away, as it didn't suit our tastes. Our friend, Bolle, said that the smoking process can alter the taste of smoked eel greatly so we should give it another try sometime.

Several other dishes which I favor but leave to the professionals follow. **FRENCH APPLE TART** is readily available in most *patisseries*. My one and only attempt did not turn out as well as what you can purchase so I leave it to the experts.

ALMOND CROISSANTS are a must for our taste-buds. We can go only so long without having them for our breakfast. As an aside, I did not realize for a while when entering a French *patisserie* that it was customary to give a greeting before giving an order. This custom was not one we were used to following in the U.S. However, it didn't take me long to realize that a proper greeting was indeed common practice in order to develop good feelings between the owner of the establishment and the customer. I now give some kind of greeting wherever I'm shopping, as I think it makes for a more pleasant day for both the clerk and myself.

CASSOULET, a dish originating in the south of France, is a stew that varies from place to place. However, the similarity among the different versions is that it's a hearty dish of beans, meats (duck, pork, or goose), garlic, onion, broth and herbs. We have tried it in restaurants as well as the commercially, canned variety. For the professional chef, it requires investing lots of time and energy.

There are some foods that just taste better when someone else prepares them. If I crave **TREACLE TART** when in England, I search it out at a restaurant. It becomes a special treat. In all our visits in English homes, we have never been served treacle tart. For those of you who have not heard of this tart, it is a sugary, sticky pie made with golden syrup and breadcrumbs.

We were served **PAVLOVA** once by Sue Apperley in her English home but have often ordered it in a restaurant. It's special and I'm not sure that I would be able to make the meringue suitably, as it must be moist on the inside and hard on the out.

I once drooled over **STEAK AND KIDNEY PIE** but would never try to make it myself. Sometimes the kidneys served are disgusting. They can taste totally different, and I would not know how to select the right ones.

I could sit down to a serving of **EMPANADAS** once a week, I think, and probably would not grow tired of them. They are a speciality in Argentina, probably as common as the hamburger is to the U.S. They are oh, so good. Just this year a restaurant in

Georgia has been advertising them on their menu, and our car will obviously head in that direction one fine day.

I'm not sure just how common it is, but the following dessert can be purchased at some food stores in England. Friends of ours brought it to the dessert table and for a chocoholic such as myself, **DEATH BY CHOCOLATE** was a risk I was willing to take.

PROFITEROLES, which I once tried to prepare, has a note written beside the recipe. "Don't bother to try again." I may someday try a different recipe. Not too long ago, however, I was enthralled by a serving of these at a French restaurant not far from where we were building Oasis. The profiteroles were filled with vanilla ice cream, not whipped cream which is often the filling used. Personally, I don't care for lots of whipped cream but ice cream is another story. Beside the individual serving was a small pitcher of hot fudge sauce. After this treat, every time I would pass by the restaurant on shopping trips, I wanted to pull to a stop. However, I just relied on my good memories and saved consuming lots of calories. And, as I write this, I'm thinking to myself, "What is wrong with you?" I used to have a card at my desk that was a quote from a woman (I have forgotten her name.) but not her advice. If she had her life to live over, she would go barefoot more often and eat more ice cream cones, among other things. I should have stopped for another profiterole.

To me, this dish did not sound enticing. However, it was a Burgundy region restaurant's specialty and again, "Try it; you may like it." **OEUFS EN MUERETTE** is different but nice. For one of Hal's birthday gatherings, our friend, John Nye, served this as the first course. It can be the main course and we have often made it so at various restaurants. For the gathering, our hostess, Sheila, prepared the main course of lamb with mint sauce, and I brought the carrot cake. John would probably walk a couple of miles for a serving of the carrot cake just as we would cover that same distance for his rendition of poached eggs prepared in red wine. If it's on a restaurant's menu, we usually choose it.

Another French culinary delight is **ESCARGOT** (snails). Probably it's the butter and garlic that make the dish such a popular one. And, it's not just the French who favor them; there used to be a restaurant a mile from my home in Maryland that offered them as an appetizer. Like most things in this 21st Century, more and more food items are becoming common in many countries of the world.

Friends, Bolle and Carla, from the Netherlands, spend many hours in their kitchen preparing a meal called an Indonesian rice table that beats all. In restaurants all over their country, one can order Indonesian foods. But, we have never had such an array of meats and spices as our friends put on the table. Though it's all very well seasoned and melts in your mouth, we especially like the **CHICKEN SATAY.** Maybe it's because it has some good-ole-peanut butter in the sauce. One can buy the satay sauce in a can in the Netherlands but, of course, it's not as good as homemade.

Here are the many dishes written in Dutch and English set on the table at the Verweij household:

Sate Babi	Pork sate kababs
Katjang saus	Peanut sauce
Nassi Putih	White rice
Rendang padang	Beef simmered in herbs
Ajam ketjap	Chicken in sweet soy sauce
Ajam rudjak	Chicken with coriander and peppers
Smoor pedis	Ground beef with spicy herbs
Gado gado	Soy sprouts with peanut sauce
Mihoen goreng	Baked noodles with vegetables
Seroendeng	Fried coconut with peanuts
Kentang goreng	Sweet, spicy potato chips
Rempejeh	Hot peanuts in spicy pancake
Kroepoek oedang	Shrimp bread
Emping blado	Sweet, spicy chips of nuts
Sambal badjak	Puree of pimiento
Sambal oelek	Hot red pepper condiment

The last seven items can be purchased from shops and would be difficult to duplicate in the home kitchen. The others, however, were prepared by Carla and took most of a day and a half. Bolle helped with putting the kababs together. He said that Indonesian restaurants might serve as many as 26 items at their rice table. Preparing and enjoying this meal came from life experiences gained by an uncle of Bolle's family.

I have no intention of trying to duplicate all of the above but am eager at some point to be able to serve the chicken or pork kababs in the peanut sauce.

FRIED OYSTERS are a special item on restaurant menus in the U.S., especially in the south. I have a real fondness for them and if available, will order. I do not practice deep frying food in my various kitchens for two reasons. We choose not to consume fried foods frequently, so they are limited to restaurant meals. Secondly, I don't like the idea of deep, hot oil on my cooking stoves.

I am quite fond of **SZECHUAN** and other **ORIENTAL FOOD** but find that I am never able to collect all the ingredients to make dishes that I like. So, I save eating those foods for when I am dining in a restaurant.

I mentioned before that one of the dishes served by Diana was **STUFFED HAM.** I look forward to having it when we are in southern Maryland. My best memory of eating it was as a sandwich made from the leftovers as we headed home after a family visit.

IX

Kitchen Utensils

For the total knife drawer, I use the following:

Saw-tooth paring knife
Large saw-tooth bread knife
Large chopping knife
8 to 12 steak knives

Scissors for chopping food products, everything from lettuce to bread for croutons to almost anything that needs cutting into pieces though we seldom prepare roasts of any kind that require a carving knife, I do add an electric knife when in the house for slicing and a regular carving knife for elsewhere.

I use the following utensils in whatever kitchen or galley I work:

Pans: 3 saucepans and 1 large Dutch-oven pan with lids

Special-designed microwave bowl for steaming vegetables
Special microwave spatter cover

Strainers, small and large

Bowls: 2 to 3 large made of glass
1 set of 3 (variable size) in glass

Place Settings for 8 to 12:

Stainless ware, including serving spoons (I refuse to spend my time shining silver.)
Spatula (2 sizes)
Rubber spatulas
Wooden spoons
Soup ladle
Wok or large skillet
Skillets: 1 set of 3 (variable size)

Mouli Jr. (hand grinder that does many of the jobs of a food processor)

Baking dishes, various sizes

Casseroles for oven-to-table use
Cookie sheets
Cutting boards
Electric, hand mixer
Pizza pan(s)
Tea kettle

Microwave
Toaster

Items used in home, not on boat or camper:
Bread maker, Slow cooker, Pancake grill, Waffle iron, Food Processor

You will notice that all measurements are given in ounces, for both liquid and bulk. If you have an 8-oz. measuring cup and a Tablespoon/teaspoon measurer that you can buy everywhere, this is all that you will need. Also, "t" represents teaspoon, and "T" represents a Tablespoon.

I refer to medium-size cans (14 to 16-ounce range) and large cans (24-ounces).

X
Family Members and Friends

Hal's daughter Sarah Foligno, husband Andrew (Andy), and daughters Rebecca (Becky) and Colleen

Dorothy's daughter Diana Kraft and husband Thomas, Sr., deceased, and their daughters Christina and Karen, son Thomas, Jr. (TJ)

Hal's son James (Jim) Stufft, wife Mary Jane, and son, Samuel (Sam)

Hal's sister, Anita Straume, deceased

Hal's sister, Ruth VanAkin and brother-in-law, Gerald (Jerry)

My sister, Kathryn (Kate) Jackson and deceased brother-in-law, Howard

My brother, Lynn Leitnaker and wife Marjorie (Margie)

My mother, Dorothy and father, Paul Leitnaker, both deceased

Hal's mother, Lenore and father, Paul Stufft, both deceased

Family covering four generations has been the source of many of my favorite recipes. I am grateful to have such good cooks about me. All of the above have been helpful by graciously giving me their recipes and comments.

But, I am especially lucky to have had a mother who served as a good model in many ways. Most of us love and admire our mothers though I have had friends over the years who thought their mother was their enemy and spoke negatively of her.

My mother was born in 1900 so I could easily relate her age and life to mine. It was required that she return from her university studies to take care of her ill mother and siblings and was unable to return to conclude her degree. However with advanced courses, she qualified to teach. She taught her younger sister but changed grade levels when I came along. She was so well liked by my friends that they complained to me when they missed out on her instruction.

She married my father at age 24; they had three children. She helped on occasion to milk cows, gather eggs, and butcher chickens for Sunday dinner. She painted farm buildings when Dad went on vacation to Canada with his fishing buddies. She put her three children in paint clothes and gave us a bucket of paint and a brush. She always wore dresses and wore high heels when away from home, including all day in the classroom. She did have assistance from two women who cleaned the house and ironed our clothes.

She helped the poor students by giving them odd jobs on our farm and she taught them responsibility and cleanliness. She provided them with clothes. I continue to meet her students who remind me of new dresses she bought for them or how she was responsible for much of their success in life. I admire her continually; she would give me and the younger generation some stiff competition.

I must not exclude my father as he was my excuse to get out of the house and into the fields. He was the primary income earner. He modeled that you should be immaculate in everything you touch. If a stray stock of corn appeared in the soybean field, he called this succotash and walked far to pull it. The roads passing his land were always trimmed and mowed right up to the field crops. To this day, I admire this quality and am often disappointed in what I observe along country roads.

I'm very indebted to my parents and realize it more and more with each passing year. Each of us probably carries on activities that our parents modeled; think about it.

Friends, including their nationality and place of residence, who have had an impact on my travels and entertaining:

Anne and Robin Stevenson, Scotland

Carla and Bolle Verweij, The Netherlands

Gwenda and Bruce Roberts, Australia, living in Spain and other places

Jo Parfitt, England, living in France

Peter Mastenbroek. The Netherlands, living in France

Roger and Sue Apperley, England

Sheila and John Nye, England, living in France

Ursula and Mike Baroi, Switzerland and India, living in France and England

Friends who have contributed their recipes:

Barbara and Mike Tittensor, England

Paulette and Al Ricciuti, France

Louisa Guzzetti, Massachusetts

Mary and Tom Cox, Florida

Muriel and John Gealer, England

Reube and Doc Moorehead, Pennsylvania

Tere and Roger Davis, Argentina and England, living in Buenos Aires

XI

Oops and Aahs and Ughs

Picture this! You prepare a special lunch for a couple. You wait a couple of hours for them to arrive. You don't eat. They arrive very late; say that they became hungry on the way and stopped to have lunch. UGH!

You have planned the week's meals for guests. The refrigerator is packed. Friends arrive. Their dog food requires refrigeration. UGH!

English friends invite you to "tea." After several years living in their country, you didn't pick up on the meaning of "tea." Eventually, you learn to ask if you are invited for the 4 o'clock tea and a biscuit or for an early evening meal referred to as "proper tea." OOPS!

You have prepared the weekend menus for the family's visit. In the refrigerator are two oven pans the same size covered in foil--one containing the layered salad and the other, a main course. After the pan has been in the oven a short while you realize that you put the salad in the oven. UGH! What happens here is that I so enjoy visiting with the family that I make the kitchen time secondary in my thoughts.

Recipes often call for using either butter or margarine. But, not in one instance that I learned the hard way. When preparing the French toast, I substituted margarine. The bread stuck to the pan; the toast was edible but the pans had to be thrown away. UGH!

Another couple invited for lunch just didn't show. We worried that something had gone wrong on the highway. The wife was driving her husband. He had made a special piece of amateur radio equipment for us and he wanted to give it to us personally. They were on the road some three hours, came within a couple miles of their destination. The wife became disgusted when she chose the wrong turn. She turned around and returned home. It wasn't until much later that day that we learned they were safe back home. That was a relief to hear, then, we became angry that she had given up so close, two miles away, to where we were building our boat. UGH!

You are making pumpkin cobbler. When it comes out of the oven, it tastes flat—not like what Ruth had served. Then, you find out that you used plain pumpkin and not pumpkin-pie filling. You try sprinkling the top with seasonings, but it just doesn't taste as good. UGH! Then, if that mistake wasn't enough a couple of years later, you grab a can of pumpkin from your cupboard and proceed to make the cobbler. Not again! I think I have finally learned my lesson.

I was ready to serve the final course, my ice cream cake, to some eighty-five guests when I realized that the cakes were so hard that a knife, even warmed, would not cut it. So, the guests were asked to be patient, that dessert would be ready in twenty minutes of so. It probably took longer than that. UGH!

Here's the scene. Guests are outside on a lovely summer's evening along the canal bank. They have noticed the steaks that are coming out of their marinade and being readied for a barbecue. We light the charcoal but nothing happens. We add wood chips to encourage the heating, but we have no luck. The steaks have to be brought into the boat and put in a skillet for frying. UGH!

The recipe, "Chicken Divan," calls for "cooked chicken. And the chef wonders why it is taking so long for the chicken to become tender. It's a longer wait for dinner as I forgot to use cooked chicken. OOPS!

We are watching our first granddaughter for the day; she is around 11 months old. She is sitting on the kitchen counter while Grandma puts a Dutch Apple pie together. AAH! It isn't until the pie is being removed from the oven that Grandma notices a little bowl of ingredients sitting on the counter. The spices for the pie were not included but it didn't turn out too terrible. We now call the Dutch apple pie "Christina's apple pie," though all ingredients are included. OOPS!

A friend has invited us to a restaurant meal in Paris. Now, that's a special treat. You want to order something very wonderful. You select as part of the plate *ris*. It sure doesn't look like rice when it is placed before me. Rice is *riz, not ris*. It turns out the dish in front of me is poached sweetbreads. UGH!

We now carry with us a proper food dictionary when dining in French restaurants. After all the many visits to Paris on our five boats you would think I would be more on top of food items; however, just last summer I ordered what I thought was a pastry crust over chicken *(en croûte)*. Having failed to read the menu carefully and being so sure of myself that I didn't think it necessary to check the dictionary, I was served *choucroute,* sauerkraut. UGH! The good news is that it turned out to be a tasty meal. Here again we were in company with daughter and her mate and the conversation took precedence.

I once learned that I had been served new potatoes in an English home and had failed to mention how unique and lovely they were. Back then, a potato was a potato, and its size was not of importance. As a kid helping my father harvest potatoes, the little ones were a negative—the bigger the better. Since then in my reading of cookbooks (Yes, I'm guilty of spending hours perusing cookbooks.), I realize that new potatoes are something different. In England, especially, they are a big deal and the cook goes to some length to prepare them. I still do not fully appreciate their uniqueness and it's obvious I have more to learn. OOPS!

The Kraft family and I were enjoying a typical full-breakfast at a country bed and breakfast in Ireland. The woman of the house was serving the plate of eggs and toast, etc. and on the plate was something round that none of us recognized. TJ, age 11, inquired about it and the woman explained that it was a sausage made from pigs using the pig's blood. TJ managed to swallow hard and remain silent until the woman returned through swinging doors back to the kitchen. Then, he proclaimed: "Uuuuugh."

XII

Index for All Recipes by Category

APPETIZERS

Black bean ...39
Blue cheese crisps ...109
Cheese & artichoke dip ...4
Chicken livers wrapped in bacon, *Rumaki* ...147
Chili con queso ...16
Frosty sours cocktail ...192
Ship's drink ...47
Shrimp ball ...3
Wine cocktail, *Kir* ...100

BREADS, BREAD DRESSINGS, AND PIZZAS

Calzones ...79
Cheese pizza ...78
Cinnamon rolls ...185
Corn bread dressing ...183
Cranberry nut bread ...5
Cuban bread ...184
English muffin bread ...183
French toast ...13
Garlic bread ...184
Pizza with feta and shrimp ...80
Tea Scones ...57
Thanksgiving dressing ...182
Turkey stuffing ...181
Yankee oyster dressing ...182

CAKES

Angel food, plain or chocolate ...177
Apple ...179

Carrot cake and icing ...38
Devil's food chocolate with penuche icing ...176
Ice cream cake with chocolate syrup ...12
Ice cream cake with hard meringue, *Vacherin* ...44
Lemon pudding cake ...107
Pineapple downside-up ...75
Plain cheesecake ...179
Pumpkin cheesecake ...180
Strawberry shortcake ...177
Sour cream and walnut coffee cake ...17

COOKIES

Almond cocoons ...4
Blonde brownies ...165
Cherry & almond shortbread ...187
Coconut ...17
Heart cookies ...185
Peanut butter and chocolate ...6
Tri-level brownies ...62

DESSERTS

Apple dumplings ...11
Baklava ...164
Blueberry-peach cobbler ...73
Crème caramel ...169
Date pudding ...168
English trifle ...167
Floating island, (MW) *Ile Flottante* ...170
Hot Fudge Pudding ...27
Peaches in sherry ...60
Pumpkin cobbler ...163
Sticky toffee pudding ...32
Tiramisu ...166
Vanilla custard, (MW) ...190

EGG DISHES

Breakfast casserole ...13
Egg casserole ...14
Omelet for lunch or dinner ...146

Quiche ...124
Scrambled eggs (MW) ...93
Scrambled eggs with smoked salmon and chives ...93

BEEF

Beef lasagna ...7
Beef pie with mashed potato topping, Shepherd's pie ...76
Beef stew in a pumpkin, *Carbonada* ...34
Braised Swiss steak in a slow cooker ...126
Cranberry meatballs ...130
Eggplant *Moussaka* ...143
Meatloaf in pastry, *Lihamurekepiiras* ...15
Meatloaf with tomato ...125
Portable meat pies, *Cornish pasties* ...23
Roast beef hash ...22

CHICKEN

Chicken casserole ...123
Chicken crepes ...138
Chicken curry ...119
Chicken Divan ...136
Chicken with dried beef ...146
Chicken enchiladas ...115
Chicken in garlic sauce ...123
Chicken Kiev ...121
Chicken lasagna ...10
Chicken livers sauté ...118
Chicken livers supreme ...118
Chicken noodles au gratin, (MW) ...129
Chicken in pastry shells, *Vol-au-Vent* ...122
Chicken parmesan (MW) ...97
Chicken in phyllo, *Kotopits* ...142
Chicken *Saltimbocca* ...120
Chicken with wine from Burgundy, *Coq au Vin* ...71
Cluck-cluck stew in slow cooker ...126
Sweet and sour chicken ...128
Teriyaki-glazed chicken ...91

HAM AND PORK

Glazed baked ham in orange sauce, *Jambon a la Orange* ...56
Ham loaf ...145
Paella, Portuguese-style ...140
Pork chops in French mustard cream sauce ...134
Pork roast, festive ...133
Pork and sauerkraut ...137
Stuffed pork chops ...137

FISH AND SEAFOOD

California grilled fish ...135
Crab cakes ...55
Fillet of fish with almonds (MW) ...73
Party seafood ...132
Salmon patties with mango chutney ...46
Salmon with leek sauce ...72
Scalloped oysters ...128
Scallops in wine sauce, *Coquille St. Jacques* ...92
Seafood lasagna ...8
Teriyaki salmon ...72

PASTAS

Cheese enchiladas ...116
Macaroni and cheese with prosciutto ...134
Summer pasta with brie ...58

PIES

Blackberry and apple ...52
Chocolate and peanut butter ...171
Chocolate and pecan ...174
Dutch apple ...174
Pecan ...174
Pie crust ...172
Key lime ...175
Strawberry ...173

SALADS

Apricot ...103
Avocado and shrimp ...154
Broccoli ...106
Brown rice ...70
Cauliflower ...153
Chicken gizzard, *Salade Gesier* ...158
Cranberry Jello ...157
Egg and beet ...159
Fresh fruit, (Waldorf) ...156
Goat cheese with dressing, *Chevre Chaud* ...102
Greek ...157
Green salad with tuna ...155
Layered salad ...155
Mexican fruit ...117
Pasta salad ...156
Pineapple cheese ...104
Potato ...70
Side salad, smoked salmon ...154
Tomato salad ...43
French dressing ...43
Twenty-four hour salad ...102
Yogurt ...152

SANDWICHES

Egg salad pitas ...150
Hamburgers with blue-cheese dressing ...106
Muffaletta ...148
Pork barbecue ...148
Shrimp on croissant ...149
Sloppy Joe's ...151
Tuna franks ...150
Turkey patties ...150

SAUCES AND DRESSINGS

Barbecue sauce ...191
Blue cheese dressing (See 106.)
French dressing (See 43 under Tomato Salad.)
Honey-mustard salad dressing ...83

Marinade for steaks ...18
Stir-fry sauce ...191
Sweet & sour dressing ...192

SOUPS

Chicken and rice ...161
Chili ...162
Crab chowder ...160
French onion ...99
Potato ...159
Vegetable and pasta, *Soupe au Pistou* ...161

VEGETABLES

Brussels sprouts with onion and bacon ...19
Carrots, glazed ...63
Cauliflower, baked ...27
Cheesy potatoes ...59
Corn casserole ...64
Lima beans in tomato sauce ...18
Peas and potatoes ...61
Scalloped corn ...64
Scalloped potatoes ...65
Snow peas & tomatoes ...94
Sweet potatoes, candied ...66
Sweet potatoes with streusel ...66
Sweet potatoes, stuffed ...67
Tomato halves with herbs ...69
Tomato-zucchini grill ...40
Vegetable lasagna ...9
Vegetarian spaghetti ...131

ECLECTIC

Caramel popcorn, (MW) ...186
Peanut butter fudge ...188
Rice pudding ...186
Tiger butter candy ...189
Waffles ...190

---Dorothy Young, Hal Stufft

Imler, PA---Jekyll Island, GA---Aboard Oasis in Europe

November 4, 2009 to February, 14, 2011

CPSIA information can be obtained at www.ICGtesting.com
261928BV00003B/1-100/P